sensational knowledge

Tomie Hahn

Sensational Knowledge

embodying culture through japanese dance

WESLEYAN UNIVERSITY PRESS

MIDDLETOWN, CONNECTICUT

Wesleyan University Press
Middletown, CT 06459
www.wesleyan.edu/wespress

© 2007 by Tomie Hahn
All rights reserved

Printed in the United States of America
5 4

Library of Congress Cataloging-in-Publication Data
Hahn, Tomie.
Sensational knowledge : embodying culture through Japanese dance / Tomie Hahn.
p.   cm.—(Music/culture)
Includes bibliographical references and index.
ISBN-13: 978–0–8195–6834–2 (cloth : alk. paper)
ISBN-10: 0–8195–6834–1 (cloth : alk. paper)
ISBN-13: 978–0–8195–6835–9 (pbk. : alk. paper)
ISBN-10: 0–8195–6835-X (pbk. : alk. paper)
1. Dance—Japan—Study and teaching. 2. Japan—Social
life and customs—Study and teaching. I. Title.
GV1695.H24 2007
793.3'1952   2006038728

The author gratefully acknowledges the following for
permission to use previously published material:

Tomie Hahn, "Emerging voices—encounters with reflexivity," *Atlantis: A Women's Studies Journal/Revue d'Etudes sur les femmes* 30, no. 2, 2006. Institute for the Study of Women, Mount Saint Vincent University, Halifax, Nova Scotia B3M 2J6 Canada, www.msvu.ca/atlantis

Tomie Hahn, "'It's the RUSH': Sites of the Sensually Extreme." The Drama Review vol. 51, no. 2 (T190), Summer, 2006. The Drama Review, The MIT Press Journals, Five Cambridge Center, Suite 4, Cambridge, MA 02142–1493

Online video examples referred to in the text are available at:
https://www.weslpress.org/readers-companions/
password: SK68359

In memory of Tachibana Hiroyo.

*Dedicated to Tachibana Yoshie and
all who have shared their sensibilities
with me over these many years.*

contents

illustrations

figures

photographs

online visual examples
(available at: https://www.weslpress.org/readers-companions/)

x » Contents

Online video examples referred to in the text are available at:
https://www.weslpress.org/readers-companions/
password: SK68359

a note on names and media

The East Asian convention of placing the family name before the given name has been followed for Japanese names. I refer to Tachibana Yoshie as "Iemoto" (headmaster) and Tachibana Hiroyo as "Soke" (previous headmaster) because this is how we refer to them in our dance school. When these titles are used as names I have capitalized them. In contrast, when the terms *iemoto* and *soke* designate (social) positions, the words appear in lowercase. As a courtesy, the names of students have been changed. Because I have selected photographs and video passages in which students needed correction, these are not necessarily excerpts of which they would be proud.

All video documentation included with this text was shot by myself at the Tachibana School in Tokyo. Photographs are also my own unless noted otherwise.

preface

I remember my first dance lesson with Iemoto (Headmaster) Tachibana Yoshie in Tokyo. She took my elbow and led me across the studio, pointing at the impeccably clean wood floor. Nothing seemed unusual. "See these marks . . . ," she said, kneeling down on the floor and still pointing here and there. As I bent down to sit by her side, minute water stains and nicks on the floor's surface came into focus. "Those stains are from all of our sweat and tears here together," she continued, sweeping her arm across the room toward the half dozen onlooking students. "All these marks are from our hard work together every day—dancing." I looked up from the floor to the students and down to the floor again. My eyes, now wide open, saw how speckled the floor was.

Throughout this book I refer to Tachibana Yoshie as "Iemoto" (the word for headmaster) and her mother, Tachibana Hiroyo, as "Soke" (previous headmaster) because this is how we refer to them in our dance school. Dancers affectionately call the Tachibana dance studio in downtown Tokyo "Hatchobori," the name of the subway stop across the street. Hatchobori often becomes a metaphor for our dance lives, relationships, obligations, and the Tachibana dance tradition. I have revisited early memories like the one above many times over the years, considering how Hatchobori embodies our dance, and how each of us contributes to the physical form of the studio. The surface nicks and stains, while insignificant in themselves, are a tangible result of meaningful physical exertion during lessons—generations of dancers' marks layered upon each other.

Hatchobori, witness to the daily transmission of moving art and embodied cultural knowledge, stands as both a symbolic and a very real structure of edification. In this lesson the message of Iemoto's work ethic was very clear. I realized with awe the magnitude of energy that had been expended on this dance floor. When Iemoto's arm stretched out toward the students, Hatchobori became personified for me. Dancing bodies had inscribed these marks on the hard floor, contributing symbolically to the larger representation of the school body, and an instantiation of our strong bonds. The students observing my lesson were only a handful of the many generations of bodies that had created these patterns I was kneeling on. I felt included in the group, nervous, yet ready to dance. And so, Iemoto's illustration served a purpose.

Years later Iemoto again anthropomorphized Hatchobori. She said, "You have changed, in your walk, look, and manner at Hatchobori. These are things I have not taught you. Hatchobori taught you how to enter the *keikoba* [practice hall or dance studio], sit, bow, and behave with others. Because you have spent time here you have learned the feeling of Hatchobori. Learning quickly is not good—you cannot force your mind or body to remember properly. Living in Japan and being in the studio every day has taught you more of the lifestyle, people, and dance."

These lessons of the body deeply inspired my ethnographic pursuits. I have studied Japanese dance since the age of four. This book is my attempt to comprehend how my body has come to *know* this movement. It is, then, a more general exploration of how movement is transmitted and embodied, using Japanese dance as a case study. My own experience has both enriched and problematized my ethnographic process. My analysis of the learning process proved to be elusive; the art form and its transmission left no trace other than my growing proficiency; there was no "concrete" object to grasp. Ironically, the very "data" I sought were deeply entrenched in my very body—ready to be mined. However, as embodied knowledge, it became a puzzle for me to excavate. My field site eerily appeared and disappeared before me. My body became one of my primary field sites. I soon realized that, beyond Hatchobori, the dancers moving around me were in fact my field sites, and my own body a terrain to survey.[1]

acknowledgments

If I could, I would kneel, gently place a closed fan before me, and bow deeply with gratitude. I have had the great fortune of receiving sensational knowledge from many people. I realize I will never be able to repay what I have been given, yet I feel fortunate to have the ability to express my sincere gratitude here. I thank the Asian Cultural Council, the American Association for University Women, Tufts University, and Rensselaer Polytechnic Institute for their generous funding of my research. Thanks to Suzanna Tamminen and Eric Levy at Wesleyan University Press, who had faith in this text.

Learning embodied practices is a moving experience that has enriched my life. Transmission flows in time and resides in a living tradition. I am indebted to Iemoto Tachibana Yoshie and Soke Tachibana Hiroyo, who opened their hearts and the *keikoba* (dance studio) to me, passing down a lineage of movement that inspired this ethnography. As will be apparent in the pages to come, Iemoto's passion for dance and art expanded my awareness, now instilled in my everyday life. I owe her a depth of gratitude for the many years of inspiring lessons. To my childhood teacher in New York, Tachibana Sahomi, who will forever be a part of my dance, thank you. To all the Tachibana teachers and dancers in New York—Sahotoyo and Sahotae—and in Tokyo, where there are too many to list here, I send my utmost gratitude.

In my first semester in graduate school Kay Kaufman Shelemay's fascination with transmission systems was infectious, and through the years she has continued to inspire me in innumerable ways. Kay and Mark Slobin have been true mentors, encouraging my diverse interests, from Japanese dance to Monster Truck rallies to computer music. For years Cynthia Novack (Bull), now passed away, urged me to keep returning to the sensate body, the experiential essence of movement, to respect what the body knows, and to be determined to articulate this knowledge in as many forms (text, dance, teaching) as possible. Thanks to Lori Anderson-Moseman and Sean Williams for urging me to experiment, be playful, and let my voice tell this story.

Foremost, to my husband Curtis Bahn I owe a truckload of thanks for his undying support that has kept me dancing, playing music, writing, and laughing. His voracious curiosity has been inspiring. My Hahn and Bahn families have provided me with a wealth of support— I could say that my father and mother initiated this ethnography, since they started my sister Kimiko's and my *nihon buyo* lessons in Tokyo when we were children. It was my father, Walter Hahn, who inspired my curiosity about teaching practices. His enthusiasm as a creative artist and teacher never ceases to amaze me.

There have been great losses during the process of researching and writing this book. The tragic loss of my mother during my graduate years was unbearable, yet somehow returning to the countless Japanese (and Japanese American) women around me eased my journey. Both of my husband's parents, who were such pillars of support, also passed on at this time. During the final edits of this manuscript Soke passed away, and I am saddened that she never held the book that she inspired.

sensational knowledge

unfurled

I recall the initial struggle of opening my fan as a child.
Closed, the fan was stick-like and strong. It seemed unwilling to unfold.
My teacher's arms enclosed me and her hands guided mine into position.
She showed me how to push my right thumb against the outer "bone"
to pry the fan open,
unfurling each panel.
We repeated this over and over—
a dance we privately shared within the lesson.
Though I have witnessed many students' first fan lesson over the years, I know it is a
duet that will never be performed in public.

one

introduction — sensual orientations

"Know with your body," headmaster Tachibana Hiroyo said during my dance lesson, as she gently drew her hand to her chest. In this fleeting moment she succinctly imparted a cultural sensibility, a Japanese way of knowing, that moved beyond these few words and gesture. Curious about my own understanding of such moments, and the embodiment of such sensibilities conveyed during lessons, I was drawn to research how culture is passed down, or embodied, through dance.

This book is an ethnography that focuses on dance transmission and how cultural knowledge is embodied. I strongly believe that an observation of how dance is taught reveals a great deal about that culture as well as the individual dancers practicing the tradition. This ethnography is based on my fieldwork and experiences studying Japanese dance (*nihon buyo*) for over thirty years. I do not intend this book to be a comprehensive introduction to *nihon buyo* or its history, nor is it a record of specific dances. It is about process. I employ *nihon buyo* lessons at the Tachibana School in Tokyo as a case study to shed light on transmission and embodiment. For most performing arts traditions around the world, the general public sees only staged, or "finished," performances. Rarely does one have a chance to witness behind-the-scenes activities such as lessons or rehearsals. Compared with *kabuki*, *noh*, and *bunraku*, the genre of *nihon buyo* remains relatively unknown outside Japan. Further, outside *nihon buyo* dance studios, it is rare to have the opportunity to observe the process of dance training, where culture flows.

framing sense

I find that an ethnographer's academic discipline often imposes a privileging of one sense — "blinding" (deafening, numbing, muting, etc.) the ethnographer's experience of the lush sensory environment. Our academic disciplines in the arts appear to be organized by the specialization of sensory mode (departments of art, dance, and music, for example), but at the expense of a holistic analytic and experiential perspective. What theoretical, metaphoric sieves do we carry when we go to the field?[1] What slips through the sieve because we are screening for "answers" on a specific issue or our attention is keenly focused on a specific sensory/artistic practice?

For this very reason, and because dance transmission is a multisensory experience, I have drawn from a number of disciplines for theoretical and methodological guidance — most prominently, ethnomusicology, dance studies, anthropology, performance studies, and Asian philosophies of the body. Each offered a different approach for unfolding the complex process of dance transmission.

I use the word *transmission* in this book for several reasons. First, this word calls up the well-established scholarly history of transmission systems, such as oral/aural transmission in ethnomusicology, dance studies, and oral history. Second, I view transmission as a process that spans the practices of both teaching and learning. To study transmission is to view a process that instills theory and cultural concepts of embodiment. In this book, transmission concerns the information flow between teacher and student — the sender and receiver cycle — and embraces the personal relationships that evolve.

As is generally known, philosophically, theory and practice are not separated in Japan — the mind and body are not considered to be separate entities but are instead regarded as interdependent (see the work of Yuasa 1987, 1993; Nagatomo 1993b). Theory thus arises from practice. We embody the essence of theory when presence and thematic articulations of physical movements arise through practice. This approach contrasts with other methodologies in which theoretical concerns initiate the work and practice is a vehicle for "proving" certain theories. As dance scholars have long argued, the body does not intellectualize theory before it learns — rather, theory arises from engagement in body practices (Foster 1997; Bull 1997).

When I observed and experienced corporeal lessons during fieldwork, the senses emerged as the vehicles of transmission and the connection to embodied cultural expression. The senses reside in a unique position as the interface between body, self, and the world. They are beautiful transmission devices, through which we take in information, comprehend the experience, assign meaning, and often react to the stimuli. Not only do the senses orient us in a very real, physical way; they enable us to construct parameters of existence—that which defines the body, self, social group, or world. Simply, we are situated by sensual orientations. In my eyes, transmission systems are valuable to observe as processes of embodiment, effectuated via the senses, that encode and convey cultural meaning to reveal a particular (sub)culture's sensual orientation in the world.

The work of Cynthia Bull (Novack) has been influential in my conceptualization of the socially, sensually situated body in dance. She concludes her article "Sense, Meaning, and Perception in Three Dance Cultures":

> I am proposing that the particular characteristics of each dance form and its unique manner of transmission and performance encourage priorities of sensation that subtly affect the nature of perception itself. Dance finely tunes sensibilities, helping to shape the practices, behaviors, beliefs, and ideas of people's lives. (Bull 1997: 284–285)

Considering the senses as the vehicles of dance transmission, I began to ask: How does culture shape our attendance to various sensoria, and how does our interpretation of sensory information shape our individual realities? How are cultural systems of teaching bound to sensoria and the constructedness of awareness? Can some transmission practices incite transformative effects? Further, how does the culturally constructed process of transmission influence our sense of self?[2]

My basic framework for how dance transmission processes orient the body/self stems from the research on the anthropology of the senses, particularly the collections of articles edited by David Howes, *Empire of the Senses: The Sensual Culture Reader* (2005) and *The Varieties of Sensual Experience: A Sourcebook in the Anthropology of the Senses* (1991), Constance Classen's (ed.) *Worlds of Sense: Exploring the Senses in History and across Cultures* (1993), and Anthony Synnott's *The Body Social: Symbolism, Self, and Society* (1993). These works propose fascinating models for the sensoria in culture, not only the idea of the cultural construction of the senses, but the existence of a hierarchy of the senses in each culture that reflects their worldview, cosmology, or "world of sense." Running with this basic premise, I propose that an investigation of how art is sensually transmitted within its cultural context can reveal how the senses shape our understanding of what exists outside the body (and its relationship to the interior body), and can foster the construction of sensible worlds of shared cultural meaning.

Performance studies provided one of the most diverse perspectives for performance analysis, and offered me a range of insights. For example, Richard Schechner wrote:

> Performances are actions. As a discipline, performance studies takes actions very seriously in four ways. First, behavior is the "object of study" of performance studies. Although performance studies scholars use the "archive" extensively—what's in books, photographs, the archaeological record, historical remains, etc.—their dedicated focus is on the "repertory"—namely, what people do in the activity of their doing it. Second, artistic practice is a big part of the performance studies project. A number of performance studies scholars are also practicing artists working in the avantgarde, in community-based performance, and elsewhere; others have mastered a variety of non-Western and Western traditional forms. The relationship between studying performance and doing performance is integral. (Schechner 2003: 1)

For my work I would add "sound" to Schechner's first two sentences above, to clarify that sound is a part of the "object of study," although it is certainly clear in subsequent passages that he includes this sensory parameter. Schechner's substantiation of the values of the practitioner-scholar relationship reinforces participant-observer methodologies long practiced in ethnomusicology and anthropology.

Transmission via the senses instills profound cultural beliefs in the body, and contexts of dance transmission are rich settings for observing culture in action, especially the shaping and orienting of the body/self for artistic expression. I believe performance provides a special metaphoric space often revealing how people make sense of their lives and community (Schechner 2003; Fine and Speer 1992). Through fieldwork we are offered a glimpse at a subculture's performance practice and "techniques of the body" (Mauss 1979; Foster 1997) as shared cultural knowledge. Susan Leigh Foster underscores what observations of such techniques might uncover:

Any standardized regimen of bodily training, for example, embodies, in the very organization of its exercises, the metaphors used to instruct the body, and in the criteria specified for physical competence, a coherent (or not so coherent) set of principles that govern the action of that regimen. These principles, reticulated with aesthetic, political, and gendered connotations, cast the body who enacts them into larger arenas of meaning where it moves alongside bodies bearing related signage. (Foster 1995: 8)

As a window to embodied expression, fieldwork in music and dance can reveal how a community attends to the world and constructs its identity and art from shared sensibilities, shared sensual orientations. Fieldwork can be a dance of disorientation. In the field ethnographers immerse themselves in another culture's world as an attempt to comprehend how that culture constructs and makes sense of what's "out there." Fieldwork experiences often directly reveal contrasting constructs of reality that challenge our core sensibilities, changing the way we orient ourselves in the world.

In this book I hope to reveal how a culture's transmission processes prioritize practitioners' attendance to certain sensoria (even particular qualities of sensory experience), and how the transmission of sensory knowledge can shape dancers' experiential orientation. Through practice, systems of transmission structure experience so that, within the social group, the world appears similarly constructed and members know how to interact within it. I will illustrate how the entire setting and ritual of dance lessons conveys a Japanese sensibility—from bowing, to where one stands during a lesson, to attire, interactions, voice, gaze, spatial negotiations, and even touching.

inscribing sense

I have been fascinated by the presence, or absence, of the body in dance scholarship. Curiously, in many texts the body has been left entirely off the page. Scholarship before the 1970s primarily focused on contextualizing the dancing body, dance history, theory, and on documenting choreography. But specific cultural references to, and analysis of, the body itself were few. I believe this is in part due to the difficulties of analyzing movement, as recording technologies for moving images were not accessible or affordable for the general public to document dance in a format that enabled repeated viewings for detailed analysis. While film was available, it was costly. Video technology changed dance scholarship. Although several notation systems existed (such as Labanotation, developed by Rudolf Laban in the early twentieth century), dance has primarily been an art form passed from body to body, and not inscribed in a universally accepted standard notation system.

Since the 1970s scholars have written meticulously about the body, culture, and embodiment. The study of the body in society has received increased attention in such diverse theoretical disciplines as feminist theory, social psychology, cognitive psychology, anthropology, philosophy, performance studies, communication theory, medical anthropology, politics of the body, and aesthetics. This interdisciplinary interest, alongside rapidly advancing computer and video technologies, and developing dance and performance studies scholarship, fueled a diversity of exciting research on the body. Joann Kealiinohomoku's landmark article "An Anthropologist Looks at Ballet as a Form of Ethnic Dance" (1969) spoke volumes, critiquing previous dance scholarship without a grounding in culture or the body. Then, in 1974, Allegra Fuller Snyder proposed dance as a "way of knowing"—a concept that significantly changed dance scholarship, specifically, notions of embodiment.

From the mid-1980s dance ethnologists took a momentous leap, presenting movement *as* culture (Novack [Bull] 1990; Cowan 1990; Ness 1992; Sklar 2002) and bringing the moving body to a central position in their critical analysis. *Sensational Knowledge* continues on this historical path. With its fleeting presence, the dancing body has turned out to be an elusive informant to research. I crave specificity and a semblance of physical presence in dance scholarship. Limbs. Breath. Shoulders. Muscles. Gaze. I notice that the body appears in text when particular aspects of dance are considered, such as detailed descriptions of movement, choreography, learning, and personal accounts. When I read passages narrating the dancing body, a kinesthetic sensation comes over me, even though my eyes alone are moving from line to line. For example, in *Samba*, Barbara Browning brings the reader to the body in motion. An excerpt from Browning's description of the Brazilian orixa (Yoruba god) Oxossi dance ushers forth the feeling of movement quality: "When the right foot is stepping, the body is directed crosswise on a left diagonal, and vice versa. On the lifting beat just before the change in direction, the dancer often spins around full circle, to the back, such that her feet and the angle of her body are already in preparation for the next step" (Browning 1995: 62). Even though I am unfamiliar with this dance, the text provides a depth of kinesthetic information so that I can imagine the moving body, perhaps somewhat empathetically. Browning's theoretical offerings are only richer as a result, because the theory is embodied in the dances she describes. Dance scholars have found marvelously playful ways to push the boundaries of inscribing dance. Who can forget Julie Taylor's magical flipbook imagery in *Paper Tangos* (1998)? The moving body emerges in tiny photographs, her graphic tales of dancing in Buenos Aires, and passionate poetry.

Scholars of dance have chosen their themes, or conceptual frames, to stage dance in text. Sometimes the description of movement and embodiment of theory is not the primary concern. For example, in *Tango and the Political Economy of Passion*, Marta Savigliano ingeniously composed unusual text formats to narrate her multivoiced commentary on tango. Several sections are organized to resemble theatrical scripts, complete with stage directions. Dividing the page into two columns enables multiple voices to simultaneously speak to the reader. I found her text brilliantly creative, especially her challenge of paradigms for academic texts. However, with each page I turned I longed to read about the intimacies of moving bodies and the specificity of embodying tango. But this is not the point of her book. I am certain some readers will be frustrated at the conceptual frames that I have chosen to focus on—the embodiment of culture via sensual orientations and lived experiences of transmission, rather than historical or theoretical matters. Each writer, each dancer, is inclined to reveal the nature of dance from a particular perspective. My impulse is to contribute to dance scholarship by writing what I know, what I have embodied, inspired by ethnographic practices.

For me, theory unravels in moments of experience—in music, dance, and in fieldwork. In lived experience we find the essence of our humanity, of our varied cultures, and individual desires. I have been influenced by ethnographies that intimate the personal and transformative experiences of fieldwork (among them Shelemay 1991; Kisliuk 1998; Ness 1992; and Sklar 2001). I find that these works strategically expose the ethnographer, clarifying gaze and identity within lived moments. They also challenge ethnological discourse, including personal experience as a dialogical, and very real, part of the theoretical framework. They are bold works. For example, in *Seize the Dance!* Kisliuk even included her personal poetry, offering us her creative writing from the field to expose emotions and a broader sensibility of the BaAka people. Similarly, in *A Song of Longing* Shelemay revealed her more personal, emotional ethnographic journey. Shelemay wrote:

> I began working on *A Song of Longing* in 1986, at first planning to write a more accessible account of my controversial findings about the Falasha religious tradition. But almost as soon as I began to write, other issues began to surface. To speak honestly about my Falasha research, I realized, I had to explore the relationship between my personal and professional experience in the field and the manner in which the two were inseparable.
>
> From the start I struggled with the fact that I wanted to write a book that would not fit into an established literary or scholarly category. The problem had implications for both publication prospects and my career. (1991: xii)

Texts such as these encouraged me to experiment, writing about the moving body in an attempt to offer a way for the reader to vicariously "know with the body" through text and other media. Have you ever had the feeling of vicariously moving around in an author's shoes? When ethnography is written from a reflexive voice, this type of experience can arise. I do not believe that writing reflexively is always appropriate, but for my aim of conveying dance transmission as physically close to the reader as possible, I knew I needed to narrate *sensational knowledge*.

sensu—unfolding site

Nihon buyo dancers spend countless hours moving with fans. This personal object has inspired the organization of this book. Let me explain. Splayed across the floor, my field notes, letters, and sketches appeared fanlike and moved me to employ its familiar structure. The word for the common dance fan is *sensu*. These fans are an extension of dancers' bodies and essential to our expressive art. "Dancers live through *sensu*," I heard Iemoto say to a new student as she held out an open fan. Snapping it closed, she continued, "As the *samurai* has a sword, this [fan] is our weapon." *Sensu* spring to life in dancers' hands. Through daily practice we learn to manipulate *sensu* to tell stories. Amusingly, *sensu* is the word for dance fan and the loanword for "sense."[3] Though the character for *sensu* is written differently to convey the different meanings, the coincidental wordplay offers a meaningful metaphor for this book's structure and how embodying dance is a gradual unfolding process. Also, the aesthetic of folding, or wrapping, has been a thematic thread in Japanese culture (see Joy Hendry's book *Wrapping Culture: Politeness, Presentation and Power* [1995] for insights into real and metaphoric wrapping in Japanese culture).

Fans have been a part of Japanese dance history for over four hundred years. While fans vary in shape, size, and material, there is a standard *sensu* that dancers are most familiar with—constructed of paper, bamboo, and metal.[4] It is a simple object. Like two hands held together with fingers outspread, ten blond bamboo *hone* (bones) radiate from an intersection to expand nineteen folds of paper facets. The paper is glued to the bones and, on the outermost bones, secured with thread. A metal finding fastens the bones tightly at their point of crossing—the *kaname* (pivot point)—and lead weights are discreetly tucked within the outer bones for balance. Often the paper folds display beautiful designs, ranging from abstract shapes to intricate depictions of scenes. Like the individual sections of a Japanese screen or scroll, panels or sections of the fan's artistic design can be appreciated as complete units when the fan is partly closed or, with the entire fan unfolded, can be viewed from the larger context of the nineteen-panel composition. Similarly, small vignettes on individual leaves of this book can be appreciated as a peek into a very personal scene—but when these vignettes are viewed in the context of the full panorama, the composition reveals social dynamics of the group. My hope is that this ethnography unfolds much like *sensu*, with vignettes drawn from my personal lessons and fieldwork to unfurl intimate panels that contribute to my analysis and the larger picture of embodied cultural knowledge in the context of the Tachibana community.

reflecting bodies

Because *nihon buyo* has been a part of my life since childhood, it was a clear candidate for a case study on the transmission of cultural sensibilities. I decided to write this ethnography with a reflexive voice because my body physically experiences and informs my perspective on transmission, and ignoring this embodied voice would have been disingenuous. An author's voice always provides point of view. I believe each research project sits in a different location on the continuum of qualitative versus more objective research methodologies. Reflexivity will arise in varying degrees in our ethnographies, and I believe that each project calls for a unique approach, or methodology of reflexivity. If appropriate for the project, reflexive presentation, or display, of identity in ethnographic narrative can utilize the researcher's self, the complex process of comprehending the relationship of self to other, and the embodied knowledge of the participant-observer-researcher, as a resource within the research. But, as a practice, reflexive writing leaves us exposed and vulnerable. It can be difficult and often painful work. Each ethnographer has a different level of comfort with reflexive disclosure.

If we are able to reveal and monitor our vulnerabilities, the dynamics of power and control issues that play out in ethnographic practice can be incorporated as part of the work. In her book of essays *The Vulnerable Observer: Anthropology That Breaks Your Heart*, Ruth Behar reveals the diversity of vulnerabilities encountered by anthropologists and writes:

> Anthropology . . . is the most fascinating, bizarre, disturbing, and necessary form of witnessing left to us at the end of the twentieth century. As a mode of knowing that depends on the particular relationship formed by a particular anthropologist with a particular set of people in a particular time and place, anthropology has always been vexed about the question of vulnerability. (Behar 1996: 5)

In the ten pages following this quote Behar provides examples of vulnerable moments exposed by reflexivity, and then cautions, "Vulnerability doesn't mean that anything personal goes. The exposure of the self who is also a spectator has to take us somewhere we couldn't otherwise get to. It has to be essential to the argument, not a decorative flourish, not exposure for its own sake" (15). There have been many vulnerable moments for me during fieldwork and in the writing of this ethnography, revealing a deeply physical, personal process of embodiment. I feel exposed in these pages, yet desire to convey the transmission process from this embodied place of understanding. That said, I hope that my reflexive presence in this ethnography sheds light on embodied transmission practices (for more on reflexivity see Hahn 2006a).

While my embodied field site inspired this research, it would also position obstacles before me to contend with. Several dualities run through my life—I am biracial (Eurasian); a performer and researcher; a dancer and musician. These dualities have influenced my perspective and relationship to my work. Nearly all ethnographers face issues of negotiating multiple identities in the field and at home that heighten their cross-cultural understanding and in turn affect their work. While the dualities in my pursuits exist by choice, the physical nature of my biracial identity poses an inextricably embodied duality that inherently shapes how I comprehend the world and how the world sees me.

I am perceived contextually by others—an identity situated by how I sound, my attire, actions, the surroundings, or the performance style I practice. These issues have surfaced through my ethnographic experiences and growing up biracial.

embodying fields

My parents, both visual artists, took my sister and me to live in Tokyo for a year in 1964. My father, a German American born in Milwaukee, studied Asian art, and produces Asian-influenced art. My mother was a Japanese American *nisei* (second generation) whose parents immigrated from Hiroshima to work on a Maui sugarcane plantation. Living in Japan was far from my mother's own desire. In the United States she strove to fit into American culture, which was difficult during the war. As she said to my father when we traveled to Japan, "You brought me back to everything [Japanese] I spent most of my life escaping from." In Tokyo my mother was faced with the duality of looking Japanese but being Japanese American. My sister, Kimiko, and I were placed in a public school in Setagaya-ku. We both studied *nihon buyo* each week for that year.[5]

I have vivid memories of our Tokyo experience—interesting sights, foods, smells, sounds, friends, and family. I also recall people pointing at me and calling out in boisterous voices, *"gaijin!"* (foreigner, or outsider). Sometimes small children would wander over and try to touch me or stroke my brown hair.

Upon returning to New York my parents placed us in Japanese school on Saturdays at the New York Buddhist Academy in New York City, where we studied calligraphy, Japanese language, and dance. We lived in Pleasantville, a town sixty miles north of the city, and attended the public school there on the weekdays. In the sixties and seventies few people of color lived in Pleasantville. Kimiko and I were taunted with name-calling—"Jap," "Chink," "Nip," or "Ching Chang Chong," to name a few. Classes in school focused on Western history, literature, and sports and only occasionally ventured to the "exotic" East.

On Saturdays at Japanese school we were among Japanese and Japanese Americans who "looked" Japanese and who attended the Buddhist services on Sundays. Dance lessons were special weekly events. I felt a focused attention from my dance teacher Tachibana Sahomi, a sensibility so different from my public school week. It is difficult to nail down the exact essence of that sensibility—perhaps it was the way she sang the music while we danced, or how she would slightly adjust my fan position.

In hindsight I see that both communities were important to my well-being and understanding of my mixed-heritage identity. The survival tools I developed in my childhood included codeswitching abilities for smooth navigation between communities. Wearing tattered, embroidered, bell-bottom blue jeans and listening to rock and roll during the week contrasted with the *yukata* (cotton *kimono*) and *obi* (sash) I would wear while dancing to *nagauta* (music for *kabuki*-style dance) on Saturdays. However, these two sides of my life never intersected. The parsing of my week starkly juxtaposed my biracial halves. At that time I believe I appreciated this compartmentalization of my identity—the two halves were clear and separate.

I studied *nihon buyo* at the New York branch of the Tachibana School (at the New York Buddhist Academy). I met my teacher, Tachibana Sahomi, when I was nearly six. Each Saturday I danced by her side, imitating every gesture. I recall her saying—"When you're dancing you can be anyone." In context she meant that I needed to focus on embodying a particular character for the dance I was learning, but also hinted that dance could enable me to experience a variety of identities. Even within dance, abilities to switch between characters and styles were honed and honored. Shifting between identities was an activity I learned both in and outside the dance space.

My formal initiation into the Tachibana dance family in the late 1980s marked yet another level of symbolic duality. From the moment of my *natori* (stage title) ceremony, only my performance name—Tachibana Samie—would be known in the *nihon buyo* world. Acceptance into this dance family changed my life. However, because of the hierarchical (*iemoto*) guild system, it also excluded me from researching and studying at other dance schools. In discussing ethnography, Clifford notes the problems and advantages of studying one's own culture: "Insiders studying their own cultures offer new angles of vision and depths of understanding. Their accounts are empowered and restricted in unique ways" (Clifford 1986: 9). I found myself situated in an interesting, yet often frustrating, state of betweenness that offered multiple perspectives, advantages, and disadvantages.

I am an insider and outsider to Japanese culture and *nihon buyo* tradition—not "native" yet not a stranger. While this peripheral existence deeply influenced my ethnographic research, it also problematized the emic/etic research dichotomy. I found that, in order to convey embodiment in dance and the situated body in fieldwork, I would need to comprehend and voice my multiple "other" perspectives as scholar/dancer, musician/dancer and biracial woman (Motzafi-Haller 1997; Mendoza 2000). Yet the intimacy of my embodied field site often encumbered the research. When I wore the hat of dancer, the scholar's analysis interrupted the flow of movement. Conversely, as I analyzed dance transmission I was frustrated that my body "knew" a movement yet I could not articulate it in text. Much like investigating whether the light remains on when a refrigerator door is closed, stopping to examine my embodied data rudely disrupted the continuity of my realizations.[6]

I have seriously taken heed of Lila Abu-Lughod's reflections on ethnography, particularly since I am one of the "halfies" writing ethnography that she refers to, defining them as "people whose national or cultural identity is mixed by virtue of migration, overseas education, or parentage" (1991: 137). She notes the problematic nature of halfie and feminist ethnographic perspectives—"when they present the Other they are presenting themselves, they speak with a complex awareness of and investment in reception. Both halfie and feminist anthropologists are forced to confront squarely the politics and ethics of their representations. There are no easy solutions to their dilemmas" (142). Directly confronted by this predicament in writing, I realized that my challenge would be to actively disorient my very insider, outsider, and "different" perspective in order to articulate embodied, sensory knowledge. Abu-Lughod proposed strategies in which to purposely write "against culture," or disturb the problematic construct of anthropological discourse built on cultural difference—through creating "ethnographies of the particular." "By focusing closely on particular individuals and their changing relationships, one would necessarily subvert the most problematic connotations of culture: homogeneity, coherence, and timelessness" (154). The backbone of this ethnography reclines upon a "particular," personal, approach—in hopes of avoiding those generalizations that breed stereotypes. Moving forward from Abu-Lughod's strategies on writing against culture, I have purposely written some text to disorient readers. I juxtapose different kinds of texts and voices to playfully suggest new ways to perceive relationships, similar to the way that uncommon juxtapositions chaotically appear in our daily lives and challenge our understanding of associations.

The works of Cynthia Novack (1990) and Zoila Mendoza (2000) provided insights into balanced involvements in dance, music, research, and writing—inviting me to draw from my sensory knowledge to inform the writing and, in turn, allowing the writing to inform my body. I found that this stance blurred my notions of interior/exterior, insider/outsider, ethnographer/dancer dualities, yet drew together personal experience, fieldwork, and analysis. Because of this complex dialect of particular bodies, field sites, and identity, I have chosen to write this book from multiple voices—from a body that knows several worlds and appears in the text in different roles to convey how we learn and sensually orient our bodies/selves at Hatchobori.[7]

fanning stereotypes

The vignettes appearing in this book are meant to resemble scenes on paper fans, revealing private moments at Hatchobori drawn from my field notes, conversations, and dance experiences. I find that the detailed minutiae of dancers' daily lives are held fast to the *sensu* "bones" supporting the structure—the transmission of dance.

Nihon buyo repertory is filled with dances in which the fan must, in the mind's eye, continuously transform into various objects or scenery throughout a performance—a *sake* (rice wine) cup, a pine tree, or a leaf in the wind. Fans also impart intangible aspects of dance, such as emotions or atmosphere. The prop can playfully obscure, highlight, and reveal images of the dance narrative and, literally, the dancer's body—covering a smile, partitioning off faces in conversation, or framing an exposed neck. Metaphorically I employ this same unfurling of the context, dancers' movements, and bodies to show how we embody dance at Hatchobori. I simultaneously wish to reclaim the trope of the fan as a lure—to reappropriate the exotic mystique of the "fan dance" stereotype of the demure "Oriental lady" who entices the onlooker's gaze by revealing and concealing her body. Yes, the performing body commands attention with its presence, yet the fan trope I aim to present in practice reveals the tough, flexible reality of women practicing Japanese dance.

The recent flow of popular books on *geisha* (Yoshikawa Mako's *One Hundred and One Ways* and Arthur Golden's *Memoirs of a Geisha*, for example) has been astounding. Each text provokes discourse on the entire trend, particularly the depiction and exoticism of women performers. Feminist, Asian, and Asian American writers critiquing these books, as well as the fashions that they launched ("*geisha* glam," revealed by the popular use of chopstick hair ornaments and white makeup), have mourned the reinforcement of "exotic" and erotic stereotypes of Japanese women and have loudly questioned the authority of voice and character portrayed in text. *Geisha* stereotypes extend onto the big screen as well. Many Asian Americans and Asians living in America mobilize when films depicting Asians with Orientalist stereotypes debut. In an article titled "The Mystique of a Geisha Packaged, Available for Sale" in the October 21, 2005, issue of *The Pacific Citizen, The National Publication of the Japanese American Citizens League*, Lynda Lin writes, "Two months before the film version of 'Memoirs of a Geisha' is scheduled to open in theaters nationwide, studio executives and retailers are already making it possible to dress, look and even smell like a geisha" (Lin 2005: 1). Lin is referring to Sony Picture Entertainment's marketing deals with Fresh, Inc., for the product "Memoirs of a Geisha Eau de Parfum" and Banana Republic's "Memoirs of a Geisha" clothing line. Lin quotes John Tateishi, executive director of the Japanese American Citizens League: "What strikes me is a curiosity that the producers of these products seem to want to reflect admiration for Japanese culture and those things that exemplify its beauty and serenity . . . But in reality, what they've done is to bastardize those qualities by a kind of stereotyping that pretends to capture the essence of beauty in Japanese culture" (4).

Though this book is not solely about gender, one of my aims has been to reappropriate the fan, *kimono*, and hair ornaments to tell a very different story of Japanese performing women.[8]

arranging folds

My hope is that the text unfolds and enfolds an array of sensual elements—personal moments interspersed with analysis, orientations, and video documentation—displaying an expansion of embodiment grounded in the everyday experience of movement and sound. There are five chapters, fanning out as fingers. The first is here, in the opening of the outer ethnographic bone—"sensual orientations"—an introduction to the characters in the folds of stories to come. The second, "moving scenes," supplies a basic overview of early *nihon buyo* history and the social structures supporting transmission. "Unfolding essence," chapter 3, approaches the energetic qualities of dance, including Japanese concepts of the body/spirit and examples of aesthetics.

Chapter 4, "revealing lessons," occupies the largest amount of space and is itself composed of five sections, creating folds within folds. We begin at Hatchobori with an introduction to lessons, including a typical day and the modes of sensory transmission. Section two is focused on the primary mode of teaching—visual transmission. Next we move to tactile transmission in section three, and the impact of touch on learning. Oral/aural transmission is presented in section four, then section five turns to notation and video media as a means for transmission. In these five sections of chapter 4, I showcase the minutiae of everyday transmission at Hatchobori with case studies (and A/V examples) to offer concrete examples of how dancers come to embody *nihon buyo*. Individual dancers and lessons appear in this section, providing a rich source of information to experience and analyze the practice of dance.

I must stress that the segmenting of the senses into discrete units in this section is for my analytic purposes only—within actual lessons the senses are not disjointed from one another in such an orderly and separate fashion but are wholly interrelated. However, through this analytic dissection I hope to reveal the complexity of one subculture's multisensory transmission structure. Chapter 5, "transforming *sensu*," draws the disconnected senses together again. This chapter explores presence in performance as an embodied sensibility that is transmitted. I also present transformative experiences in fieldwork as a means for comprehending varying perspectives of "knowing," or situating, the body. In the outer bone of this book-as-fan I close as I began, with reflexive thoughts on my personal experiences studying *nihon buyo* and dancing fieldwork.

dis-Orient

It is through culture patterns, ordered clusters of significant symbols, that man makes sense of the events through which he lives. The study of culture, the accumulated totality of such patterns, is thus the study of

the machinery individuals and groups of individuals employ to orient
themselves in a world otherwise opaque. (Geertz 1973: 363)

The irony of "flattening" embodied experiences of dance and fieldwork by transliterating lived experiences into text inspired me to consider ways to sensually outfit readers through inciting interactivity. If
we were in the same room, talking about embodiment, dance transmission, and the ethnographic experience, I imagine the nature of our
discussion would be quite active—passionate even. In fact, it would be
much easier for me to show you a gesture, a video, or to sing a musical
passage than to write a text about the practice of this lively, sensuous
art and my ethnographic engagement. My aim is to playfully arouse
understanding through activity—in the text and the online companion—to pose a sensual *dis*-orientation through presenting another subculture's practice of sensual orientation.

The text and the online companion might seem experimental at
times. This is my attempt to see if there are ways within ethnography to convey the experiential, ineffable aspects of fieldwork by inciting interactivity. Throughout this book there are short sections
titled "orientation" that are meant to stimulate activity and provide
a "mindful," visceral quality to the text.[9] For example, at the close of
this section you will find the first "orientation." Here I invite active
involvement to directly raise questions considering the situated body
in performance and in text. Similarly, in "orientation—a virtual lesson" I encourage readers to take a lesson by following the video footage of headmaster Tachibana Yoshie teaching dance. Since the footage
was shot from a student's perspective (behind the teacher), this simu-
lated gaze attempts to capture the feeling of participating in a lesson at
Hatchobori. Although nothing compares to the lived experience of a
dance class and a fully embodied engagement of the senses in a new
experience, these orientations are meant to inform through practice,
and to perhaps trigger active associations for the reader.

I consciously employ the word *orientation* to reference sense and embodiment but, simultaneously, to strategically reappropriate "Orient."
My reappropriation is in the spirit of Henry Louis Gates, Jr.'s, play on
Standard English "Signification" (1988). For some readers the word *orientation* may create an association with *Orientations: The Magazine for
Collectors and Connoisseurs of Asian Art*. I hope to redirect any such association. If anything, this is another case of reappropriation, taking the
word from its art-collecting and connoisseurship realm to one of comprehending the situated body within culture. James Clifford, citing

Edward Said's *Orientalism* (1978), speaks to the power dynamic in the ethnographer's gaze: "This Orient, occulted and fragile, is brought lovingly to light, salvaged in the work of the outside scholar. The effect of domination in such spatial/temporal deployments . . . is that they confer on the other a discrete identity, while also providing the knowing observer with a standpoint from which to see without being seen, to read without interruption" (Clifford 1986: 12). The entire passage is interesting, as Clifford presents the Orient as a performance site:

> The Orient functions as a theater, a stage on which a performance is repeated, to be seen from a privileged standpoint. (Barthes [1977] locates a similar "perspective" in the emerging bourgeois esthetics of Diderot.) For Said, the Orient is "textualized"; its multiple divergent stories and existential predicaments are coherently woven as a body of signs susceptible of virtuoso reading. This Orient, occulted and fragile, is brought lovingly to light, salvaged in the work of the outside scholar. The effect of domination in such spatial/temporal deployments (not limited, of course, to Orientalism proper) is that they confer on the other a discrete identity, while also providing the knowing observer with a standpoint from which to see without being seen, to read without interruption. (1986: 12)

My ever-present voice and body throughout the text aims to expose Clifford's "to see without being seen" dynamic. Said has directed us to acknowledge the domination of the Orient by the West. I embody both geographies. In this text I deploy my biraciality as an embodied subversion of fixed East-West boundaries, distinctions of "other," and to give voice to a reorientation of artistic expression.

Stories about learning, dance, fieldwork, the body, and dance narratives are folded into the text to connect vital narratives as they are superimposed on the everyday experience at Hatchobori. The disorienting sensibility of this organization is intentional. In a way, orientation is gained through a process of "making sense" of disorienting experiences. This kind of structure poses mindful "groundlessness" in everyday experience that is revealed "in knowing how to negotiate our way through a world that is not fixed and pregiven but that is continually shaped by the types of actions in which we engage" (Varela, Thompson, and Rosch 1991: 144). I hope the juxtaposition of stories, voices, and senses encourages active orientation through disorientation, or the appearance of order within chaos.[10]

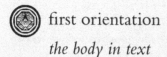 first orientation

the body in text

Imagine taking a drink of water from a glass *as* performance. I employ this engagement to locate a regularly repeated experience shared by readers to be utilized as a unit of observation. How can we convey the essence of movement, sound, and the lived experience of culture? How do we write the body into text?

Probably you raise the glass and drink "without thought"—without the need to consider or analyze each action methodologically. But if this ritual were a research project, those unconscious aspects held in your embodied knowledge would hopefully surface as your examination progressed and as you found empirical substance in the activity.

First, let's consider the unit of observation, or, define the edges of this ritual. In your eyes, when does the "performance" start and end? Does it begin when you enter the kitchen (if this is indeed where you perform "the act")? How often do you repeat this ritual? Is there a pragmatic aspect to this performance? When did you learn this behavior and from whom? What are other considerations? Finally, and my point behind this exercise, *how can you convey the enactment* of the ritual to an outsider of this tradition so that she can deeply comprehend it? If the outsider were standing next to you, wouldn't it be easier to take her to your special ritual area and show her? How about conveying the experience in text? Not as easy as demonstrating, right?

Imagine your water ritual as a deeply moving artistic "tradition" that you need to transmit through writing. How would you convey, not only the rudimentary steps of the ritual, but the context and embodied experience of the art? Consider the negotiations of turning on the faucet and filling the glass with water—how do you coordinate the movements? Can you describe *in detail* your grasp and coordination of the glass as you bring it to your mouth? Then, do your lips move in preparation as the glass approaches? Do your glands react in expectation? How do you draw the water into your mouth and then swallow? Can you describe the movement quality? How about the feeling of the glass in your hand and the water flowing into your mouth? Has the visual focus of the water now vanished, as the water travels to a hidden vessel? What takes over after vision? Is the water cold? Are there smells, tastes, or sounds assisting you to engineer this performance? How do you coordinate your breathing with this flow of water in your body? There are countless minutiae to detail this "simple" performance. As an insider to this ritual, which aspects do *you* believe are *essential* to impart, in order to convey the vital core of the tradition?

Nearly every task we engage in is multisensory. The next time you take part in the water ritual, notice how your observation of this act has transformed simply because you are thoughtfully considering it. Also, the (self-)conscious "thinking through" of the process might change your ritual precisely because you are aware of the observation process. Participation informs and makes conscious concepts of performance, and, should you write a detailed description of the process, most likely many unconscious aspects would arise. Participation also reinforces the practice of the enactment within the body, solidifying the memory and embodiment of the act.

If you were to compare your ritual experience with that of a friend, undoubtedly the experiences would differ, partly because you drink water differently, but also because each of you experience the grand event differently, notice particular characteristics, or make contrasting assumptions regarding what is necessary to convey the essence of the ritual. Each person's account depends on that person's perspective, and is informed by past experiences, by enculturated sensual orientations.

A clear and detailed description of even a simple experience is endless. My point here is that conveying lived experience is challenging, particularly if it is a performance practice you "know" in your body but do not regularly transmit to someone else—either through demonstration or through writing. This has been one of my fascinations in writing about dance transmission. Originally, when I set out to conduct research, I asked dancers how they learned, or how they knew a particular movement. They rarely responded with more than a handful of words, such as—"I follow" (in lessons), "I watch," "I listen," or, taking my hand, said, "let me show you." The truth is, *I* didn't know how I embodied the art, which is why I stubbornly embraced the topic. Since I had danced for thirty years prior to considering this question, I needed to take the stance of an ethnographer, collect "data," and traverse the analytical space between my embodied knowledge and collected field data to find the essence of the dance transmission.

Hopefully, this orientation reveals the challenges of ethnographic and artistic sensibilities. One of my concerns in the process of conducting fieldwork, analyzing the "data," and writing has been to understand the essential elements that I believed needed to be imparted to convey concepts of transmission and the embodiment of art. I have been fascinated by what sensory modes different people privilege in the transmission of their art or within their discipline of choice. Their/my sensual orientation influences the end product. Through fieldwork I came to understand that we inhabit very different worlds.

folded in

When I was ten Sahomi told me about Saho, her childhood teacher in Fukushima.
I did not realize at that time that I would later bear the name Samie—
a name built on "Sa" that would tie me forever with both women.
I would never meet Saho.
Years later, dancers would say my movements bore certain tendencies,
certain qualities of Saho, passed down through Sahomi.
I wondered about inscriptions—not messages written and handed down—
but inscriptions folded into the body through experience.
Artful moments, tucked into every leaf of the body, like bookmarks
placing experience and time.

two

moving scenes—history and social structure

While introducing Japanese dance to a workshop audience in New York City, Iemoto explained, *"Kabuki* gave birth to *nihon buyo"*—she took hold of her abdomen and gracefully swept her hands downward, in a rather humorous pantomime of giving birth. In this swift gesture she told the tale of history. Because this ethnography focuses on transmission (and historical and technical considerations such as costuming, props, and scenery are widely available), I will not detail the history of the genre but rather point out several key transitions in history that have influenced *nihon buyo* transmission. Current scholarship on a number of contemporary Japanese "traditions" claims that their histories have been re-created to suit the contemporary reinvention of tradition and ties to a sacred mythic past (Yamazaki 2001). Similarly, dancer/scholar Ananya Chatterjee has noted the retrospective creation of Odissi's history to attempt "to project a continuity of 'tradition' and establish a strict code of 'classicism'" (Chatterjee 2004: 144). *Nihon buyo* does not escape such reinventions; in fact, the nostalgia behind *nihon buyo*'s origins reveals a great deal about the contemporary practice.

Japanese dance originates in colorful mythologic times. The *Kojiki* (A.D. 714) and *Nihon Shoki* (A.D. 720), Japan's earliest known written documents, tell the famous tale of the Sun Goddess—Amaterasu-no-omikami. Insulted by the mischievous pranks of her brother Susanoo-no-omikoto (guardian of the underworld), Amaterasu hid herself within a cave. Darkness immediately fell upon the heavens. This greatly troubled the gods, and they summoned Ama-no-uzume-no-mikoto (a lesser goddess). Scantily dressed in only a few tree branches near the cave opening, Ama-no-uzume-no-mikoto performed a comical, erotic dance for the gods on an overturned tub. The gods' uproarious laughter soon aroused the Sun Goddess' curiosity. Amaterasu wondered what the commotion could be, peeked out, and instantly her brilliant rays spread out to the world. The gods had also placed a mirror at the mouth of the cave, and Amaterasu, seeing her own luminous beauty, was easily coaxed from hiding.

The history of Japanese dance through the ages metaphorically mirrors this myth of the Sun Goddess. Long periods of war starkly mark Japan's history. According to Nishikata Setsuko, after such dark, depressed periods of war, Japanese dance flourished (Nishikata 1988). There is a saying in Japanese, *odori agatte yorokobu* (to dance [jump] for joy)—expressing the human nature to dance and be exuberant during good times.

displaying time

Japanese traditional dance is often classified into four categories—*kabuki odori* (*kabuki* dance), *goshugimono* (or *su odori*, dance with spiritual roots stemming from religious ceremonies), *kamigata mai* (pieces from the *geisha* tradition, most often including a fan), and *sosaku buyo* (pieces outside the three categories above, such as newly created choreography). The study of *nihon buyo* must include an awareness of the variety of influential genres such as *bunraku*, *kabuki*, *noh*, and folk dance. However, historically the roots of this genre are most strongly tied to *kabuki* and *furyu* (popular dances). The "birth" of *nihon buyo* from *kabuki* that Iemoto referred to lies in their common origin history—the famous story of the renowned seventeenth-century priestess of the Izumo Shrine named Okuni. Despite the lack of specific accounts of Okuni's life, she continues to be hailed as the originator of *kabuki* dance.

After the *Sengoku jidai* (the "One Hundred Years War" in the late sixteenth century) the Japanese people, tired of fighting, needed entertainment to express their joys. In the bustling city of Kyoto, street performers set up makeshift shops and small stages along the Kamo River between Shijo and Gionsha avenues. Here a *miko* (temple priestess) from Izumo named Okuni created a stir with her style of *nembutsu odori* (Buddhist dances). Apparently these performances were far from religious and often tended toward wild and erotic themes. Okuni donned unusual costumes, carried a sword, and danced in a style foreign to the district. This drew crowds of onlookers, and her dance became widely known as *kabuki odori*. The word *kabuki* at this time meant "wild," "avant-garde," or "unusual" dance. In the late sixteenth century *kabuki* was an everyday word for things that were uncommon or that departed from the norm. Later in time the word *kabuki* was written with different *kanji* (Chinese characters adopted by the Japanese) breaking down to *ka* (song), *bu* (dance), and *ki* (skill).

The history of *kabuki* is traditionally broken down into periods. The early years are referred to as *onna kabuki* (women's *kabuki*). Apparently at this time the relationship between the theater and illicit activities (such as prostitution) was growing. There are numerous accounts of the questionable character of performers, who were treated as outcasts.[1] The popularity of *kabuki* dance grew rapidly, and performances soon spread to other metropolitan centers, such as Edo (Tokyo). The Tokugawa government was concerned with the developing trend, especially its associations with prostitution, and banned women from the *kabuki* stage in 1629. This closed the era of *onna kabuki*. Although women were forbidden from performing at this time, ironically the "birth" of dance is attributed to a female goddess and the origin of *kabuki* to a woman performer.

The style of *kabuki odori* that followed was called *wakashu kabuki*, or "youth" *kabuki* (also known as *yaro kabuki*). Young boys assumed the roles of women, and the audience became enamored of their portrayals. Perhaps too enamored. *Wakashu kabuki* also flourished but lasted only until 1652, when young boys were also prohibited from taking the stage. This time the government's reform attempted to halt homosexual prostitution. The government's seventeenth-century interventions in the practice of *kabuki* led to the establishment of an all-male theatrical genre and the development of the *onnagata* (female impersonator) tradition. In contemporary Japan, *kabuki* remains an all-male genre.

moving women

Despite the Tokugawa edict banning women from the stage, women had plenty of opportunities to continue to practice dance. The professional tradition of *geisha* performing dance and music never ceased. *Geisha* were not the only female performers, however, for women from the middle class also continued to study dance as part of basic etiquette training. The various "practice" or "rehearsal arts" (*okeikogoto*), from tea ceremony and flower arrangement to dance, were considered a means of developing a woman's social graces. In a society that placed great value on deportment, women's manners signaled rank and upbringing. In the mid–eighteenth century small neighborhood schools (*terakoya*) not only taught reading and writing but also dance and *shamisen* (a three-stringed lute) for etiquette. It was thought that if a woman's manners were proper, then her family could arrange for her to marry into an affluent family. Her chances of gaining employment, moreover, would be far greater with suitable etiquette training.

It was during the Edo period that the merchant class became overwhelmingly powerful. Wealthy merchants, wanting to elevate their social status, enrolled their daughters in dance and music lessons. Since private dance and music performances were often presented at the homes of *samurai*, these merchants hoped that a powerful official would employ their daughters.

According to Nishikata, dance schools for women were particularly popular during the mid–nineteenth century. She cites one publication, *Kamikuzu kago* (The Waste Paper Basket), that mentions the popularity of women dancers in the Nakamura and Iwada schools.[2] Nishikata also reveals that while the legitimate (all-male) *kabuki* performances continued on the "surface" (*omote*) to be publicly quite visible, lesser-publicized performances by women were also to be found within a "hidden side" (*ura*) of society. Furthermore, she states that, by the Meiji period, women performers greatly influenced the *kabuki* world from this seemingly weak position (Nishikata 1988). Although women or men do not exclusively practice Japanese dance, women currently dominate the *nihon buyo* dance world, and *nihon buyo* performances are not as widely publicized as *kabuki*.

The difficulty of defining and categorizing *nihon buyo* generally gives way to extraordinary lists of influential genres and their techniques. The various arts in Japan are not as segregated from one another as in the West. Distinctions between theater, dance, and music are often blurred, and practitioners frequently have strong backgrounds in several disciplines. In addition, specific performance genres have intertwined; they have influenced one another so greatly over time that it is difficult to unravel and differentiate one from the other. These genres, such as *noh, kyogen, kabuki, bunraku, minzoku geino* (folk or popular arts), and *nihon buyo*, have a complex historical relationship, in which they have borrowed stylistic features, movement vocabulary, musical styles, and story plots from one another. References can be as subtle as a gesture within a phrase, or as overt as the appropriation of full narratives. Quoting or referencing another genre reinforces stylistic borrowing between these genres, but further complicates the distinctions between them. For audience members and performers, however, this eclecticism is an exciting aspect of the performing arts.[3]

In general, the performing arts in Japan that include vocal lyrics are hinged on a narrative form. The centrality of storytelling is fundamental to understanding how these performance genres have deeply influenced each other through history. The vocal text is primary. Essential to all aspects of performance is the expression of the text, its nuances, puns, metaphors, and emotional content. It is at this narrative and thematic juncture that *nihon buyo* overlaps with other theatrical genres.

Early on, *kabuki* performances were in the form of rather short dances accompanied by *kouta* (or *hauta*) "short songs," performed in a folk- or teahouse-style structure. Eventually, particularly during the Edo period, thematic material and compositions were extended and became known as *nagauta* or "long songs." This latter vocal style was accompanied by *shamisen* (three-stringed lute), *taiko* (stick drum), *ko tsuzumi* (shoulder hand drum), *o tsuzumi* (side hand drum), and various types of flutes (such as *noh kan, takebue,* or *shinobue*).[4] The Edo period is also the era when narrative theatrical forms developed and solidified in Kyoto, Osaka, and Tokyo. During this period makeshift stages gave way to licensed theater buildings that became increasingly permanent structures. *Bunraku* (puppet theater) was flourishing, and the influences between genres mentioned above were constant.

Prior to the introduction of foreign dance styles in the twentieth century, there was little need for a generic term for Japanese dance. Rather, dance pieces were distinguished by the basic terms *mai* and *odori. Mai* refers to a refined, reserved, expressive style of dance with few jumps or quick (folklike) movements. On the other hand, *odori* refers to a lively style, displaying some leaps and quick, energetic movements. Although aspects of both *mai* and *odori* are exhibited in dance from Tokyo and the Kansai (Kyoto-Osaka) regions, *mai* is more closely associated with Kansai and *odori* with Tokyo. The differences in the two styles reflect the character of the two areas in Japan—Kyoto has long been considered the seat of the reserved, older cultural traditions, while Tokyo is associated with an up-to-date, modern, and lively style. In present-day Japan this continues to be the distinct nature of the two regions' aesthetic tastes.

The three dance elements of *nihon buyo* are considered to be *mai*, *odori*, and *furi* (the pantomime movements from *kabuki* dance). Combinations of each of these stylistic ingredients are what flavor particular genres and dances. Each genre may emphasize one of the three styles, but in general these are the basic elements that characterize Japanese dance. An important point is that, through *furi*, "the body can reveal its true inner self" (*katachi ni arawasu*).[5] Interweaving the qualities of pantomime (*furi*), *mai*, and *odori*, *nihon buyo* has inherited a wide palette of physical vocabularies to express the narrative. The subtleties are endless.

The history of stylistic borrowing between *kabuki*, *nihon buyo*, and other genres does not end in the Tokugawa period. Ever since the early twentieth century the influence of Western theatrical styles and dance, from ballroom dancing to ballet, modern dance, and folk dance, for example, has been a significant historical development. During the Meiji and Taisho eras a fascinating tension arose—a tension between Japan's rush to modernize, on the one hand, coupled with a desire to uphold "traditions," on the other hand, that prioritized particular aesthetic ideals and reinforced Japanese etiquette. Modernization, in the early 1900s, was equated with Westernization. Both Gunji (1970) and Yamazaki (2001) emphasize critic Tsubouchi Shoyo's great influence on *nihon buyo*, particularly as a visionary for constructing a national theatrical genre bridging modern and traditional ideals that would appeal to the general public at the time. Yamazaki claims that it was Tsubouchi who, in 1907, first used the term *nihon buyo* (Yamazaki 2001: 186–187).

Modernization and tradition did coexist, but as an interesting dance of selection and prioritization. The strict, hierarchical *iemoto* social structure provided for a highly selective transmission process for inclusion or exclusion of specific influences on dance within a particular school. This created myriad dance style nuances or an individual school taste with varying degrees of Western influences (Western is often synonymous with modern). A number of schools became well known for their spectacular modern styles. Western influences also created tensions among the dance community, as these new styles were seen as diluting the carefully transmitted Japanese dance tradition. Today there remains a wide variety of dance styles associated with different schools. Some have continued to perform the traditional repertories in addition to creating new works that reflect contemporary society. The Tachibana School teaches traditional and contemporary choreography; however, the dance vocabulary of the contemporary pieces remains within "traditional" *nihon buyo* vocabulary and consciously does not include Western dance vocabulary.

unfolding houses

A look at the historical roots of dance schools reveals that many stem directly from *kabuki* lineage, or have some close contacts with *kabuki* families. From the early eighteenth century actors and choreographers of the *kabuki* stage established schools of dance. Soon dancers from these schools established their own groups, branching out further from the *kabuki* stage. The Tachibana School descended from the *kabuki* tradition in this manner, and in this section I use the story of this school as a case study in dance history.

The founder of the Tachibana School, Tachibana Hoshu, was born in the Nihonbashi District of Tokyo in 1894. As the pupil of the famous actor Ichimura Utaemon (the fifteenth-generation headmaster of the Ichimura *kabuki* family) he took the name of Bando Utazo. He also studied with the sixth-generation headmaster of the Fujima *kabuki* dance family, Fujima Kanjiro, and attained the title Fujima Kansuke. He actively acted, danced, and choreographed for *kabuki* performances. With actor Nakamura Genzaimon he established the "Sakura kai" (cherry blossom performance group) at the Zenshinza theater company, performing its newly created style of *kabuki*.

Tachibana Hoshu established the Tachibana School in 1938, naming it after Tachibana Sakon, an expert in *komai* (short dances) in the Horeki era (mid–eighteenth century). Tachibana Hoshu's skill as a choreographer was recognized as one of his strengths, drawing performers from other schools. To this day the Tachibana School is known for welcoming students from different schools (Mizuki and Azumaji students regularly take lessons at Hatchobori, for example).

Tachibana Hiroyo was born in Tokyo's Fukugawa District in 1916. In her teens she joined a women's singing and dancing group, the Shochiku shojo kageki dan, led by Fujima Kansuke (Tachibana Hoshu). She also performed with the famous actor Enomoto Kenichi's Ichiza dance group. At nineteen Hiroyo became choreographic assistant to Tachibana Hoshu for the Shochiku women's group and began choreographing for other dance groups as well.

In 1939, one year after the Tachibana group was founded, Tachibana Hoshu and Hiroyo married. The dance studio was located in Asakusa, a lively district in Tokyo that was the center for performing arts at the time. Both husband and wife taught students and continued to choreograph. They had two daughters, Akiko and Yoshie. In 1946 the Tachibana School (and residence) relocated to Hatchobori in the Chuo District. The school expanded and grew as *nihon buyo* became more and more popular with the general public. In 1962 the headmaster position was passed to Hiroyo because of Hoshu's failing health, and one year later he passed away.

Tachibana Hoshu and Hiroyo's younger child, Yoshie (b. 1941), grew up among artists and performers. She studied dance with her parents from the age of five. During a conversation I had with Tachibana Yoshie she reminisced about her early years growing up in Asakusa: "*Geisha* would hold me in their arms and talk to me while they bounced me up and down on their knee . . . those kinds of experiences helped me to know the inner qualities of these women and a part of that lifestyle. I really like *geisha* and I go to visit them, to watch and learn" (Hahn field notes, November 30, 1993). In fact, *geisha* are among the students that study at the Tachibana School. Since she was brought up by dancers, Yoshie's everyday experiences fed the expression of her personal style of dance—what critics call "Yoshie's world." In 1979 the headmaster position was transferred to Tachibana Yoshie.

As mentioned earlier, the regional character associated with a school's dance style strongly colors that school's personality. The three generations of Tachibana headmasters were born in downtown Tokyo, or *shitamachi*. This area of the city was particularly famous during the Edo period as the heart of its artistic, creative community. Visitors to the city were attracted to the colorful area, where vendors and performers entertained customers on the streets. The character of the metropolis, including fashions, styles, etiquette, and behavior, became strongly associated with the downtown area. It is this Edo character that the Tachibana School maintains as the inspiration for its dance style, one that is both lively and reserved. This is reflected in distinct dance movements that are often quickly executed, then held in a posed position, and in rhythmic diversity. There is an elegance to the school's style, yet the choreography also reflects the lively character of the city life.

The Tachibana repertory primarily consists of *kabuki* dances, *suodori* (dances performed in a plain-style *kimono* rather than full *kabuki* attire and props), and *shinsaku buyo* (newly created choreography). Both Soke and Iemoto continue to choreograph new works. Iemoto has included contemporary as well as experimental performances in her current endeavors, such as sports-event programs, choreography and

performance for television, opera, and musical productions. Collabora-
tions with a wide variety of artists from contrasting disciplines (theater,
music, modern dance, and folk dance, for example) provide her with
a vehicle to express the inner heart of contemporary Japanese people
through movement.

Organizations for the arts, such as the Nihon Buyo Association,
are very powerful in Japan. This membership solidifies a school's position within the larger dance community and provides a degree of
status. The Nihon Buyo Association presents forums for dance performances and lectures that inherently shape relationships between
various schools. Soke and Iemoto have been active for many years as
advisers for the Nihon Buyo Association. Soke has been the district
head for the Chuo District of the association. Both Soke and Iemoto's
strong interest in traditional arts, including performance, fine arts, and
folk arts, is reflected by their long-term involvement on committees to
promote the traditional arts.

Nihon buyo is one of the many traditional *okeikogoto*, or "practice
arts," that provide physical training for amateurs in addition to professional practitioners. Other *okeikogoto* include tea ceremony, flower arrangement, archery, *koto* (a thirteen-string zither), and *noh*. In addition,
there are a wide variety of modern practice arts that have been added
to this category, such as piano, tango, and ballet. The majority of dancers who study with Iemoto are *nihon buyo* teachers and advanced students. On occasion intermediate and beginning students who have
studied with their local branch teacher travel to Hatchobori to experience lessons with Soke and Iemoto.

The stereotype of *nihon buyo* held by Japanese who are not practitioners is that it is an art of the elite (housewives) who pay enormous
sums of money to study and perform. To a degree this is changing, as
the concern for the preservation of traditional performing arts is growing among Japanese artisans. In the public schools Western music and
dance are regularly taught, while the traditional arts are given only a
brief introduction at best. Also, there is great pressure on young people
to advance in business, science, and technology. Iemoto, reflecting on
this modern-day dilemma, said, "Life changes quickly. Today young
people in Japan have no connection to the [older] Japanese traditions
. . . they know *coffee!* not the way of tea, *kendo*, how to put on a *kimono*,
wear their hair up, how to put on traditional makeup. Through dance
we learn about many of these things" (Hahn field notes, October 9,
1993). I found that dancers come from diverse backgrounds, including college students, teachers, aerobics instructors, *geisha*, housewives,

and actresses. Conversations between classes can be fascinating, as these backgrounds intersect in casual chats on anything from the taste of seaweed from a particular region to health, television shows, and of course dance.

The main Tachibana School (now "Hatchobori") remains in Tokyo but is located in the Chuo District. Branches in Japan located outside Tokyo include Fukushima, Akita, Tohoku, and Shikoku. There are also schools in Australia and the United States (in New York City and Portland, Oregon). The New York branch was established by my childhood teacher, Tachibana Sahomi, in 1966. Sahomi, a *nisei*, was born in California. Her parents were amateur *kabuki* actors who encouraged her to study the traditional arts, particularly *shamisen* and *nihon buyo*. In the 1930s young Sahomi was sent to live with her grandparents in Fukushima. Here she studied with Tachibana Saho and received her *natori* (attainment of a professional stage name). During this time the tension of war threatened non-Japanese residing in Japan. Sahomi was put on one of the last ships returning to the United States to join her family in California. In 1945 she was interned with her family at the Topaz Relocation Center in Utah for three years. During internment, Sahomi taught and put on performances in the camp with other Japanese and Japanese Americans, using makeshift stages, props, and costumes. After the war, Sahomi traveled to New York. Here she actively performed Japanese dance and studied a wide variety of dance styles. From 1966 to 1990 Sahomi led the school and dance group at the New York Buddhist Academy on the Upper West Side of Manhattan. In 1990 she moved to Portland, Oregon, and began a new branch of the Tachibana School. The New York Tachibana School now continues under Japanese American teachers Tachibana Sahotoyo and Sahotae. The focus of this ethnography is on transmission at Hatchobori, so I have not included examples from the Japanese American context. See the book by Barbara Sellers-Young, *Teaching Personality with Gracefulness: The Transmission of Japanese Cultural Values through Japanese Dance Theater* (1993), for an interesting account of *nihon buyo* transplanted and taught in Oregon.

structuring fans

A social structure referred to as the *iemoto* "headmaster" system governs many of the traditional arts in Japan, in which the headmaster has formative control of the definitive transmission of the genre. This hierarchical structure both preserves and regulates the transmission of the art form within a school of practice. Strikingly, the *iemoto* system is prevalent throughout such diverse practices as tea ceremony, *nihon buyo*, musical genres, *noh*, horsemanship, flower arrangement, and martial arts. For a culture that values the continuity of its traditions, the *iemoto* structure provides a strict and reliable system to cautiously regulate the definitive practice of a tradition. Discipline is vital on several levels—on a microscopic level for the transmission of individual dance steps, choreography, costuming, music, and so forth; on a middle level for the negotiation of hierarchical designations of students and teachers within the school; and for the large-scale organization of a tradition's continuity to future generations. The very existence and preservation of a school's artistic tradition relies on such systems of transmission.

An examination of the etymological elements of the two *kanji* characters for *iemoto* yields insight into concepts embedded within the *iemoto* system. The word *iemoto* breaks down to *ie* (house, family, household) and *moto* (foundation, origin, beginning).[6] *Iemoto* is both the name of the person who holds the "headmaster" title and the name of the pedagogical system. Only one *iemoto* leads a particular school at one time. The position is traditionally passed down through inheritance. However, when there is no successor, a top student is usually chosen and even legally adopted into the family to continue the artistic lineage.

The *iemoto* system is one of the many family social systems in Japan related by the concept of a household system (*ie*, which is the first *kanji* character with the term *iemoto*). Social anthropologist Nakane Chie points out the importance of the *ie* concept in Japan:

> The essence of this firmly rooted, latent group consciousness in Japanese society is expressed in the tradition and ubiquitous concept of 'ie,' the household, a concept which penetrates every nook and cranny of Japanese society . . . In this ideological approach the 'ie' is regarded as being linked particularly with feudal moral precepts; its use as a fundamental unit of social structure has not been fully explored. (Nakane 1970: 4)

The efficient *iemoto* social structure was established in the Tokugawa period (1615–1868), when highly organized Chinese social systems were influencing Japanese society. During this period formal systems for organizing institutions, as well as strict social ethics based on Chinese Confucian teachings of loyalty, were impressed by the *bakufu* (shogunate) on Japanese society. This Tokugawa regime was a strong militaristic, feudal, patrilineal society in which hierarchical structures provided a systematic form to support such loyalty. Within the context of government, effective and loyal transmission was essential, including the transmission of war strategies, plans for organizing society, and commerce for basic living necessities. The powerful *bakufu* government shaped the principles of virtually every facet of Japanese life—bonds of duty and obligation between a *samurai* (warrior) and his master, man and woman, husband and wife, parents and children, teacher and disciple. To this day the *iemoto* system relies on members' tenets of loyalty, obligation, and respect. Social bonds between members are the living thread of a tradition's prosperity, transmission, and continuity to future generations. Because artistic traditions are transmitted through lineages of artists primarily via oral transmission, qualified practitioners are highly esteemed as culture bearers within Japanese society.

The direction of transmission flow is clear within an *iemoto* system. The headmaster delegates all that concerns the school. This involves training teachers, distributing teaching licenses and *natori* (professional stage names), determining the repertory, the current artistic style of the school (for *nihon buyo*, the choreography), the authoritative interpretations of pieces, overseeing public performances, and selecting the school attire and other signifiers (such as *kimono*, fans, and crests). As the headmaster of the school, the *iemoto* is revered as the definitive expert of the tradition. Transmission, in the most general sense, is logistically controlled single-handedly by the *iemoto*. The organizational structure of the *iemoto* system may appear unbearably confining to non-Japanese; however, I hope to reveal the variety of realities in life within this family system.

In 1979 our *iemoto*, Tachibana Hiroyo, passed the headmaster position to her daughter, Tachibana Yoshie. Tachibana Hiroyo is now referred to as Soke, or "previous headmaster." This is an interesting shift of positions. Here the dynamics of mother–daughter and *soke–iemoto* are inextricably linked. Although Iemoto is effectively the headmaster of the school, Soke's presence is a manifestation of Tachibana continuity. At the time of my fieldwork Soke continued to teach and be quite involved in everyday activities at Hatchobori. Soke's interpretations of the repertory have been highly respected, and I noticed that Iemoto consulted her from time to time for various dance considerations, from choreography to costume and spiritual matters. *Nihon buyo* is not a static form, however—subtle choreographic changes do occur between generation and generation, preventing stagnant artistic expression. With Soke attending lessons, dancers had an opportunity to compare the two masters' personal styles and dance spirits. It has been interesting to observe and experience the interpretations of a dance taught by Soke and to review this same dance years later with Iemoto's interpretations. The high respect of Soke's senior position is further illustrated in seating arrangement, program booklet order, and other representations of ranking. Soke is always presented first, then Iemoto, then senior teachers, *natori* students, and non-*natori* students.

The level below Soke and Iemoto at the Tachibana School includes board members/supervisors (*kanji*), directors (*riji*), and licensed teachers (*shihan*), who in turn train the various levels of students. The creation of a Tachibana board (to handle the treasury and various organizational duties and decision making) is a bit more democratic in structure than a traditional *iemoto* structure, altering the strict hierarchy dominated by a single headmaster.

The subtler ranking of teachers basically falls into levels of seniority and ability. The *iemoto* system thus provides an arrangement of interpersonal mentoring relationships centered on the transmission of a specific art. In this sense, the similarity of the group's social structure resembles that of a family unit, with ties of common interest (rather than strictly blood relations).

The sense of family is clearly embodied in the tradition of bestowing the family name, or *natori*, on qualified students. A *natori* is an artistic (stage) name presented to a student who has passed the school's qualifying examination. After initiation, the student enters the artistic family unit, receiving the surname and a newly created first name. This personal name is generally comprised of the *kanji* character(s) (or sounds of the characters) of the current *iemoto*'s first name and/or the student's teacher's name, as well as a personal *kanji* character for the particular student, reflecting a quality that the student embodies. When selecting a name for a student, teachers consider the student's history, personality, and talents.

As an example, my own *natori* name is Tachibana Samie. The *Sa* character derives from my childhood teacher's name, Sahomi; the *mi* is the sound of my mother's name, Miyako; and the *e* is from my Iemoto's first name, "Yoshie." Saho taught Sahomi, who in turn taught Sahotoyo and Sahotae and myself. Many names are composites of Soke's first name, Hiroyo, such as Michiyo and Yoshihiro. This latter name also derives from Iemoto's name, "Yoshie," as do the students' names

Yoshiaki and Mie. These examples illustrate how students of the same teacher(s) often share common *kanji* characters and similar-sounding names, uniting them in a familial manner. The names themselves link together, embodying the lineage of the school. The *natori* naming process marks dancers' entrance into the artistic family unit. Once given the *natori*, one's original (biological family) name is never used within the school. Often dancers know only each other's *natori* name.

A ritual of family lineage was enacted each time I met a Tachibana dancer at Hatchobori. I recall being introduced to Sato. We smiled at each other knowingly. Although we had never met before, the similarities of our two names—Sato and Samie—was no coincidence. We suspected that we, or our teachers, had shared a common teacher. Confirming this, Sato nodded at me and said, "Sa-to. *Sa* like Samie," as she gracefully traced our identical "sa" *kanji* character on her palm with her finger. This type of endearing intimacy was not unusual. I recall kneeling in the dressing room at Hatchobori in 1993, folding my *yukata*, when Mie sat close and introduced herself: "My name is Mie, the 'mi' of Samie and Yoshie's 'e.' We share two *kanji*." These everyday rituals of lineage, packed with powerful emotions of bonding, further reinforced our embodied traditions.

Sharing the story of one's name in such a manner illustrates the Tachibana lineage and sisterhood/brotherhood embodied within the naming process—having Yoshie's "e" symbolizes that one has received a part of Iemoto's name and spirit. Relating the similarity between names when meeting for the first time breaks down barriers, instantly identifying one another as relations within the family. Each time this greeting and unfolding of names occurred, the extended Tachibana network became clearer to me, as well as the feeling of kindred bonding.

Several symbolic markers of a student's new life as a Tachibana arise during the *natori shiki* (name-taking ceremony). The student receives a document declaring his/her new name, and the Tachibana family *mon* (crest) from Iemoto and Soke (see figure 1). Family crests appear on items such as documents, formal school *kimono,* and fans. At the ceremony a *sake* cup is passed between Soke, Iemoto, and the student in a

FIGURE 1. Tachibana *mon* (crest), based on a citrus fruit design.

fashion similar to the passing of cups in a wedding ceremony (the cup, shaped like a wedding *sake* cup, is later given to the student). The ritual symbolically unites these new "family" members and marks the student's initiation into the artistic family.[7]

Accreditation rituals within various *iemoto* systems symbolize the agreement of mutual obligation between master and student. Hsu explains this "return value relationship" (*taika kankei*):

> (a) The master will give his disciple professional protection and advertise him professionally. (b) The disciple must fulfill his duty of faithful service to his master. This is a highly personal relationship. He can not change masters. (Hsu 1975: 64)

Paramount to all the relationships within the group is the commitment to the *iemoto*, school, transmission, and art. As Hsu writes above, one never changes masters. Because practitioners embody a teacher's "house" of dance, correct transmission is vital. Fundamentally, transmission depends on mutual commitment. Because dance is learned primarily via oral and physical instruction, students must rely on the teacher for new dances, clarity of the form, and general direction.[8] On the other hand, the teacher transmitting the dance extends the art to other locations and into the distant future, beyond his/her lifetime. In order to keep the school's tradition alive, a teacher's major commitment is the transmission of the art.

The structure of the *iemoto* system effectively provides each member with a clear concept of his/her place within the family. In general, all members of a group dedicate themselves to the *iemoto*, school, and transmission of the art. This dedication predominates over all else, such as personal matters and individual needs, or taste. Members subordinate and discipline themselves for the solidarity of the group. This can present conflicts for those members with spouses and children, pressuring members to prioritize time, engagements, and affiliations. Within the group, the structure of the *iemoto* system presents clarity of roles for each individual member. In many ways the group provides a known system for interaction that can be a comforting aspect of belonging to such a group. Hsu expresses this relationship further:

> . . . the iemoto, large or small, is not merely an organization. It represents a way of life, a structure in which Japanese men and women see themselves and the world around them organized, a key to problem

PHOTO 1. Talking about dance. Tachibana Yoshie and author. PHOTO: WALTER HAHN

solution, and a map for dealing with internal dissension and external pressures. The iemoto tells us something about how the Japanese relate to each other and to the non-Japanese world at large. (Hsu 1975: x)

The master-disciple teaching system inherently transmits the deep value of experience and respect for elders. In Japanese traditional performance circles (unlike Western dance genres, such as ballet or modern dance), dancers continue dancing to advanced ages. A performer is considered to be at his/her prime from the age of thirty and, basically, continues dancing until he/she passes away or can no longer move. It is believed that, while youthful beauty can capture an audience even without refined technique, a mature dancer has experienced and embodied more of life and this essence can be imbued in her dance.

Respect for elders can be seen throughout Japan in many forms. Within the Tachibana School the seniority and mentoring structure within the *iemoto* system reinforces this reverence. Daily I witnessed great affection between young and old. For example, younger dancers gladly (and quickly) moved from comfortable sitting areas when an elder member entered the room. Younger dancers look to their elders with intent admiration and sit respectfully in a humble posture while they speak. Elders convey aspects of lived time that younger generations respect and, through shared lessons, can learn about—a time prior to their birth. Further, all dancers can observe a wide age range of students throughout the day, encompassing generations of Tachibana family members. The *iemoto* system, then, becomes a way of life, a way of relating to one another and sharing *nihon buyo*.

From a very young age dancers learn to take care of their fans. I recall stepping over a sensu when I was a child and being immediately instructed to walk around it, never over it. This is a taboo related to cleanliness and etiquette in Japan—particularly a concern regarding contact with the feet (or objects that have touched the feet), considered to be an unclean area of the body. We are taught that fans are to be respected and looked after as we would our own bodies. Both fans and bodies are considered tools of our art.

Every few years the Tachibana School issues a new school fan. These sensu are used for lessons, and naturally become ragged with use. I still keep sensu I practiced with over the years, though many are hopelessly tattered and unfit for use. On some fans the paper, long faded to pale tints, is barely attached to the bones. I periodically notice these older fans lined up in rows, tucked away on a shelf; each one stores a host of memories—particular teachers, lessons, and dances. There is the red and white one I dropped countless times while I practiced flipping it in the air. Bones split and weathered, it is over thirty years old. That sensu endured weekly torture, but, like a soldier, saved future fans from similar inflictions. In gentler times it portrayed cherry blossom petals falling, or undulating waves. I clearly recall my teacher Tachibana Sahomi clasping my hand and fan in hers to impart the energy of flowing water.

The bamboo bones on some of my sensu soldiers seem to take on a subtle luster at the base where they were held, which I imagine comes from the oils and sweat on my hands seeped in over time. I think back to my lesson with Iemoto when she showed me the dance floor marks at Hatchobori—how the places and objects around us often embody the history of our dance. A part of me permeated the sensu bones, while learning to tell stories through them. We practice manipulating fans as extensions of our bodies in dance; at the same time they also come to resemble us individually.

three

unfolding essence—energetic sensibilities and aesthetics

During a visit to New York City in 2005 Iemoto explained to several beginner students why a fan is placed at arm's length on the floor when bowing to a teacher. She said something to the effect, "It is a kind of metaphor. The fan creates a line between the student and teacher, and draws attention to that space. The line symbolizes the spiritual boundary (*kekkai*) located between the two individuals, honored as a kind of devotional space. When you are bowing you are demarcating and acknowledging the distinction between your teacher and yourself, but your bow respectfully honors both of you." In the following days a fellow dancer and I corresponded via e-mail about this lesson, and she pointed out the importance of Iemoto's use of the word *kekkai*, a word with spiritual overtones that carries the meaning of boundary or barrier.

Nihon buyo lessons often seem spiritual in nature, extending beyond the rudiments of dance steps or music. It is not uncommon for Soke and Iemoto to speak about learning dance as a process for understanding self and spirit. They often stress the value of learning through the body and speak of *kokoro* (literally—heart, soul, spirit), an expressive essence projecting from one's inner self within the body. After a lesson one fall day Iemoto spoke informally to me about learning dance and *kokoro*:

IEMOTO: Dance should be here [she put her hand to her breast]. First comes the body. The most important thing is *kokoro* . . . without this there is nothing. When I teach students they think it's strict sometimes and they cry and cry. But this [correction] must happen for change to take place. You will really remember clearly, fully, if I make corrections—and then the dance will be performed in the proper manner, not just any way of dancing.

TH: [*nodding*] Yes, I have cried here too . . . seeing other dancers and wanting to learn to dance like them, I cried in frustration because I can not do it yet.

IEMOTO: [*nodding*] I understand.

TH: But this makes me practice harder, although I am tense . . .

IEMOTO: The head [mind] and body are imbalanced sometimes . . . [she held her cupped hands up as if holding a large ball before her— one hand, palm down, at her brow and the other, palm up, at her breast] . . . but after practicing for a time you will feel more and more balanced [as she said this, her hands gradually came together until they gently touched]. The best is to be equally balanced—then you can dance from *kokoro* . . . without experiencing life, without personality, you have no dance, no *kokoro*, and you are invisible. But if you have a sense of self, then you can become any character on-stage—a woman, a young boy, an old man.

Iemoto's words and actions revealed the "mindful" practice of dance and its ability to enable personal growth through a disciplining of the body. Her words and gestures unfolded concepts regarding the transcendence of the physical through dance to enact something beyond the limits of the individual self—a transformation of the body for artistic expression. This transformation resides beyond a fundamental recall of individual dance steps and artistic techniques (*kata*) to become the essence of *kokoro* in the art, perhaps similar to what Dorinne Kondo found in her research on tea ceremony: "it is by becoming one with the rules that the possibility of transcendence lies" (Kondo 1985: 302). Iemoto's words unmistakably stated the value of correct practice—"You will really remember clearly, fully, if I make corrections—and then the dance will be performed in the proper manner"—and that "not just any [arbitrary] way of dancing will balance the body/mind." My interpretation of Iemoto's words is that artistic discipline fosters a flow of *kokoro*, or the ability for one's inner physical/spiritual energy to flow freely in creative expression.[1]

In most cases, traditional artistic training is prescribed—from individual steps to choreography, or the process of transmission. These prescribed artistic techniques (*kata*) are an important part of a performer's technical, expressive vocabulary. Although one school may have a system for teaching that is very different from the system of another school, cultivation and training is taken seriously as a significant process of developing character and spiritual strength (*seishin*). It is believed that the body's actual form and actions embody the inner nature (or spirit) of the person. Consequently, the transmission process is crucial because training the body to conform to set patterns (*kata*) "shapes," develops, or "cultivates" the character of individuals as well as that of the school.

Concerning the idea of artistic training and the body's form, Yuasa Yasuo proposes that "the theory of artistry derives from cultivation theory, the idea that one's bodily form directly expresses the mind." In his chapter "Theories of Artistry," Yuasa posits that artistic cultivation practices stem from Zen meditation:

> In Zen cultivation, whether one is engaged in seated meditation or in everyday chores, one is instructed to assume a certain "form" (katachi) or posture for meditation, eating, worship, or working in compliance with the monastic regulations. At any rate, Zen corrects the mode of one's mind by putting one's body into the correct postures. (Yuasa 1987: 105)

It is believed that regular practice of prescribed dance poses and movements reinforces artistic skills in the habitual body, and as movements become embodied, an experience of freedom and realization may occur. From a highly disciplined and structured pedagogical foundation it is thought that the skills of an artist can flow "naturally" or effortlessly from the well-trained body. This fundamental concept of training can be found in artistic practices throughout Japanese history, from theater to calligraphy to woodworking (see Coaldrake 1990). Perhaps the most well-known treatises on training in Japanese performing arts are the writings of Zeami (the professional name of Kanze Saburo Motokiyo, 1363–1443). His texts offer an abundance of information on *noh* and its transmission during the early fifteenth century:

> A real master is one who imitates his teacher well, shows discernment, assimilates his art, absorbs his art into his mind and his body, and so arrives at a level of Perfect Fluency through a mastery of his art. A performance by such an actor will show real life. (Rimer and Yamazaki 1984: 66)

Though centuries apart, there is a strong similarity between Zeami's statement and what Iemoto conveyed to me in our conversation. Both reveal that the spirit (or life) of art can exist only through disciplined practice of the mind/body with a teacher. Also, both connect the "balance" of mind/body and "fluency" of artistic practice.

Learning dance is a lifelong endeavor of embodying the tradition— a concept of practice that is strongly rooted in the *iemoto* social structure as well as Buddhist approaches to practice. I hesitate to place too much emphasis on Buddhism and Japanese philosophy as the foundation of transmission processes. *Nihon buyo* itself is certainly not explicitly a religious practice. However, the roots of nearly every traditional art in Japan are in some way indebted to the overwhelming influence of Buddhism during its formative eras. Japanese philosophers themselves directly draw a deep correspondence between the traditional arts and Buddhism (see Yuasa 1987, chapter 5).

Because *nihon buyo* repertory often depicts life in Japan, Buddhist overtones in pieces range from strongly thematic to subtle metaphors. Some dances, such as *goshugimono* (a formal, congratulatory dance genre), are derived from religious ceremonies and embody spiritual practices.

The pedagogical practices of many Japanese traditional arts, coming from a society where the disciplined irrationality of Zen Buddhism formed the dominant religion, incorporate a reverence for what is inexpressible through words. Learning through practice is vital. Transmission processes place value on the experiential and the heightening of awareness. Through repetition and practice it is believed that one may experience a different level of understanding. In this manner the body itself is seen to locate the deeper meaning of the practice, the transmission process, one's relationship to the practice, and the form itself. Because of this basic pragmatic approach to life as process and practice, it is easy to comprehend why such a straightforward approach to life and practice could pervade Japanese sensibility.

Buddhism, particularly Zen philosophy, stresses the value of direct transmission (teaching without words) that manifests itself through the active body. A moment's thought and further intellectualization are seen to interrupt the direct process, creating (unnecessary) mediation and a loss of clear transmission. Countless stories within the literature reflect this emphasis, such as Takashina Rosen's "Sermon without Words":

There is an ancient saying: "Better an inch of practice than a foot of preaching." It refers to the sermon preached by the body itself, through action and without speaking.

The sermon of words and phrases is the finger pointing to the moon, the fist knocking at the door. The object is to see the moon not the finger, to get the door open and not the knocking itself; so far as these things do achieve their objects they are well. (Takashina 1988: 177)

Another saying, "To know for himself what is cold to be cold, what is hot to be hot," is explained by Yuasa Yasuo: "[This] is a common Zen expression meaning that cultivation can be understood only by personally experiencing with the whole mind-body; it cannot be grasped by the intellectual understanding of books" (Yuasa 1987: 103). This last statement echoes what some dancers have questioned about my research, including such comments as, "Why are you studying *how* to learn? Just dance." For me, the idea of knowing the essence of cold or hot directly relates to questions raised in the "drinking water" orientation—reality is in the physical engagement and sensational knowledge of experience, a reality embodied in Iemoto's fleeting gesture while she said, "first comes the body. The most important thing is *kokoro*." Theory lies in the practice of embodiment.

Buddhist concepts concerning the body reveal a great deal about Japanese praxis. Thomas Kasulis' interpretation of the writings of Kukai (774–835 C.E., the founder of Shingon Buddhism), concisely imparts how enlightenment is embodied through practice. Kukai stated:

The reality-embodiment preaches the Dharma (*hosshin seppo*). (1993: 308)

One becomes a buddha in and through this very body (*sokushin jobutsu*). (310)

Kasulis' reading of Kukai's words are:

Our bodies, just as they are, are already expressions of the cosmic buddha's enlightenment . . . We only need to realize it. (310)

The purpose of practice is to take us from belief to realization. If we have disciplined ourselves so that we enact buddhahood in thought, word, deed, we are indeed buddhas, right here and right now. The truth hosshin seppo [the reality-embodiment preaches the Dharma] is no longer a metaphysical theory, but a practical reality. We embody buddhahood. (311)

This approach to cultivating the self unifies practice and enlightenment in a pragmatic and very real, even tangible, process of embodiment. The body and its actions focus and become aware through discipline. I believe Soke's direction to "know with your body" conveys the essence of this concept concisely—embodiment and realization arise through experience and practice.

In his book *The Body: Toward an Eastern Mind-Body Theory,* Yuasa points out the locus of the body within this experiential transmission process:

> To put it simply, true knowledge cannot be obtained simply by means of theoretical thinking, but only through "bodily recognition or realization" (tainin or taitoku), that is through the utilization of one's total mind and body. Simply stated this is to "learn with the body," not the brain. Cultivation is a practice that attempts, so to speak, to achieve true knowledge by means of one's total mind and body. (1987: 25–26)

Revealed in this passage is the notion that the mind and body are conceived of as inseparable and that it is the process or development of the mind-body complex that Japanese philosophy stresses. In other words, the body is not considered to be a separate entity from the mind. There is not a dilemma, as in Western philosophy, of what the existential or physical relationship is between the mind and body. This does not mean there does not exist a duality, or tension, between the mind and body, however. It is through disciplined personal cultivation (*shugyo*, "enhancement of the personality" or "character building") that one can achieve *shinjin ichinyo* (the oneness of body-mind) and *satori* (spiritual awakening or enlightenment). I believe this coming together of the mind and body is what Iemoto conveyed with her hands drawing together while saying, "The head [mind] and body are imbalanced sometimes but after practicing for a time you will feel more and more balanced."

sensing folds

In *nihon buyo* we tell stories with the body. As in many of Japan's performing arts, the repertory consists of compositions based on a narrative and an emphasis on narrative vocal genres. Though dance movements vary according to which genre they stem from, choreography is generally tied to the narrative, however abstract. Depending on the particular piece, the narrative thread embodied in movement expression can range from realistic mimetic gestures, such as a scene from a babysitter's day, to a movement style that is only abstractly representational. In lessons at Hatchobori these mimetic actions enfold dance and our daily lives outside the studio through our physical memories and sensational knowledge.

For example, during a lesson I heard Iemoto call out from the front of the dance studio, ". . . there [in the dance passage], where the icy breeze hits your face. Next time you experience wind like this [outside], remember it in your body memory." Iemoto's direction provided an impetus for the expression of the narrative, a motivation that drew on a dancer's experience, or sensational knowledge. On other occasions Iemoto provided insights to dancers, such as, "If you live your life fully outside the dance studio, then your dancing will grow and come to life." Here dance and daily action inform each other and interconnect. The lines distinguishing them can blur and become liminal; as the movements of dance are informed by daily life, movements in life draw us to recall dance.

Performing gestures with clarity to convey a narrative is vital. For example, there is a passage in the dance "Seigaiha" where the character admires a serene seaside landscape. No scenery surrounds the performer; with just a paper fan and her body she must convey the context. In one passage a wave rushes onto the sand. In my lesson Iemoto undulated the open fan to embody the rippling water and took quick steps back, as if to keep from getting wet. In my mind the image of the beach and vast seascape came to life when Iemoto danced. In reality we stood inside the bare Hatchobori studio. How did her body evoke this dramatic atmosphere? How can Iemoto's embodiment of the character project beyond her body to stir up this seaside illusion, a corporeal impression unfolding the mise-en-scène? I admit, I was mesmerized by the vision and drawn to embody such energy.

In the dance the character of the young woman discovers an object in the sand. Iemoto's gaze and stance piqued my curiosity. What did she find? Her following gestures revealed the answer. A small seashell. Delighted, she picked up the shell and held it to the light before returning it to the sand. The vision played tricks on my mind. Fully engrossed in the scene, I found it believable, yet also knew it to be beyond the "reality" of my senses. There was no shell. No sand. No water.

PHOTO 2. Holding up a seashell in "Seigaiha." PHOTO: WALTER HAHN

When I learned "Seigaiha" Iemoto directed my focus to the seashell: "If you see the shell yourself, *really* see and feel it, the audience will believe it." I wondered, is dance an art of illusion, an artifice of staged images? If so, how is the illusion conjured by the moving body? We convey the narrative with bodies that "know," or embody, characters and emotions within dances. Again, Soke's direction to "know with your body" comes to mind, advice that privileges embodied knowledge.

I practiced "seeing and feeling" the shell, over and over again. This very point of the practice presented a fascinating yet bewildering enigma of embodiment and physical memory. How does transformation arise from the strictures of prescribed movement and choreography? There is a stylized way of tying a knot, for example, in which the movements are mimetically based on actual tying movements. However, the dance movements are not at all realistic; rather, the dancer's job is to project the "feeling," or heart, of tying. The informed body—aware of the lived experience of tying as well as the prescribed dance gestures for tying a knot—can transform the mundane to art. I wondered how (stage) presence could be taught, in an embodied sense.

I noticed that Iemoto and Soke frequently ask students, "What are you doing? Do you know? If you do not know, then how will the audience know or feel it?" Their many variations on these questions emphasize the importance of performing gestures with clarity from an informed body, imbued with a lively spirit.

During my lesson on "Komori" (The Babysitter), Iemoto burst out laughing after asking me, "What are you doing?" She continued, "Oh! Maybe you *really* don't know what you are doing!" Still smiling, she began to sing the lyrics and explain the dance movements to me. I was learning a passage where the babysitter is playing while the baby sleeps. The babysitter rhymes fish names in a song, and at one point she wriggles her entire body. In my lesson Iemoto leaned forward and asked, "Do you know what *namako* is?" I shook my head no. "It's a fish with no bones, like a jellyfish or squid, so you move like this . . . ," and she undulated as a boneless *namako*. I went home that night and looked up *namako* in the dictionary: a trepang or sea slug.

The following day I returned to my dance lesson and practiced a double-folded embodiment—enacting a babysitter playfully imitating a sea slug. We repeated the passage several times. Since the dance steps are prescribed, practice involved repetition until I could transcend the rudiments of "correct" movements while grasping for a glimmer of transformation.

During experiences of transformation like the babysitter and seashell scenes mentioned above, dance cuts to the corporeal to unfurl and disclose the phenomenal. I pondered: Considering that transmission in *nihon buyo* is based on following a teacher through prescribed movements—where is one's self, relative to transfiguration and the informed body? Where is presence in the body-character-spirit continuum? In my sea slug lesson I was imitating Iemoto imitating *komori* imitating a sea slug. Iemoto said to me, "do not just imitate me. That's boring. Learn the dance and then dance it with Samie's heart." So there is a struggle in learning. The transmission process is through physical imitation and sensory information, yet at a certain point we must embody the dance and instill our personal self through the strictures of the choreography and style. I believe this is where the body sensually situates movement to orient "self."

Rather than a masking of one's self to become a character onstage, Iemoto and Soke stress the *seishin* (spiritual strength) needed by a dancer in order for transfiguration to arise. Their concerns about training the body point to the source of transformative abilities, while also revealing Japanese concepts of embodiment. Again, Iemoto's words to me—"Without experiencing life, without personality, you have no dance, no *kokoro*, and you are invisible . . . But if you have a sense of self, then you can become any character onstage—a woman, a young boy, an old man." In a sense, the training of the body can be viewed as an enabling process, one that transforms the individual through a transcendence of rudimentary movements to a level of artistry. The leap from an embodiment of fundamental dance abilities to extraordinary artistic expression perhaps lies beyond words. It is manifest within the daily practice of dance. In chapter 5, I will return to the concepts of orientation and the artistry of transformation and presence.

moving art

The aesthetics of a genre and the process in which the art form is passed down are tightly interwoven, inseparable even. This is particularly true for the performing arts in Japan that highly value the process of learning and have a concern for the tradition's continuity. Accurately describing *nihon buyo* is nearly impossible, since the genre comprises countless subgenres and has been influenced by a wide variety of theatrical and dance styles. With this in mind, the last two sections of this chapter outline the fundamental aesthetic and physical qualities of Japanese dance in relationship to transmission.

First, let us ponder a few broad questions. What makes something beautiful, or aesthetically pleasing? What cultural insights can be revealed through observing a culture's aesthetic values? How do trends of beauty influence the arts through time? How are aesthetic values passed down from generation to generation? And finally, how does the transmission process foster aesthetic ideals? A closer look at a culture's transmission process reveals the deep connections that exist between a genre's practice, aesthetic priorities, and cultural values.

Buddhist concepts and beliefs have had a powerful influence on Japanese culture, since the arrival of Buddhism in Japan in the sixth century via contact with China and Korea. The religion spread throughout Japan, developing diverse sects and establishing a strong foundation of spiritual and philosophical principles that permeated nearly every aspect of Japanese culture, particularly transmission practices.

Enlightenment, one pursuit of Buddhism, is believed to be attained via a variety of paths, such as meditation or the diligent practice of particular art forms. In his well-known treatise *Kakyo*, Zeami (1363–1443, the creator of *noh*) wrote: "both dancing and gesture are external skills. The essentials of our art lie in the spirit. They represent a true enlightenment established through art" (Rimer and Yamazaki 1984: 90). In the journey to enlightenment, the contemplative insights gained through the struggle and suffering of attainment provide a central focus of Buddhist tradition. This fundamental emphasis on diligent practice as a process for insight is one of Buddhism's most influential contributions to the arts and is crucial to the study of *nihon buyo* transmission.

Aspects of Buddhism's spirit may be observed in four aesthetic approaches in the arts—simplicity, irregularity, suggestion, and impermanence. These four general characteristics are often used for studying the visual and literary classical arts of Japan (to name a few, Kishibe 1984; Komparu 1983; Keene 1981; Suzuki 1973; and see Addiss, Groemer, and Rimer 2006 for a valuable interdisciplinary approach to understanding Japanese arts within culture). I present these four concepts as a means of introducing the aesthetics and practice of *nihon buyo,* and to offer parallel creative trends between the arts. An overview of each aesthetic approach is followed by a mini–case study. I must admit that I myself cringe at the problematic nature of introducing such a generalized approach to aesthetics. I find it objectionable (even offensive) to reduce a culture's aesthetic approaches to only a few concepts, since not all the performing arts of Japan incorporate such an aesthetic formula. For example, some Japanese aesthetic values derive from Buddhist concepts propagated by the aristocratic nobility as early as the first century, and so these values more appropriately apply to the Japanese classical arts than to folk genres. I ask readers to please keep in mind that my purpose in the next section is to introduce general aesthetic principles at play in *nihon buyo* in order to provide a setting for transmission. My earlier question—How are aesthetic values passed down?—is a difficult one to observe. Students are not sat down and taught the aesthetics of *nihon buyo*, but rather gain an understanding of such a sensibility through practice and embodiment of the tradition—through observing dance in the studio and at performances, and through discussions during lessons. Let's take a closer look.

simplicity

The word *simplicity* encompasses several Japanese words that convey this aesthetic sense, such as *sabi* (quiet, rustic, unadorned beauty), *wabi* (poverty, simplicity), and *kotan* (refined simplicity). Simplicity is an aesthetic approach that values the use of economy in art, the shedding of superficial elements. Formal, or compositional, approaches aim to evoke the profound with minimal detail—a bird sitting on a dead branch portrayed by a few quick brushstrokes, for example. *Haiku* clearly embodies the idea of simplicity in its form, based on the verse form of 5, 7, 5 syllables. Here is a poem by Issa (1762–1826) I have grown fond of:

> Singing as it goes,
> an insect floats down the stream
> on a broken bough
> —Issa[2]

The compact *haiku* structure reveals the simplicity of the form. Subtlety is key. Removing all extraneous detail allows the simplicity, or the bare essentials, to be appreciated. Examples of simplicity may be observed in a variety of Japanese arts, such as the simple silhouette of a woman or man wearing a *kimono*, the austere linearity of traditional Japanese architecture, gardens, or the design of *sensu* (fans).

irregularity

As a creative approach, irregularity emphasizes proportions that avoid regularity and symmetry within an artistic composition. It also embraces the beauty of imperfection. An example of irregularity can be found in the art of *bonsai*, or miniature potted trees. A tree is usually not planted symmetrically in the center of the pot, but positioned off to one side or even cascading below the rim of the pot in order to emphasize the negative space within the container. This compositional structure draws attention to the tree's location in its world. *Bonsai* are encouraged to grow in gnarled and twisted forms to display their maturity as well as to draw attention to the beauty of irregularity or imperfection found in nature.

The avoidance of regularity and symmetry is thought to be rooted in nature, as well as the tendency for humans to take notice of things that are slightly unusual or uneven (as our eyes are drawn to the slightest crack in the surface of an egg, or an irregular inflection in a person's voice). For example, an artisan might select a portion of bamboo that exhibits wormhole patterns to craft a tea ceremony utensil. Irregularity may be found in poetic verse forms that employ odd numbers of lines, such as *haiku* (lines of 5, 7, 5 syllables) or *tanka* poetry (a classic verse form dating back to the first century consisting of thirty-one syllables, divided into five lines with a syllabic distribution 5, 7, 5, 7, 7).

A formal aesthetic technique called *jo-ha-kyu* (corresponding to "introduction, scattering, and rushing") is used in many compositions of music and dance. This is a tripartite structure not founded on the symmetry of musical or dance material (Western A-B-A compositional schemes, for instance) but on organizing material in an A-B-C form, emphasizing the flow of time. Dances are often composed of three sections, which in turn may be divided into tripartite subsections of *jo-ha-kyu* (or a different odd-numbered structure, to avoid symmetry). The *jo*, introductory section, opens a piece and sets the mood and artistic vocabulary. The *ha*, or scattering section, follows and gradually builds the material and momentum to a climactic point. *Kyu* (rushing) brings this climax to a rapid close, settling the intensity. The sections are not proportionally symmetrical—the *ha* section is normally the longest, and *kyu* is relatively brief. What is fascinating to me is how the *jo-ha-kyu* formal structure becomes embodied by performers. During lessons there is little discussion of compositional devices. It is thought that dancers gradually embody these structures so that phrasing is a practice that becomes physically ingrained, or flows effortlessly through the dancing body. Discussion is considered an obstacle in that it can impose a self-conscious aspect to the flow of dance or music, resulting in an apparently academic, stiff execution of the form. Inevitably such performance lacks the embodied spark, or energy, needed to enact the flow of *jo-ha-kyu*.

Tied to *jo-ha-kyu* is the concept of *ma*, "negative" or "open" space-time—a vital aspect pertaining to compositional proportions found in many Japanese art forms. It is interesting to observe how different art forms use this concept for their practice. *Ma* is a particularly Japanese aesthetic where aspects of "negative" space and time are not believed to be empty, but are considered to be expansive and full of energy. Artists employ *ma* as a vehicle to arouse a contemplative state, an awareness of expansive space and time. In *nihon buyo* irregularity and the concept of *ma* are embodied in the series of poses within a dance. Most often the body is not symmetrically "balanced" in a pose. Instead, the naturally symmetrical body is positioned so that one leg is forward or bent, each arm is held in a different position, and the torso is often turned in opposition to the direction that the feet are aligned. Not only is the body's position asymmetrical in composition; the "negative space" around the body forms interesting asymmetrical contours, such as the open area under an outstretched arm and torso. During such dance poses time freezes momentarily—a temporal *ma* that highlights a moment outside the "natural" flow of time. This expanded temporal quality is often mirrored in the music by a noticeably free tempo, implying a suspension of time through abstract punctuations of silence. Here the negative space, or *ma*, arises in the lack of sound, or silence, between notes.

suggestion

Suggestion, reflected in the word *yugen* (profound sublimity), is an art of implication and mystery. The etymology of the two *kanji* characters evokes their inner nuances: *yu* (hazy, dim, dark, quiet, otherworldly) and *gen* (subtle, profound, or dark). The Japanese love of mystery, concealing, wrapping, folding, and tying—all reflect this aesthetic in the arts. A direct presentation of a theme or artistic motif is not considered to be as engaging as that which carries a degree of mystery through implying parts of the whole. For example, the aesthetic of suggestion is embodied in the art of wearing the *kimono*. In this traditional apparel the body is completely obscured, except the neck, head, and hands. Heavy makeup and a wig normally conceal even these exposed areas of the body. The contours of the actual female form are merely suggested, leaving details of the body's form to the imagination. Compare this concealing of the body to contrasting clothing trends that enhance the voluptuous female contour, such as Victorian corsets, the sari in South Indian *bharatnatyam* dance, or even overtly stylized bras worn by American pop stars such as Madonna.

The Japanese preference for nuance and subtlety over direct communication is revealed in the aesthetic of suggestion and the ambiguity of artistic forms. Interpretation is often left for the observer to examine for herself. The structure of Japanese language is famous for demanding interpretation—the lack of subjects or plural forms, for example, oblige listeners to focus and contextually interpret the speaker's intended meaning. Again, *haiku* are a marvelous example of implying a scene, mood, and philosophy through only seventeen syllables.

Suggestion in *nihon buyo* is embodied in a variety of ways. The Japanese love of narrative, paired with indirect communication, provides a rich setting for theatrical works. Few props populate the *nihon buyo* stage—a simple arrangement of flowers or a screen placed to one side of the stage, perhaps. Dancers often perform whole narratives with only a *sensu* (fan) to abstractly pantomime the entire narrative. In such a case the *sensu* must transform before the audience to convey the essence of a story—the fan transforms to a rippling brook, a flower blossoming, or a mirror. The art of implication, indirectly imparting the mood and alluding to a deeper meaning, is part of the commitment of *nihon buyo* dancers.

impermanence

The notion of impermanence as an aesthetic technique is a fascinating, yet puzzling, consideration. The concept stems from Buddhist belief—the contemplation on the passing of time; the frailty of (human) existence; and the karmic wheel of life, death, and rebirth cycle. These spiritual and philosophical elements are illuminated in the arts in a variety of ways. For example, in the art of *bonsai* it is common to retain a dead branch long after it has withered. This practice is not only to suggest the age of the tree but to convey and even celebrate the frailty of the tree's existence. Japanese love of seasonal change imparts an essence of impermanence found thematically in many arts such as poetry, screen painting, objects for tea ceremony, or dance. The *haiku* composer's ability to conjure a context of time and place through merely alluding to a seasonal setting is a challenge of the poetic form. Images and sounds of summer permeate Issa's *haiku* (above), such as the singing insect and flow of water in the stream.

The evanescent quality of life is represented within dance in numerous ways. Time-based arts are naturally linked to their ephemeral existence in the present, bow to the lived experience of the moment, and revere a connection with the past in embodied memory. The transmission of dance relies on learning through doing and an active engagement of embodiment through experience with a teacher. Dance and dance training are ephemeral and necessitate regular practice to maintain embodiment, as well as social ties.

As I mentioned earlier, not all dances neatly fit into the four aesthetic categories. Consider the "wild" and busy aesthetics of many *kabuki* dances, for instance! However, despite this conflict in style, these very pieces often exhibit some aspect of these aesthetics (*ma* or impermanence, for example). I close this section on aesthetics with a case study of a dance that clearly illustrates the essence of the four aesthetics discussed above. The dance is called "Kurokami" (Jet-black Hair). The poem of the same title, written in the seventeenth century, is not attributed to a particular author. The narrative portrays a woman's longing for her lover, who has departed. In the lyrics her solitude is conveyed deeply through the stillness of images.

Kurokami (Jet-black Hair)[3]

Kurokami no	It is the pillow
musuboretaru	We shared that night,
omoi wo ba	When I let down
tokete neta yo no	My jet-black hair.
Makura koso	That is the cause of my lament
hitori nuru yo no	When I sleep alone
ada-makura	With my single robe
sode wa katashiku	To cover me.
Tsuma ja to iute	"You are mine," he said.
(*ainote*)	(musical interlude)
Guchi na onago no	Not knowing the heart
kokoro to shirade	Of a simple girl,
shin to fuketaru	The voice of a temple bell,
kane no koe	Sounds into the quiet night.
Yube no yume no	Awakening from an empty dream
kesa samete	In the morning,
yujashi natsukashi	How lovely, sweet,
yarusenaya	And helpless is my longing.
tsumoru to shirade	Before I know it
tsumoru shirayuki	The silver snow has piled up.

"Kurokami" is for a solo dancer using a *sensu*. The minimum stage space necessary for the piece is only a ten-foot-square area. "Kurokami" embodies simplicity in its concise choreography, yet the lack of extraneous embellishment requires the dancer to maintain her focused presence and develop the depth of subtle nuances in gesture.

Each phrase consists of several movements, framed by held poses that add to the feeling of stillness (*ma*) and the melancholy mood. In this deceivingly simple dance structure, every breath is apparent and, to a degree, choreographed. An inhale opens a dancer's chest above the *obi* (sash) and sends barely noticeable movement across the shoulders, neck, and torso. Her inhale is timed within the phrase, held momentarily (*ma*), and with her exhale the energy of release instigates the vitality of the next movement. This cycle of breath—from inhale, suspension of breath, and exhale—imparts a stunning flow of tension and release. Notice that the breath cycle is also an asymmetrical (tripartite) form.

In the opening of the Tachibana choreography the dancer enters slowly, yet her face is concealed by her open fan. The character's identity and emotion is a mystery, only suggested. She gracefully turns and poses holding the *sensu* before her and it transforms into a mirror. The woman adjusts her *kimono* collar and hair. Her momentary focus on her appearance early in the dance summons the viewer to observe her beauty, foreshadowing the nature of fleeting beauty with the passage of time.

Although actually sung by a vocalist, the poem text is hauntingly written from the character's point of view. Hearing the woman's internal thoughts intensifies the emotional impact for an observer—we hear her compelling lament and mournful longing in the first person, and it seems as if we are listening to her subconscious, since "her" voice emanates from the singer. Every line is heavy with double meaning and metaphor. Her first utterance (and first line of the poem), "*Kurokami no musuboretaru*" (When I let down my jet-black hair), seems unimpassioned, yet it powerfully projects a depth of emotions in metaphor. *Musuboreru* refers to knotting and, in this case, letting her hair down. In Japanese culture images of tying, wrapping, and securing something (or someone) are common, revealing metaphors of social or spiritual connectedness and bonds of love. An alternate meaning of *musuboreru* is "gloomy" or "depressed" in mood. Since the verb is linked to hair in the narrative, the emotional weight is perhaps not apparent at first. Women's hair is a potent symbol in Japan and is often used as a metaphor. There is composure and restraint in the poetic images. Letting her hair down in her lover's company implies that she also let down her emotional guard. Traditionally women arrange their hair high on the head. This contributes to the sleek, elegant outline of a woman's contour in a *kimono* but also reveals the sensuous nape of her neck. Here the *kimono* collar (*eri*) is drawn back slightly—her exposed nape line suggestive of the contours concealed below several layers of her *kimono*, *obi*, and ties.

I will not analyze the entire poem or dance, but will point out a few significant elements that embody the aesthetic techniques discussed above. The concept of impermanence unfolds in the line "*kane no koe*" (the voice of the bell) followed by "*samete*" (*sameru*, wake up, awake). This passage alludes to the Buddhist belief that spiritual awakening is possible in an instant of realization. The word *sameru*, written with a different *kanji* character, also means "fade away" or to become "discolored"—a play on words to impart the passage of time. The starkness reflected in the sparse choreography and single dancer on stage, balanced with the lush images and sounds in this passage of the poetry, also frame the temporal and spatial concept of *ma*. The music reflects this aesthetic, using a heterophonic texture of the ensemble, performed with a small chamber *nagauta* group (ensemble for the *kabuki*) of *koto*, *shamisen*, voice, and drum. The vocal and *shamisen* lines are particularly interesting. The two parts melodically mirror each other, yet each playfully stretches or compresses time in different phrases, producing integrally interwoven melodies that are similar, not identical. The lines weave together beautifully, exploiting subtle nuances of melody and timing. The most active section of the musical piece occurs in the "*ainote*," or interlude. In this section the voice rests, and the instrumental ensemble has an opportunity to play a bit more elaborately. In contrast, there are moments where the ensemble plays so sparsely that the silence, the *ma*, becomes intense, emphasizing the sorrowful, introspective mood of the dance. There is elegance in the restraint embodied in "Kurokami." The simplicity of the choreography, music, and poetry is dramatic and heightens the feelings of sadness and nostalgia.

The final poetic image of snow introduces the motif of nature but carries a low-spirited double meaning in metaphor. Snow signals the arrival of winter and the woman's awareness of time passing. Snow also embodies a metaphor of her physical changes over time. Waiting for her lover, she has endured unbearable longing, and she did not notice that "the silver snow has piled up"—that her once black hair has now turned white. In the closing passage the dancer creates a *shoji* (paper and wood) door with her fan. She slides it open to see snow falling in the garden. As she gently reaches out her right hand to catch a snowflake, she feels the chill of winter, metaphorically exposing her desolate mood. Taking the open fan with her right hand, she holds it flat and above her head to portray the eaves above the veranda. Her left hand slips into her *sode* (*kimono* sleeve) and brings it to her mouth with her fingertips. This last pose is classically asymmetrical in physical contour, from the positioning of her arms and legs, to the slight twist in her torso. Despite this asymmetrical stance, her body appears firmly grounded and compositionally balanced, as if her limbs individually create a counterbalance to ground her figure. Her final pose is punctuated with a subtle, three-part head movement that emanates from her neck—from the audience perspective: left, right, center—as she gazes longingly into the distance.

Transmission, the physical internalization of aesthetic practices, is the central focus of this book. I believe the path to comprehending cultural aesthetics, social structures, and interactions lies in the process of embodiment, or the methods of transmission. It is a cycle, however, as cultural aesthetics and interactions are also the key to understanding transmission.

As I mentioned earlier, the study of this ephemeral process challenges a participant-observer, for as the practice unfolds a myriad of cultural patterns, these very patterns become physically internalized and often seem less accessible on a conscious level. Sensational knowledge moves the dancer. It is the art, indistinguishable from the practice. The following section offers insights into how the body is composed and practices dance.

grounding the body

The way the body is presented in dance varies widely in different cultures around the world. The dancer's body in performance differs from the body in everyday life because of the intention of its display. How is the body "organized" to dance, including stance, gaze, breath, energy, weight distribution, and movement? What aesthetic cultural values might be revealed by an observation of these characteristics? . . . or by an observation of the transmission process? Although *nihon buyo* encompasses a wide variety of dance postures and movements, it is possible to outline a general character of the body.

Japanese concepts of energy flow through and around the body illuminate a great deal about *nihon buyo* and movement transmission. At the core of Japanese philosophies of the body is a concept of energy, or power, known as *ki* (in Chinese, *chi* or *qi*). In his writings, philosopher Yuasa Yasuo takes a cross-cultural approach to Japanese practices of the body—comparing Eastern and Western philosophical and spiritual paradigms—and offers key concepts, to reveal differences in cultural practices. Yuasa's writings include references to specific practices such as martial and performing arts, making his work particularly valuable for Western theorists studying Eastern performing arts. Nagatomo Shigenori, introducing Yuasa's research on *ki*-energy in *The Body, Self-Cultivation, and Ki-Energy*, writes, "According to acupuncture medicine, an invisible psychophysical *ki*-energy circulates within the interior of the body, while at the same time intermingling with the *ki*-energy pervasively present in the environment including that of other persons" (Nagatomo 1993a: xii). *Ki* remains a somewhat elusive concept, however:

> The scope which this concept covers is very comprehensive; it can include, for example, a climatic condition, an arising social condition, a psychological and pathological condition. It also extends to cover a power expressed in fine arts, martial arts, and literature . . . Yuasa, while confining his use of the term "*ki*" to human beings and their living environment, defines *ki*-energy as a third term with a *psychophysical* character that cannot be properly accommodated within the dualistic paradigm of thinking . . . it is not arrived at merely through intellectual abstraction, but is derived also from observation of empirical phenomena detectable both experientially and experimentally in and around the human body. (Nagatomo 1993a: xi–xii)

Awareness and control of *ki* through the body fosters the flow of movement, enabling dancers to move with a spirited energy that radiates from the body through dance. As stated by Nagatomo above, awareness of *ki* is developed through experience, rather than intellectual pursuits. I believe that this is one reason why active (dance) practice is privileged over discussion during lessons—*ki* is considered to lie beyond what words can supply. Only through the gradual process of practice and observation can the development of *ki* awareness and embodiment be gained. Yuasa proposes the idea of training the body via self-cultivation, or *shugyo*, as a path for developing *ki* awareness:

> I have developed a special interest in the problem of self-cultivation [*shugyo*] as found in various Eastern religious traditions. In Japan self-cultivation methods have been established and transmitted to later generations ever since Buddhism's acceptance in ancient times . . . a

connotation of the term "*shugyo*" or simply "*gyo*" (self-cultivation) is that of training the body, but it also implies training, as a human being, the spirit or mind by training the body. In other words, "*shugyo*" carries the meaning of perfecting the human spirit or enhancing one's personality. Therefore, it seems to imply that mind and body are inseparable. (Yuasa 1993: 7–8)

Yuasa's work imparts the profound significance embodied in self-cultivation and *ki* energy. Embodying practices are a deeply personal and spiritual engagement, a challenge of the body and mind. However, the path to understanding is through the body and experience, a concept Soke stated so clearly in my lesson—"Know with your body."

Training of the body is key for *ki* to flourish and develop. Specifically, a disciplined routine of specific movement and sound patterns must be practiced in order for the body to move freely with the spirit of *ki* energy. Yuasa wrote:

> when there is repeated training in the practice of performing techniques, the body-mind is disciplined, then the state of conscious movement changes into one which the hands, legs, and body unconsciously move of themselves. This is the state of "no mind." (Yuasa 1993: 31)

The performing techniques Yuasa refers to are *kata*. *Nihon buyo* dances consist of *kata*, formalized body movements that greatly aid the memorization and embodiment of pieces. *Kata*, or "precise exercise forms" (Singleton 1998), are a distinctly Japanese formal device found in nearly every artistic practice, such as tea ceremony, archery, theater, *enka* (popular song, see Yano 2002), and martial arts. Because most of the traditional artistic practices in Japan are taught through active engagement, *kata* are vital as the foundation for training. In *nihon buyo,* *kata* function as the fundamental building blocks for the foundation of dance expression. Rather than learning the discrete forms individually first, as is the case in ballet training, *kata* are learned gradually and contextually within dance pieces, but also from observing *kata* during other students' lessons. In a sense, this is similar to children's acquisition of language vocabulary; new words are heard and incorporated as they are needed.

Kata operate as artistic motifs that are standard and repeatable. They are also flexible. Structurally similar *kata* may appear in a variety of pieces, yet for each dance, and even within each phrase, a *kata* is performed with the nuance, or flavor, of that particular context. For example, a seated bow is a *kata* performed in many dances. However, the specific character the dancer portrays in a dance will modify the basic bow, depending on the character's gender, social status, age, mood, or the social context of the bow (who s/he is bowing to). Formal bows in a classic dance will differ from a bow in a dance based on a folk dance. It is important to keep in mind that there are *kata* for each movement unit. *Kata* are named and so have a pragmatic purpose in lessons, as teachers can call out a *kata* during a lesson. In this section I will be describing only the general manner in which the body is organized to move. For a wonderfully clear and organized description of the specifics of dance movement see Hanayagi Chiyo's *Jitsu nihon buyo no kiso* (The Practical Skills of Basic *Nihon Buyo* Movement).

The concept of a dancer's form, or posture, is expressed in the word *katachi*. This word does not simply translate into "posture"; it represents a structural system for cultivating the body, and, as Komparu Kunio points out, there is a connection between *kata* and *katachi*:

> Two Japanese words, *kata* and *katachi*, are closely related. *Kata* corresponds to pattern, model, or mold; it refers to set movements in the martial arts and to dance patterns in Noh. The word *katachi* means shape, form, or condition, as perceived by the senses. We can generally translate *kata* as pattern and *katachi* as shape or form, but the terms may be very close in meaning. According to etymological dictionaries the word *kata* derives from *kami* (god) and *ta* (paddy or hand). Thus *ka-ta* involves god, agriculture, and the hand of man, and indeed the basic movement patterns of Noh are related to agricultural activities and sacred rituals . . .The *chi* of *katachi* apparently is an indication of mystical powers and often appears written with the character for soul or spirit. (Komparu 1983: 221)

Katachi is the form that the body assumes while dancing—the structural source for the flow of energy and movement. For dance, the notion of flow is apparent in a physical sense as well as in the sense of an inner, contemplative energy. *Nihon buyo* movements derive from a strong core centered in the abdomen, or *hara*, where the body's energy and spiritual center resides. The body moves with a firmly grounded stance derived from a lowered center of gravity rooted in the *hara*. The basic stance reinforces this foundation—feet are firmly planted on the ground; the tailbone is tucked under so that the hips appear level with the floor; and the knees are always bent. Movements emanate from the *hara* region and radiate outward through the torso and limbs. The connection of the feet to the smooth wooden floor plays a vital role in a dancer's carriage, balance, and movement vocabulary. More importantly, the connection of the body's *ki* energy to the earth is via tactile contact with the soles of the feet. This is an energetic transmission flow between the dancer and ground.

Apart from a few exceptions, *nihon buyo* dancers perform in traditional socks, or *tabi*, when dancing. *Tabi* enable dancers to glide smoothly along the wood floors in a commonly performed style called *suriashi* (a "sliding feet" walking style). They are made of finely woven cotton with metal tab findings sewn vertically on the inner side of the ankle to secure them on the feet. In a mittenlike fashion, the large toe is enclosed separately from the others, enabling *zori* (a thong sandal) to be easily put on or taken off. Also, the isolation of the big toe allows it to spread out slightly from the other toes to grip the floor, greatly aiding stability by creating a stronger base. *Tabi* fit tightly around the foot like a second skin, sculpting the foot into a single sleek shape. I detail *tabi* here because dancers rely on firm contact with the ground, and *tabi* are the only thing that comes between feet and floor.

Foot and leg positions vary according to the character role a dancer is portraying in a piece. In general, legs and feet are discreetly turned inward for female roles, which keeps the *kimono* composed during walking. Thighs and knees are held together with knees bent. The dancer walks with small, controlled steps, not strides. The leg and foot positions of male characters, on the other hand, vary from a straight, forward position to one that is turned out from the hip, somewhat like a shallow ballet plié. Of course there are countless variations depending on the character's age, social status, gender, or the genre of the dance. In fact there are many pieces in which a dancer assumes several roles to convey the narrative. In such dances she must shift, or codeswitch, between the variety of characters in such a convincing manner that the audience can fluidly follow the story (see chapters 4 and 5). For dances that involve codeswitching between contrasting characters, the physical portrayal of the personae is vital.

For all character roles, the slight bending of knees grounds the body and also supports a manner of shifting weight often incorporated into dances. Because *tabi* allow feet to slide on the floor, the body can easily change directions by shifting weight while rotating the feet. The firmly grounded nature of the lower body secures a flexible foundation from which to move. Above the navel a dancer's carriage is upright—neck and head erect, chest and shoulders held back and broad. When teaching posture, Iemoto often tells us to imagine a thread emanating from the crown of the head that is pulled upward as the tailbone is simultaneously pointed down, creating a sense of rootedness to the floor. The basic carriage is interesting because it polarizes the body so that from the navel to the floor a dancer is grounded, and from the navel up she extends upward. The key here is the midpoint, the *hara*—safeguarded below layers of costume. The strength and life of movements radiates from this central core.

I recall that during one lesson Iemoto began to swing her arms like a propeller while commenting to a new student how easy but senseless it is to just swing the arms into place. "That's not dance. The movement must come from here," she instructed as she embraced her *obi* with her hands, then fluidly slid them up along her torso and shoulders, until her arms were outstretched high in the air. Again and again I have seen her "dance" this basic lesson of the body—each time with animated vigor and enthusiasm, revealing how essential the flow of energy is in *nihon buyo* movement. This brings our focus to the shoulders, arms, wrists, and hands.

Shoulders perform an interesting role in *nihon buyo*. They are quite active, as they provide a crucial link between the dancer's strong torso, head, and her highly expressive hand and arm movements. In this capacity they physically support the arms, but, more importantly, they convey the energy outward from the torso through the arms, wrists, fingertips, and fan or other prop. Iemoto often reminds students that shoulders need to be drawn down and back. A slight tap between the shoulder blades during a lesson signals that the muscles here must firmly support and control the shoulders.

On the surface, *nihon buyo* can appear as if the hands and arms take on the majority of activity. As Iemoto implied with her "propeller" arm lesson, this perspective is misguided. Movements of the arms alone will seem lifeless and disembodied. When an experienced dancer moves, the flow of *ki* energy from her body's core outward is apparent in a fully embodied sense, and the animated energy only heightens the articulation of the hands and fingers. The entire body radiates with energy, whether moving or still.

Shoulders carry an emotive role as well. Considered to be a sensuous area of the body, the shoulders press downward with every step a dancer takes. Each (vertical) half of the body is coordinated such that, for example, when the left foot moves forward, the left shoulder simultaneously moves downward. For female characters, depending on the particular dance and role, the undulation of the shoulders can range from subtle to overtly sensual. Shoulder movements for male roles are also varied but generally reveal the degree of strength, or virility, of the role—from a swaggering, domineering character to a more light, or humorous, role. Of course the expressivity of the shoulders is connected to that of the entire body. As a link between torso and arms, their role is significant.

As mentioned above, on first glance *nihon buyo* appears to prioritize hand and arm movements. Because gesture plays a vital part in the narrative, the hands often appear to function as the primary communicators of movement articulation. Compared with female characters, the arms for male roles are generally held away from the body with the elbows turned outward (again, depending on the character's social status and age). In contrast, female characters keep their elbows close to the body, turned downward. This is culturally considered to be more composed and reserved but also ensures that the underarm and breast area are discreetly hidden from view. However, keeping the elbows in this reserved position does not mean that a woman's arms do not stretch out, away from the body. They do, but elbows remain pointing downward.

The flow of energy from the *hara* rises up the erect torso, across the shoulders, down the arms and wrists, through the hands, and extends out through the fingers. If there is a prop in the dancer's hand, then the energy must then be conducted across the fingertips and out through the prop, as the prop is employed as an extension of the body.

Because there are countless ways of positioning the hands, I will provide only a general description here. Female characters' hands move almost as if they are one complete, simple unit. Fingers are held together, with the thumb tucked slightly into the gently cupped palm. Individual fingers do move separately, however. There are many gestures that require an extended index finger or pinkie; it depends on the context of the movement and the specific movements choreographed into the narrative. Hands for male roles range from a cupped hand, similar to the hand for a female role, to a boldly extended hand with fingers splayed. In the case of both male and female hands, movements of wrists, hands, and fingers are interconnected and maintain the flow of energy from the body. The use of the hands in this way also maintains the simple, clean-line aesthetic form valued in Japanese arts.

Returning to the shoulders, let's move up the spine to the neck and head. With the torso and shoulder area providing a strong yet supple foundation, the head and neck are able to move freely. Like the shoulders, the female neck is considered to be highly sensual. Though generally concealed under makeup, the neck, face, and hands are the only areas of the body that are exposed to view. The collar of the *kimono*, or *eri*, is drawn down the back to reveal more of the female contour for more provocative characters, such as *geisha*. In general, the neck is held erect and long—extending the crown of the head upward. The neck moves the head in a variety of ways, from straight back to forward and side to side. A characteristic movement in *nihon buyo* occurs at the end of a phrase, where the head, shoulders, and neck punctuate a three-movement closing unit. For example, the head remains relatively upright and turns to face right-left-center, as the shoulders and neck undulate in the same direction to emphasize the movement. Supported by the back, the neck does the majority of the work to support the head in a level position while the shoulders are moving. For female roles this action necessitates the ability to execute the sequence in a graceful, smooth manner. To complicate matters, if a wig is needed for a particular role, then the neck must take on the added challenge of the weight while maintaining an outwardly elegant appearance. Shoulders do not move as gracefully for male roles. As male characters walk their shoulders move, but instead of undulating softly they remain broad to open up the chest cavity. The upper torso and shoulders can emphasize a strong male character's swagger, for instance, by shifting the corresponding shoulder forward and down as the leg steps ahead.

A dancer's gaze and facial expression convey considerable information about the character being portrayed. Facial movements in *nihon buyo* tend to be reserved relative to other Asian dance styles, such as Peking opera, South Indian *bharatnatyam*, or *kabuki*. Although gaze and facial expression in *nihon buyo* may appear subtle, this is a very powerful aspect of the dance. Generally a dancer's gaze moves in sync with her head, or slightly leading her head movement. For example, if a character looks across the horizon slowly from left to right, her eyes continue scanning the horizon with a straight gaze as her head moves, or just prior to her head in anticipation. If there is a fan pointing to the horizon, then her eyes must be drawn to the same location. The gaze is focused and directs the body to the following gesture.

While facial movements vary from dance to dance, by and large facial demeanor is relaxed and calm in an introspective sense, often letting the body, rather than overt facial expressions, convey the emotional impact. Of course there are dances in which a character's emotions are distinctly portrayed—such as a mother smiling as she holds her baby, an evil villain showing contempt, or a comic character bumbling along a country road.

Taking a step back, we can observe how Japanese aesthetics and concepts of the body are integrally linked. Learning dance by following a master allows for a gradual acquisition and enculturation of aesthetics via the body. Embodying a wide variety of ideals and philosophical concerns, the animated body acts as the living art form, narrator, individual, and social metaphor representing the "house." The *ki* (core energy) located within the *hara* (abdomen) empowers the individual to flexibly perform as these various markers of identity. In the *keikoba* (practice hall or place of practice) we take part in *keiko* (practice), a word that carries associations with *shugyo* (self-cultivation) and training of the mind-body complex. In English the word *training* has strong connotations with a regimented program of activity devoid of emotion or compassion. While many of the arts in Japan are strictly overseen, *keiko* is considered to be a process in which the body endeavors to reach a level of technical mastery so that the mind does not hamper the expressive body, which can then move fluidly—without thought.

Soke and Iemoto's intense focus and awareness attracted me to research the pedagogical system of *keiko* at Hatchobori. As I unraveled their teaching methods I realized that a large part of what they teach through dance is focused apperception—*haragei*, or the art of using the energy and strength of one's personality. The very word *haragei* incorporates *hara*, the area of the abdomen where *ki* energy resides. The *kanji* for *haragei* provides insight into its embodied meaning: *hara* is the common word for abdomen with alternate meanings of mind, intention, courage, spirit; *gei* means art. Francis Hsu directly relates *haragei* to transmission: "The central core of teaching is *haragei* (literally, abdomen technique) through which the disciple learns not by receiving explicit instructions but by unconscious imitation of the master" (Hsu 1975: 63).

The various interpretations of the word *haragei* supply plenty of insightful metaphors inspired by the body. Lakoff and Johnson (1980: 25–32) and Fernandez (1974: 124–125) posit that temporal and spatial orientation are partly constructed for us culturally, via metaphor. Specifically, structural metaphors within rituals and other shared cultural experiences assist individuals in constructing ideas of structural spaces. I believe that such metaphors and orientations structure not only the spaces for the body to inhabit but also interior physical space *as* the body. As a philosophy of the body, *haragei* points to the *hara* as the source of energy—the *hara* is an area within the body but also interacts with exterior space and the individuals located outside the body. The *keikoba* is a private space inhabited by students and teachers, a place that stages the narrative of transmission. It is a narrative comprising similar episodes of the articulate body, repeatedly displaying the practice of aesthetic cultural values and social bonds through fragments of dance. The bodies in this narrative are in transition, gradually embodying knowledge through practice. The metaphors connecting the practice with the physical and spiritual not only surround the dancer as she learns to move—she appropriates these metaphors until they become embodied.

outspread

Stretching your fingers out as wide as possible, your hand transforms to a paperless
sensu. This corporeal fan embodies stories raised in gesture and sound.
An open palm, fingers cupped, can beckon for food, catch a raindrop, or make a
connection with another hand.

        . . . and how did you learn to use this fan?

four

revealing lessons—modes of transmission: visual, tactile, oral/aural, & media

Japanese traditional dance training is an extremely personal learning process. It continues to be based on a master-disciple (one-on-one) transmission process in which the student follows the teacher through the movements and sounds of the dance. The nature of the teaching process is personal and touches on nearly every corporeal and emotional aspect of the individual in order to pass on the tradition. Through analysis I hope to elucidate this sensate, intimate quality of the transmission process.

Lessons are, for the most part, clearly defined units that are convenient to observe. They are repetitious. This includes recurrent patterns of the overall day, individual lessons, as well as methodical units of teaching. Lessons formally begin with a bow to the teacher followed by a review of the section of the dance a student is learning. The dance passage is repeated several times until the teacher is confident the student has a grasp of the movements introduced thus far and can proceed with the dance. At this time new material may be introduced and reviewed several times. If this is the case, then the teacher generally begins the dance from the opening of the dance and through the new section. The lesson closes as it began, with a bow to the teacher.

There is comfort in the regularity of this ritual lesson composition, as it meets students' and teachers' expectations of what constitutes a lesson and the relationships between individuals. The entire structure, including subtleties of manner, sequence, and use of space, become part of a dancer's lesson vocabulary. On a purely pragmatic level, the regu-

larity of systematic movement (and sound) patterns within a dance lesson helps students to embody the dance and musical structures. On an
ethnographic level, the consistency of the repetitious teaching unit and
method is conducive to analysis. Further, the abundance of similar data
from lessons substantiates assumptions concerning the structures of the
transmission process.

The following case study begins with a guided tour of my field site
and the everyday events of transmission experienced there. It is written through my eyes in the present tense—constructed from my field
notes, video footage, and memories—in order to provide a peek into
our lives at Hatchobori. The symbolic nature of space arises throughout, as well as how dancers are enculturated in the ritual traditions
of these spaces. Embedded in this narrative are the elements of transmission that are isolated and analyzed in more detail in upcoming
sections.

entering Hatchobori

Like most students, I ride the subway to dance class. Just across the
street from the Hatchobori Subway Station in central Tokyo stands
the Tachibana dance studio and home. Dancers casually refer to this
modern black building as "Hatchobori." I carefully slide the opaque
glass front door to the right. This motion instantly automates a familiar chime melody, announcing my arrival. I swiftly enter, as the ring-
ing will not cease until the door is closed.

Three pairs of shoes are neatly arranged in lines to my right and left,
indicating that several students have already arrived. I include my own
in the row next to the lacquered wooden tub filled with fresh bitter-
sweet flowers. In the small niche on the opposite wall sit several small
objects—a wooden elephant memento from Iemoto's dance trip to
Thailand and a single flower floating in a miniature glass bowl. This
simple vestibule reveals Soke and Iemoto's great regard for the art of
display, in this case the welcoming effect of arranged flowers in beautiful containers. The aesthetic of simplicity is reflected in the stark, clean
line of the flower arrangement as well as the traditional architecture,
which contrasts with that of the city street I left moments ago. I take
two steps up from the tiled foyer to a smooth, natural wood floor. To
my right is the dressing room, straight ahead are stairs to the Tachibana
family home, and to my left is the *keikoba* (dance practice area). The

keikoba is the beehive of Hatchobori, socially organized, spatially defined, and buzzing with activity and the sounds of teaching. Soke and Iemoto are both in the studio, focused on a student dancing. I kneel and, during a pause in the lesson, bow to greet each of them.

This customary formal bow signals the first of many during a day of dance. No matter what time of day or night dancers arrive, "*Ohayoo gozaimasu*" (good morning) is the first greeting. This custom has historical roots. In the theater world, work hours often ran counter to the workday of the general public. Soon this greeting became customary between performers to mark the "morning" of their professional day.

Changing from street clothes to *yukata* (cotton *kimono* worn in the summer, around the house, and for dance practice) follows. Brushing through an indigo *noren* (a cloth doorway partition), I enter the small dressing room to the right of the foyer. *Tatami* (straw matting) covers the dressing room floor. A wall of wooden shelves brims with bundles of dance clothing wrapped in colorful *furoshiki* (wrapping cloth). Just to the left, twenty or more *yukata* hang, waiting to be worn. After lessons *yukata* are often damp, so instead of being folded, they hang here to dry. On the wall, a sheet of rice paper bearing Iemoto's calligraphy displays the current schedule of lessons.

This room feels like a haven between two worlds. It embodies spatial and temporal liminality, a place neither in nor out. Two opaque windows face the bustling Tokyo street. City sounds: office workers shuffling by, high heels hitting pavement, the hollow pitch of *geta* (wooden clogs), the harsh blast of an occasional car horn, and the enthusiastic chatter of shopkeepers filter in. In contrast, from the dance studio drifts in traditional music from the cassette player, mixed with Soke's or Iemoto's voice singing the music, dancers' conversations, and general household sounds. The combined sound is a mix of hundred-year-old music with the lessons of the day. I find this room an exciting spot to compose myself and make the transition from the hectic city landscape to my dance lesson/fieldwork site. Also, since all the dancers briefly stop in this room, away from the larger group in the dance studio, it serves as a location where I can enjoy casual conversation and inquire freely about dancers' lives and their personal thoughts about dance. The dressing room can also be lively, bustling with dancers dressing, preparing for class, applying makeup, or changing back into street clothes.

Walking into the dance studio, I notice a lesson is about to begin, and I sit on the *tatami* floor at the front of the room. The entire room is constructed in a traditional Japanese style—natural wood walls, floor, ceiling, and *tatami*. A large mirror hangs on the right wall, and along the left wall windows extend just above eye level. The dance area has a sprung wood floor, giving it bounce. Since *nihon buyo* requires dancers to stamp, this resilience is kinder to the body. But equally as important, stamping reverberates the floor and creates a distinct hollow percussive sound. The floor is smooth, allowing feet to slide smoothly in a movement called *suriashi*.

A wooden cabinet in the corner houses contemporary audio equipment. A small bamboo bench stands near the sound system against the wall. Iemoto pointed out that this bench had been added to the room because many of the elder dancers' knees and ankles troubled them, making it impossible for them to rise and take part in dance class. Most dancers choose to sit on their heels in the traditional *seiza* style, in front of this bench. A Western-style rosewood chair sits to the right of the room and is reserved for Soke, now in her eighties.

Michiyo is just beginning her lesson when I enter the studio. She kneels in the center of the studio floor, slides her practice *sensu* (fan) out from her *obi* (sash), and places it horizontally at arm's length in front of her on the floor. She fixes her gaze at a spot on the wall high above our heads where several large black-and-white photos of Tachibana Hoshu, the first Tachibana *iemoto*, are displayed on the wall. Michiyo places slightly cupped hands on the floor before her and bows respectfully to these images, then bows to Soke and then to Iemoto, who stands off to the right. Iemoto nods.

Michiyo rises and slides open her fan as she walks to the far corner of the studio with Iemoto and they both assume the opening dance position. From my seated perspective, Michiyo poses one step behind and to the left of Iemoto—the customary place for the student during lessons. Iemoto nods her head to the student operating the cassette player, and the music begins.

They move in graceful, synchronous steps. Michiyo clearly knows this section of the dance, yet it is obvious that she is fully aware of Iemoto's every move. Subtly gazing to her left, Michiyo catches Iemoto in her peripheral vision. She maintains her position relative to Iemoto as they dance. Iemoto sings the mnemonics and vocal lines to highlight the cues while they dance the opening passage. After ten minutes they stop at the end of a phrase and Iemoto turns to Michiyo saying, "We went to here?" Michiyo nods. They turn and walk back to begin the dance again.

After reviewing the opening passage three times Iemoto continues dancing, introducing a new section of the dance. Michiyo immediately drops to the floor; she kneels, bows, and stands again, then promptly resumes following Iemoto's movements. This bow symbolically thanks a teacher for proceeding to the next level. Michiyo's continuous sweep of action passes so swiftly that an observer might miss the ritual. In this gesture, Michiyo's quality of movement changed as she shifted out of a dance persona into a student's role, returned fully composed, and continued her lesson with ease.

Michiyo's body movements now reveal she is entering an unfamiliar section. While I am certain she has previously seen this dance at performances and during other students' lessons, her body reveals a quality of uncertainty, showing that she has not yet physically come to know the choreography in full. She concentrates on Iemoto's every move and attempts to imitate each step. Iemoto's movements now appear somewhat more distinct and punctuated, without the subtle nuances of the previous section. This shift in movement quality and interaction is not dramatic, however. Iemoto sings the mnemonics of the musical instruments and vocal line along with the taped music to cue the dance steps. She also interpolates between the mnemonic cues and emotive explanations, revealing a dancer's inner incentive to move—"Oh, how beautiful the snow is . . ." Iemoto holds out her hand to catch a snowflake, quickly drawing it back as she mimes a cold shiver within her body. The illusion convinces me, yet the temperature in the dance studio is a balmy eighty-seven degrees.

Suddenly the front door chime rings out. We hear the quiet shuffling of shoes and bags coming from the hallway. Iemoto, so deeply focused on Michiyo's lesson, is not distracted. Soon the visitor appears from around the corner, and we see that it is Hosen. She steps into the studio, kneels on the floor, bows to Soke and Iemoto, and then to the students sitting to the side. Iemoto smiles and bows her head in greeting yet does not break the continuity of Michiyo's lesson.

At a certain point Iemoto turns to Michiyo and says, "Let's stop here," marking the end of the new dance section she will introduce today. Michiyo smiles and nods. Iemoto then looks up at the ceiling, humming to herself. Catching the opening musical phrase of the new dance passage in her memory, she begins to sing and dance without the taped music. Michiyo follows carefully behind her. The new section walk-through serves as a demonstration. Iemoto dances each step with meticulous attention to clarify each movement. The step-by-step progression slows down or accelerates as Iemoto elastically modifies the time with her movements and singing. She gauges this time change according to Michiyo's response. If Michiyo seems to be picking up the steps with ease, then the phrase proceeds. In the spots where she appears to be struggling even a little, Iemoto accommodates by retarding the tempo subtly.

After walking through the new section, they run through it with the taped music. Iemoto continues to narrate phrases, including mnemonics and song. After two or three repeats Iemoto says, "From the beginning," and Michiyo walks back to the entrance position while the person cueing the music rewinds the tape. This time Iemoto stands in front of the dance floor and watches Michiyo perform the first section alone. Iemoto points to the upper right corner during one of Michiyo's poses, directing her gaze. A moment later she raises Michiyo's arm a few inches by gently tapping the underside of her wrist with her right hand. Then, just as the new passage begins, Iemoto joins Michiyo in the dance. At the close of this run-through the music is turned off and Iemoto says, "*hai*" (in this context, "that's all" or "that's fine"), signaling the close of the lesson. Michiyo closes her fan as she moves to the center of the floor, kneels, places her fan before her again, and bows. She exits the dance floor to the left and, kneeling on the *tatami*, bows to the student who ran the tape recorder for her lesson.

At this time everyone greets the newly arrived student, and they chat for a considerable time about the weather, family, recent trips, and health. Michiyo discreetly slips out a cotton handkerchief from inside her *yukata* and dabs the sweat from her face and neck. She turns to the cassette player and cues the tape for the following lesson. Meanwhile, the next student prepares a prop for her lesson and walks to the center of the dance floor. Kneeling down to bow, the cycle of a new lesson begins.

unfolding space

How we inhabit Hatchobori, or rather how we are enculturated in the ritual of orienting ourselves within this space, reveals a great deal. In this section I return to a dancer's passage between rooms to unfold the symbolic house. The space is typically Japanese—every square meter of space is efficiently utilized; the interior design is traditional yet blended with a modern, sophisticated style; and natural building materials such as wood and stone are used. In addition, each room clearly demarcates boundaries of private versus public social space that are actively negotiated in a Japanese manner.

The vestibule symbolizes a distinct boundary between private versus public social space and is an area where transitions or exchanges between these social groups occur. Transitions come about in a literal sense, as visitors remove shoes and coats and prepare to be seen in the household, but also in an abstract, existential sense, as visitors transition into the Tachibana dance family social space.

The vestibule, while tiny, secludes visitors from the main areas of the building, such as the dressing room, *keikoba* (dance studio), or Tachibana family home, which is upstairs. Further, visitors must take off shoes and step up into the inner sanctum of the Tachibana dance household. This is also an area where greetings take place. Salutations and farewells are important social interactions in Japan. These moments offer marvelous opportunities to observe markers of Tachibana familial relationships, hierarchical boundaries, and even emotional outpourings. So the vestibule serves not only as a protective spatial buffer to the house but as a rich social space.

Social bounds and transitions take place in the vestibule on three basic levels. The first is the distinction between outsiders and those Tachibana members in the house, such as the arrival of a delivery person at the front door. The outsider is greeted at the front door or in the vestibule, and from this vantage point the outsider cannot see into the *keikoba* or living space. There is no transition for these individuals, just a perfunctory exchange of business, and then they depart. Another level of entry is when dancers arrive for their lessons. Students enter the Tachibana School with only a front door chime announcing their presence. They have a brief moment of transition to remove shoes and prepare to enter the household. If a lesson is already in progress, then there is the "dance" of announcing one's arrival in the more populated *keikoba*—through bows and greetings. Only after one has shown her face in the *keikoba* can a student gracefully depart to the dressing room, a private sanctum in which to relax and perform yet another transition: putting on a *yukata* and preparing for a lesson. The third kind of transition is the one between dance students and the Tachibana living quarters on the floors above the ground floor. In order to traverse this boundary one must climb the stairs directly across from the vestibule. But at the top of these stairs one is in the Tachibana family kitchen and dining room, a private living space. Members of the dance group are oriented within Hatchobori in this way, fully enculturated as to how to traverse private and public areas, while outsiders are kept at the boundary with limited access.

While the sanctity of the *keikoba* as a space of practice is symbolically represented in its physical structure, how dancers behave within this room is particularly revealing. It is a symbolic stage, where deeply intimate moments of practice, learning, and transmission are "staged." The story in the preface about the sweat- and tear-stained dance floor is one example of our staged lessons in the *keikoba*. This room is oriented in a stagelike manner, although an outsider might not notice this at first glance. Dancers are enculturated to see, use, and respect this space as a stage, as a representation of our practice, and as a symbol of the Tachibana "household." After ascending from the vestibule, turning left, you now need to descend several steps to enter the dance area, another boundary transition marked by a vertical shift. Your view into this room is from an audience member's perspective. If Iemoto is dancing she will be facing you from the dance floor, but if she is observing a student dance she will be standing at the front of the wooden floor facing the student. The "stage" or dance floor area is smooth wood, but it ends at the front of the room, an audience area with a *tatami* floor.

Boundaries between being on and being off this stage in the *keikoba* are structurally demarcated. Entrance onto the wooden floor indicates a student's intention to dance, whether it is her own lesson or she is sitting in on someone else's. Students always enter the dance floor on the far left side of the room, traveling to the back and then center stage for the opening bow. This ritual of roundabout movement acknowledges the formality of the stage, and one's respect for the practice with Iemoto that is about to begin. I witnessed a new student unaware of this custom. She wandered directly from the center of the *tatami* area to the dance floor. Iemoto intercepted and literally walked her back to the *tatami*, accompanying her along the far left wall and to center stage, where the student kneeled to bow. Later that afternoon a senior teacher chatted with me in the dressing room and marveled, "There are so many ways we move around [Hatchobori] that I don't even notice anymore. When a new student arrives I can really see it, you know?" Our daily ritual patterns and interactions are a social dance through space; they help orient us in Hatchobori.

moving closer—modes of transmission

The repetitious nature of lessons enabled me to identify the larger spatial and temporal structures of classes and how these frameworks enabled transmission. My analytic challenge was to also identify patterns of transmission on a much smaller structural level, on a personal, somatic level. Analysis of my video documentation of lessons enabled me to focus on very small units of transmission and analyze the gradual embodiment of the artistic practice. From personal experience, I "knew" how Iemoto taught dance. My body had been through the methodical repetitions of movements. Curiously, kinesthetic sensations (the sense of motion and orientation) often fell over me when I observed the videotapes, and somehow guided me through the analysis. It seemed that the field tapes were reinforcing my physical understanding of movement/sound while my body also informed the analytical process. I analyzed over one hundred videotapes. Each tape captured from one to four lessons.

The transmission structures slowly rose from the mediated data—interactions between individuals varied according to the task at hand and the individual student. Transmission, executed via a variety of sensory modes, imparted movement, sound, timing, and beyond. Specifically, visual, tactile, and oral/aural modes of transmission conveyed dance from teacher to student. The following sections are an analysis of the teaching process, organized by sense. A complete unit is devoted to each sensory mode present in the transmission: visual, tactile, and oral/ aural. Of course smell and taste are also present, though in *nihon buyo* practice they are not incorporated into the direct teaching methods. I consider media to be extensions of our senses and have included a description of how notation and video are incorporated in the contemporary pedagogical system.

Though my analytic methodology remained the same across different modes of transmission, I found that the various sensory data demanded different sets of questions. For example, vision, touch, and oral modes all presented (physical and social) relationships, yet the gaze/ contact/resonance of each of these modes implied qualitatively different interactions and ways of orienting the body. As an approach to ground the analysis within the body, I have included an "orientation" at the close of each section. The aim is to foreground the similarities and differences between vision, touch, and oral/aural experiences in the pursuit of comprehending how we learn expressive embodiment.

Fortunately, analysis did not remove the beauty or extraordinary qualities of dance for me. To the contrary, the body-to-body transfer of artistic expression was enchanting. As I analyzed the video footage I was often mesmerized by the complexity and fluidity of transmission and, luckily, could rewind the tape to revisit each moment in slow motion. The following section approaches analysis of transmission through the eyes.

masked

Holding an open fan close to me face, my eyes are hidden from view.
From this private space I can still peer out
between the bones.

appearing folds—visual transmission

When your eyes are closed, does sound move to the foreground? Are other awarenesses heightened—smell, touch, temperature, thought, taste? Then, as you slowly raise your eyelids, what appears in your field of vision? Does your gaze privilege particular visual qualities? People? Slow movements? Illuminated objects? Tall shapes? Bright or colorful objects? Then, what other qualities of visual information are subsumed by these priorities of the eyes?

We enlist sight every day constantly to assist us in a variety of activities such as navigating, organizing and coordinating objects/people, reading and writing, or enjoying art. Ironically, our dependence on vision is built on a constructed reality—deducing a three-dimensional reality by extrapolating information from light entering our eyes. Making sense of this data is a culturally constructed activity. We learn to see, to notice, to interpret what is in our visual plane, form images, and attempt to understand our relationship to what is "out there" (Forrester 2000). In a way, we sift through the rich visual data before us—the details of light, color, texture, movement, and positions of objects—to comprehend our environment. While we are oriented by sight, we also see what we want to see. James Elkins, professor of art history, theory, and criticism, provides a fascinating reflection on how we construct our world through vision:

> My principal argument has been that vision is forever incomplete and uncontrollable because it is used to shape our sense of what we are. Objects molt and alter in accord with what we need them to be, and we change ourselves by the mere act of seeing. (Elkins 1996: 237)

If we see the world according to our needs and beliefs, then understanding the role of culture and transmission is crucial for comprehending how we construct the world through vision.

Though the flow of transmission between eye and object remains "invisible," the course of vision commands attention. We have a heightened awareness of what/whom others fix their eyes on. This beacon of gaze powerfully sheds light on the dynamics of relationships between one who sees and the object of that person's gaze (Foucault 1977; Gamman and Marshment 1989). It is a perspective that raises numerous complex questions, such as: Who is watching whom? Why? Is gaze a controlling factor? How is gaze employed as a means for actively engaging with someone, or for orienting one's self in the world?[1]

In the performing arts, the audience generally watches performers who have manufactured the scene and sight line precisely for the viewers' eyes. Their gaze is choreographed to attract their attendance to the prepossessions of the performer (or choreographer).[2] The constructedness of performance appearance is clearly apparent in many cases—in *nihon buyo*, each visual detail is meticulously staged for effect. Strict rules preside over how dancers (and musicians) display their artistry in performance: they must pay close attention to costuming, physical appearance, posture, behavior, and most importantly, choreographed dance movements.

As mentioned earlier, the hierarchical *iemoto* social structure prevails over the transmission of many of the arts in Japan. Regulation of the appearance of dance is hierarchically determined, including choreography, costuming, who steps onto the stage first, or the selection of the objects onstage. The *iemoto*'s decisions on such matters greatly influence the transmission of the school's tradition through maintaining (or instituting) visually idealized conventions for the audience and performers.

Each dance has a history; when an *iemoto* determines aspects of visual presentation, his/her decisions affect how that piece will look and be transmitted in the future. Over time, dramatic visual representations become codified traditions, marking the identity of specific pieces, the genre, and the style of a particular school. Idealized conventions of the showcased body establish a shared cultural vocabulary of images that convey meaning between choreographer, dancer, and audience. Details of attire, makeup, props, stage sets, lighting, and movement are among the countless visual cues that characterize particular dances for an audience, or signal nuances of stylistic difference between dance schools. Through lessons dancers learn and embody visual conventions and, by transmitting them to future generations, maintain the historical lineage of these visual patterns, or codes, of style.

In traditional Japanese dance and theater, a character's outward appearance and action is thought to embody the identity of that persona, including social status, age, livelihood, and inner spirit. The identity of each character appearing in a dance—for instance, an aged farmer, a young child, or a playboy—is visually codified for the audience. Although there is some leeway (particularly from school to school), *kimono*, wigs, makeup, fans, and other physical attributes of a

character are prescribed, along with specific actions such as body carriage, stage positions, gaze, and movement quality. For example, in the
dance "Musume Dojoji" (The Maiden of Dojo Temple) the beautiful
"maiden" often wears a *kimono* or *obi* with an abstract design representing reptile scales, indicating her true identity as a demonic serpent who
has furtively transfigured into a maiden.

A change in a character's spiritual or emotional state is often coordinated with a visual transformation of the character's appearance—
from subtle changes in movement quality or gaze to indicate moderate
mood shifts, to dramatic costume changes informing the audience of a
character's enormous life transformation. The process of onstage character transformation is called *hengemono* (or just *henge,* transformation).
An example of *henge* is a technique called *hikinuki,* a costume-changing
technique that enables a performer (with the help of a *koken,* or stage
assistant) to shed the outer layer of a *kimono* quickly via removable bast-
ing stitches to reveal a contrasting *kimono* layer below.

One of the most famous examples of *hikinuki* occurs in "Musume Dojoji." The true identity of the temple maiden is dramatically revealed right before the audience via impressively rapid costume
changes, or *hikinuki.* The transfiguration from maiden to demonic serpent is climactic, and the audience cheers in response. Through *hikinuki,* character portrayal is marked by visual representations carefully
crafted through dance techniques.

In the dance studio proper appearance is demonstrably *performed,*
from movement, costume, facial expression, or gaze, and is a vital part
of lessons. Students' visual awareness becomes heightened over time—
honed for a wide palette of visual vocabulary that prepares them for
dance. Dancers actively learn to see and be seen. The primary mode of
transmission in *nihon buyo* is through the art of following teachers—
visually. As mentioned earlier, a student stands to the right and behind
the teacher during a lesson (see photo 3, taken from the student's perspective). At Hatchobori, we literally peer over Iemoto's shoulder to
envision and embody dance.

I often sense a feeling of dancing vicariously through Iemoto as I
gaze from this angle—a projected colocation of sorts. I believe it is this
particular view of Iemoto, while students are simultaneously moving,
that infuses a vicarious sensation via kinesthetic empathy. The practice
of learning through visual imitation, repetition, and close proximity to
the teacher reinforces imprinting—a transference and fixing of dance
information in a student's physical memory. Then there is kinesthetic

PHOTO 3. A student's perspective. Tachibana Yoshie (*left*) and Tachibana Hiroyo "Soke" (*seated*).

empathy, an empathy rooted in the body that draws on kinesthesia—the sense that comprehends the body's weight, spatial orientation, and movement of muscles, tendons, and joints. Kinesthetic empathy is mediated via visual and tactile modes of transmission (Bakan 1999: 281–291; Sklar 2001; Smyth 1984). It plays an important role in movement transference, in which a dancer, experiencing and physically identifying closely with the movements of a teacher, sympathetically coordinates her muscles to resemble the teacher's dance. The alignment between bodies via kinesthesia imprints movement and reinforces kinesthetic empathy for future lessons.

At Hatchobori we learn how to look, how to see, and how to consume movement through sight. It is through the particular angle and process of seeing that we envision and embody movement. Students are instructed to visually attend to their teachers. The dynamic in this directed gaze follows desire and authority—because the teacher embodies a dance that a student desires to learn, her perspective must pragmatically be aimed at the teacher.

The student's gaze toward Iemoto metaphorically mirrors the hierarchical *iemoto* social structure as it reenacts the historical path of transmission through daily practice. The flow of information and rules of "house" structure is governed by those in higher positions relative to those below. In the photograph taken from the student's perspective, note Soke seated in her chair, observing the lesson. Her presence illumines the historical stream of transmission in the present moment—Soke to Iemoto to student.

I believe that the focused manner of imitating what one sees is a symbolic performance of dancers' desire to learn dance. Transmission connects individuals and forms relationships; the teacher-student bonding manifests a mutual commitment to dance and a relationship of responsibility to teach/learn dance. Here learned artistic expression is intricately folded with social structures, personal desire, and the moving body.

An important feature of the teaching context is the position of a large mirror on a side wall. Because students stand diagonally behind Iemoto in lessons, it is nearly impossible to see every angle of her body. From a student's perspective, the mirror catches not only the left and front side of Iemoto's body but the student's own body as well. This mirrored view enables students to see their own image reflected back at them and to match their form to Iemoto's. In this eyeshot a dancer receives visual images from two perspectives—the natural view of Iemoto and the reflected image of her hidden side.

When dancing at Hatchobori there is a strong feeling of being watched—similar to being onstage. Classes are often observed by two to three generations of Tachibana teachers and students. There is one other Tachibana presence in the room "observing"—large black-and-white photographs of Tachibana Hoshu (the first Tachibana *iemoto*) face students taking class. I find that this display, a constant reminder of the Tachibana family descent, instills a positive sense of focus and commitment during lessons. The dance studio symbolically displays the hierarchical *iemoto* structure and the literal flow of dance transmission—the ancestral photographs hang high on the wall at the front of the room; Soke sits before this wall; Iemoto, who is teaching, dances in the formal dance area; the student taking the lesson stands a few steps behind Iemoto; and finally, any other students "sitting in" on the lesson are at the very back of the dance floor. The structures of space mirror the social organization of the fictive family and the flow of information. While this spatial organization is not directly explained to students, it reveals the depth in which the *iemoto* system is embodied in dancers' everyday practice at Hatchobori.

As I will detail in the case studies below, transmission is a profoundly personal involvement whereby seeing one's teacher dance by one's side each day imprints into visual memory images of how the dance needs to appear. The process of looking is inextricably bound to social structures and issues of desire. Teachers, as living (visual) archetypes of the art form, serve as models for students to follow and emulate. With this in mind, the next section focuses on the visual mode of transmission at Hatchobori, utilizing examples from my field notes and personal experience.

case study in visual transmission

expanded field notes

[Adjacent to the following passage are my sketches of sieves sifting stone and sand.]

I am struggling to learn a new dance now and today realized that I am only comprehending the big picture—as if I am sifting out large phrases, while the refined steps and subtle nuances escape through the sieve of my comprehension. Though I saw great detail in Iemoto's dancing today, I know the delicate nuances and subtleties are non-existent qualities in my movements. As I watched the variety of students' lessons, I realized that learning to follow (acquiring finer sieves) is a life-long challenge.

The art of following forms the foundation of *nihon buyo* transmission. Following is essential, as the rudiments of *nihon buyo* movement vocabulary are not introduced prior to learning a dance piece. At a student's first lesson she is led through a phrase of dance. This differs from other dance traditions, such a ballet or classical dance in Cambodia (Phim and Thompson 2001), where several years are devoted to the acquisition of a movement vocabulary, core postures, and forming the body. Instead, new movement is acquired gradually in *nihon buyo* through the introduction of new pieces, similar to how children learn language contextually by listening and through conversation. In this way *nihon buyo* students are dependent on teachers for new dance information. The art of following involves gaining visual acuity, kinesthetic awareness, and the ability to transfer the complexity of visual information to coordinate one's own body movements.

I found comparing a beginner's lesson to those of more advanced students insightful for understanding the gradual process of learning dance through visual awareness. Examples 1–3 in the online companion represent three levels of ability: beginner, intermediate, and advanced. In all three cases the footage depicts the student's first lesson of the same dance.

Example 1 presents a rare opportunity to examine a student's very first lesson at the Tachibana School. Just prior to Hideo's lesson the two of us chatted freely while preparing for class. He intimated that he had never studied dance before and wanted to learn *nihon buyo* as a hobby. From his comments, it was already apparent to me that Hideo was self-conscious of his (visual) appearance within this context. I wrote in my field notes:

I talked to Hideo in the dressing room. I am interested in why he's beginning dance, so I asked him questions while we were dressing. He's twenty-four. When I asked him, he told me his age and then said, "Did you think I was younger?—a teenager?"

I said, "Why?"

Hideo answered, "Because my hair is a little long now and it sticks straight up—Iemoto and Soke say I look like a boy! So, I'll be cutting my hair soon."

I asked, "Why are you taking dance . . . how did you find out about nihon buyo*?"*

Hideo answered, "My grandfather and father both like nihon buyo *and* kabuki. *My father sings* nagauta *and took* shamisen *and* nihon buyo *lessons. We both like going to* kabuki. *So, I thought I'd try taking dance. My father doesn't sing now, though. He's a* sarari-man *[a salary man, a white-collar worker]."*

I asked, "Do you have a job now?"

Hideo replied, "I have a part-time job at a big supermarket in Meguro—attending the parking lot cars and carts . . . it's exhausting work."

Soon after this conversation we entered the dance studio, and immediately Iemoto adjusted his *yukata* and *obi*, giving him pointers on how to dress properly. Watching Hideo move in his *yukata*, it seemed to me that he was not comfortable wearing traditional Japanese clothing. (This can be observed in video example 1: Hideo attends to his *yukata* during the lesson, straightening it, even breaking the continuity of his dance movements at times.) Familiarity with dance attire is one of the many dance customs that confronts a new student. This is particularly true for young people in Japan today, many of whom rarely wear traditional clothing.

a note on the online companion

The description in the following case study is not intended to be a detailed transcription of the dance. Instead, this narrative summarizes what arises in the video excerpt in order to highlight elements of the visual learning process. Movement directions provided are from the dancer's perspective: left knee, turning left, walking counterclockwise, and so forth.

It is important to note that the video footage included with this book is from my fieldwork at Hatchobori and is not staged. In my first week of fieldwork Iemoto directed me to come out from behind the camera and take lessons. Also, I found that students behaved differently if I held or even sat near the video camera while shooting. Therefore, I elected to leave the camera in one place and attended to it as little as possible. My video camera "lived" in a corner of the dance studio and captured hundreds of hours of footage during my fieldwork. This is why the camera footage remains stationary and, unfortunately, cuts off a portion of the dance space (and occasionally body parts).

The quality of Iemoto's movements during lessons is demonstrative in nature, contrasting to some degree with the expressive movement of her dance performances onstage. Since this book focuses on transmission, I have featured her teaching movement style.

Notice that Iemoto incorporates visual cues during the lessons to guide the students as they follow. These cues heighten students' visual awareness, aid their ability to follow, and draw attention to an aspect of dance that needs correction. In general, increased visual awareness helps students gain an understanding of important dance fundamentals such as the structural elements of movement, a kinesthetic sensibility, spatial awareness, the handling of props, and the custom of wearing and moving in traditional costume.

using the online companion

For each media example, I suggest reading the descriptive text, then watching the specified example in its entirety, followed by shorter viewings of specific sections so that the details can be examined. Time stamps have been included to mark particular moments in the example footage that are addressed in the text. Time stamps are yellow capital letters in parenthesis, such as (A), that appear in the lower left-hand side of the viewing window. Viewers can navigate to a time stamp chapter marker by selecting the forward/back button in the control panel or on their remote control.

online visual transmission example 1: November 17, 1993

The following passage is a description of Hideo's first run-through of the opening phrase of "Matsu no midori" (The Evergreen Pine), choreographed by Tachibana Hoshu. It is a piece from the *goshugi-mono nagauta* repertory (formal celebratory style accompanied by a *nagauta* musical ensemble). Considered to be one of the classic Tachibana pieces, "Matsu no midori" is customarily used as an examination dance within the school. Symbolically, this is an appropriate dance to introduce to a beginner, as pines are considered to be auspicious trees and are central metaphors in Japanese rituals, ceremonies, and performance. Because pine trees are always green, they are a symbol of long life. Their tendency to grow differently depending on climate, geographic context (on a rocky hillside or next to a river, for example), wind conditions, and rain demonstrates the tree's resilience. The environment, over time, shapes the contour of the tree much as experience shapes our bodies. The dancer narrates the life of a pine, anthropomorphizing it from childhood to old age, while the text plays with double meanings that reference the floating world. As a *goshugimono*, the dance wishes everyone long life and prosperity.

The quality of the movements is distinct and very precise, an embodiment of the strength and spirit of the pine as well as the formality and auspicious nature of the *goshugimono* style. Pragmatically, this clarity in movement quality introduces a beginner to many of the fundamental techniques of *nihon buyo*. Three dancers can be seen in the back of the dance space following the lesson; however, because it is Hideo's lesson, Iemoto generally does not address them.

Iemoto begins "Matsu no midori" with a formal, seated bow—hands palm down on the floor, fingers together, a closed *sensu* (fan) sitting at arm's length, and her torso is lowered. Pressing her hands into the floor, Iemoto raises up slowly with a straight back, hinging at the hips, until her arms extend completely. At the end of this movement her head continues to lift up slightly to continue the upward movement. This formal greeting to the audience manifests the strength and formality conveyed in the entire piece—embodied in a dancer's erect, broad back; strong arms; the simplicity and clarity of each movement; and focused gaze. Next, Iemoto grasps the bamboo end of the *sensu* in her right hand, turning it ninety degrees clockwise. Her body lifts up to a half-kneeling pose—left knee raised—so that her weight is distributed between her right knee on the ground and the balls of her right and left feet. Her heels are positioned directly below the pelvic sitting bones. At the same time, both arms circle gently counterclockwise until her right hand places the fan on her right thigh and her left hand, grasping the *yukata* (cotton *kimono*) sleeve opening, settles into a position extending forward with a slightly bent elbow. This last movement is rather complex—each limb moves independently as the body raises into the kneeling position.

Before proceeding to the next phrase, let's take a closer look at Hideo's lesson. In video example 1, notice how Hideo carefully observes Iemoto and attempts to imitate each move. During the curved, two-arm gesture, as the left knee shifts up to the half-kneeling position, Hideo appears to have difficulty keeping up and maintaining his balance. He raises up on his heels from the seated position and, observing Iemoto's lifted left knee, corrects his footing. His right arm coordinates with Iemoto's movement, yet the left arm falls to his lap. At this point Iemoto subtly jerks her left hand to draw attention to his incorrect arm position. Hideo catches the cue and repositions his arm. Without words Iemoto can draw a student's focus to a particular element of dance. This type of visual cueing is an important instruction and can be seen practiced often in lessons.

In video example 1, time stamp (A), Iemoto sweeps the *sensu* upward, leading the entire body into a standing position, while her left arm lowers to her side and she shifts to face left. Hideo fusses with his left *yukata* sleeve, and it seems he is unsure of how his left hand should grasp the sleeve. Once Hideo has turned to face left, note that his left arm position is still unchanged since the seated pose. Iemoto pauses briefly. She cues Hideo again by gesturing her left arm. She then walks clockwise six steps until she is facing 180 degrees opposite the preceding pose, feet together. During this walk her right hand has slowly lowered to hold the fan at shoulder height. Her right foot slides forward, and the left foot shifts to turn out. Iemoto assumes a strong, firmly rooted stance that is held momentarily: both legs are turned out from the hips, her weight falls on her right leg, with right knee bent and her left leg straight for counterbalance. Her head turns left with a distinct gaze to the distant stately pine. She holds the pose.

In video example 1, time stamp (B), Iemoto draws her feet together, left foot to her right foot. She circles her fan clockwise, then extends it out—leading her body around the space in a counterclockwise walk. Hideo's quality of movement during this walk differs greatly from Iemoto's *suriashi* (sliding feet style of walking). His gait is no different from from how he might walk when he crosses a street in Tokyo, and he looks from side to side, trying to keep Iemoto within eyeshot.

After this walk they pause, facing forward. Iemoto's right wrist and arm gently flip the *sensu* so the hand faces palm up, then draws a small counterclockwise circle with the tip of the fan and points to the left again. The point of Iemoto's fan again leads her body to turn right, and she faces backstage. They hold a pose similar to the last, right leg bent and left leg turned out and straight. Feet come together at this point, right foot to left, and they turn to the right to face stage front. Finally their arms swing in a gentle curve to the right, and they sit in the same half-kneeling position that opened the dance. Note that Hideo's gaze is continuously toward either Iemoto or one of the other students in order to follow during turns. He apparently notices that his final pose does not match Iemoto's and shifts several times to correct his knee position and balance. This concludes the first run of the opening passage, less than ninety seconds of the nine-minute dance.

In example 1 Hideo can be seen relying primarily on visual information in order to follow along. Even in this short passage it is clear that Hideo's new experience of watching Iemoto dance while coordinating his own movements is a challenging maneuver. He is honing his visual awareness skills and specific visual vocabulary. Not only is the new movement information complex; it is the process of watching and simultaneously transferring what he sees to his own body that is new as well.

online visual transmission example 2: November 17, 1993

For comparison, let us now view a more advanced student learning the same dance. Mariko lives in a northern province of Japan and cannot attend classes at Hatchobori regularly. Before her lesson Iemoto asked Mariko if she preferred to study "Matsu no midori" in female or male style. She decided on female, and her class began. While video examples 1–3 focus on the same dance, example 2 differs only in that it is performed in the female style. The choreography is fundamentally the same except the movements are stylistically gender-specific. Since an outline of the opening dance has been detailed in the previous example, only particular instances of the visual transmission process that signal a contrast to example 1 are highlighted. Several students join this lesson—Mariko is the student with the green *obi* (sash).

From the opening bow it appears that Mariko is familiar with the clothing, the dance style, and the process of following in lessons. In order to learn the new dance Hideo and Mariko both keep Iemoto within view. However, a comparison between Mariko's and Hideo's following abilities reveals aspects of Mariko's developed learning skills. Her angle of gaze is much less overt (relative to Hideo's gaze), and she apparently gleans a great deal of movement information through her peripheral vision. Her focus is clearly directed toward Iemoto. For example, in the opening bow, notice her directed gaze and careful attention to Iemoto's every action. Mariko subtly angles her body toward Iemoto for most of example 2. In several instances she checks her hand position—visibly looking over at Iemoto, then to her own hand location, and back to Iemoto. An example of this coordination is observable in video example 2, time stamp (A). Her movements during this lesson indicate that, despite the introduction of new dance information, she utilizes past dance experience to inform her present actions.

Mariko's body coordination is generally synchronized with Iemoto's throughout the lesson, and the quality of her movements, while deliberate, is generally fluid. Mariko appears to comprehend the basic movement vocabulary (*kata*) within the choreographic phrases, perhaps based on her previous dance experience, contrasting with Hideo's lesson. He follows Iemoto through the steps, yet because he has no previous association with any of the movements, the process of following is challenging.

Mariko's lesson provides a marvelous example of Soke observing lessons from her seat on the far right of the video. Although Soke remains still during a majority of the lesson, one can observe subtle cueing taking place at several points. In video example 2, time stamp (B), Soke's hands "dance" briefly, to cue Mariko. Here Soke indicates the specific hand positions and the nuance of the gesture to Mariko through visual cues. A sense of kinesthetic transmission can be noted here as well, since Soke's hands are not merely correcting the gesture, but the quality of her hand movements can be "felt" even from a distance.

Compared with the verdant quality of Hideo's movements, Mariko moves in a clearer and less tentative fashion. While Hideo's general physical coordination is undeveloped, Mariko is able to observe Iemoto's movements and gauge her own physical balance and distribution of body weight.

online visual transmission example 3: October 23, 1993

Finally, let us observe an advanced dancer's lesson. Etsuko is a *nihon buyo* teacher. While she has studied "Matsu no midori" at a different dance school, this is her first lesson of the Tachibana choreography. As a result of her many years of experience, she is familiar with the music, the stylistic features of the genre, and the particular dance. In example 3, two additional students follow in the back of the dance area. Etsuko is the student wearing the pink colored *obi* (sash) and dancing on the front left side of the dance floor.

A prominent aspect of Etsuko's lesson is her familiarity with the general conventions of dance lessons at Hatchobori. Considerations of the dance setting and process of learning that might overwhelm the newcomer do not appear to faze Etsuko, including physical comfort with the dance clothing; dexterity with props; rules of the social setting and physical space; acquaintance with the teacher and other students; the comfort (or discomfort) of being closely observed; physical understanding of the learning process (for example, following the teacher's movements and directions); and familiarity with the dance vocabulary.

From the opening bow we can observe Etsuko's clarity of movement. Although it is almost imperceptible in the example, Etsuko visually follows Iemoto with a sidelong gaze or her peripheral vision. Etsuko's movements match Iemoto's in carriage, phrasing, quality, and spatial use so closely that her lesson appears effortless. In fact, she seems to intuit certain phrases as she follows, apparently drawing from her established dance vocabulary, previous experience with this dance, and her developed visual awareness skills. For the thirty-second passage, beginning at video example 3, time stamp (A), note how Etsuko coordinates her entire body to correspond with Iemoto's movements and phrasing. This contrasts with the less experienced dancers, who must prioritize coordinating general physical movements over subtle nuance to keep up with Iemoto's pace. During this section Etsuko can be seen using the mirror to follow Iemoto's movements.

Etsuko's advanced dance abilities and movement vocabulary enable her to easily coordinate the general dance movements, balance, and shifts of body weight. This permits her to extend her attention beyond these basic dance skills to a more refined awareness of the dance. For instance, in video example 3, time stamp (B), Etsuko turns her head subtly toward Iemoto, apparently to align the quality of her fan movement to Iemoto's upward sweep. Because she is an advanced dancer, Etsuko's head turn is so subtle it might go unnoticed.

Etsuko's handling of a *sensu* reflects her familiarity with and routine use of this prop. This is clear in the video excerpt, especially when viewed in contrast to the video example of Hideo's use of a fan. Specifically, when Etsuko points her *sensu* out to the stand of pine, her movement quality reveals that the *sensu* is an extension of her own body. The movement impulse originates from her torso (from her *hara*), ripples outward along her shoulder, arm, wrist, and flows to the very tip of the fan itself. The pointing *sensu* illuminates the spirit of the pine in the imagined landscape. With the extended presence of the fan, Etsuko initiates the movement of her body from the tip of her fan, around the room to view the pine. From an audience perspective, this pointing motion directs action away from the body and to the pine in the distance. Because Etsuko regularly practices with *sensu*, she has honed the ability to control this prop as an extension of her body and a part of her dance vocabulary. Similarly, Etsuko actively employs her *yukata* (the sleeves, for example) as an expressive aspect of the dance. Compare Etsuko's dexterity with a fan and use of her *yukata* with Hideo's case in example 1. Hideo's connection with the fan and *yukata* has not formed yet, as this was his first experience holding the prop and wearing a *yukata* in a lesson.

A comparison of the three lessons discussed above illuminates aspects of the visual learning process at different stages of development. Because these students' dance experiences contrast greatly, their learning skills are dramatically apparent. What can a student grasp in the first few run-throughs of a new piece? Following a dance for the first time involves new physical experiences and awareness skills—each student's previous dance experience provides him/her with reference points for future associations. For a beginner, the dance context, movements, and music may be completely foreign. In an advanced dancer's case, individual steps might seem familiar (particularly *kata*, prescribed movement patterns), but their placement within the choreography of that particular dance positions the movements in an unfamiliar context.

Lessons provide a gradual development of awareness for students. Learning progresses in stages—from a broad overview of a phrase to a greater understanding of specific movements and a refining of subtle detail. What a beginner notices about Iemoto's movements during his/her lesson is qualitatively different from what an advanced dancer notices. Hideo, for example, seems to grasp only Iemoto's general movements (standing, sitting, turning right or left, for example) in order to keep up with her pace, but after dancing for several months he will most likely be able to make associations with certain steps and refine his own movements. Once large-scale information becomes habitual or "natural" to the student, his/her attention can turn to other aspects of the dance.

Experienced dancers, on the other hand, seem to learn new dances effortlessly. Their bodies, informed with many years of training, physically know a wide range of movements, compositional forms, the dance context, how to coordinate following Iemoto, and the conventions of dance lessons. This sensational knowledge allows these dancers to focus directly on the particular dance and its subtleties. Through this long process of acquiring skills there is also a gradual liberating process for students—as skills become habitual, a student's disorientations lessen, freeing him/her to follow Iemoto with increasing ease.

In *Flow: The Psychology of Optimal Experience*, professor of psychology and education Mihaly Csikszentmihalyi points out the (physical) human limitations for processing activities:

Unfortunately, the nervous system has definite limits on how much information it can process at any given time. There are just so many "events" that can appear in consciousness and be recognized and handled appropriately before they begin to crowd each other out . . .

> Simple functions [however] like adding a column of numbers or driving a car grow to be automated, leaving the mind free to deal with more data. (1991: 28–29)

The complex negotiation of mental and physical processing of information that a dancer attends to during lessons will be unfolded as we visit other sensory modes of transmission. I find lessons to be rehearsals of vision and visualization. To embody movement, we learn to exercise a particular way of seeing dance that is culturally constituted. What we see is not only a biological capacity for visual perception—we are trained to sort through the myriad of visual information before us to seek the vital elements needed for the task at hand or the aesthetic focus.

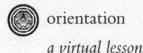 orientation

a virtual lesson

In my search for ways to convey the experience of following dance to out-siders, I shot video footage from a position diagonally behind Iemoto while she danced, to simulate a student's point of view during a lesson of the dance "Kanegamisaki" (video example 4). Although video cannot fully capture the lived experience of learning in the studio, this footage introduces the basic context of lessons from a student's perspective. Notice that the student's view of a teacher is from behind and over her right shoulder. The mirror (a rather modern addition to *nihon buyo* studios) transmits the left side of the teacher. A *nihon buyo* student's use of a mirror is considerably different from that of a ballet student, as the reflected view is not so much to observe one's own form but to see Iemoto's form more clearly or to see one's own form *relative to* hers.

I hoped to capture the essence of kinesthetic transference and the keen vi-sual awareness needed to move synchronously with a teacher via the camera angle's mime of the student's distinctive gaze. With the understanding that the art of following, so crucial to the transmission process, is merely simu-lated in this footage, I encourage readers to assume the student's role by tak-ing a virtual lesson through the camera's eye and to move with Iemoto. Since the excerpt is rather long, I suggest following just a portion of the introduc-tion and repeating just that unit several times.

In this visual orientation exercise, contemplate how your field of vision orients you, kinesthetically, in space. Through observing Iemoto dance, how is your body coordinating proportions of body space, movement quality, and timing? How does following help you to visually orient yourself? Observe your focus through several repetitions of the lesson. As you become accus-tomed to the dance and the following process, does your gaze shift from a generalized focus to one in which you notice nuances?

Finally, I'd like to add my personal experience of the transmission process to the mix. Within this section I have stressed that, to embody what one sees, acute visual awareness must be honed. Visual and kinesthetic transmission inherently produces a bonding relationship, evoked through gaze, between teacher and student. As I will point out in upcoming chapters, bonding is reinforced in every sensory mode of transmission. I believe that the relationship stems partly from the desire to dance as our teachers dance. The physical intensity and focus of repeatedly aligning one's movements to a teacher's way of dance creates an unspoken connection between student and teacher.

The visceral nature of dance transmission gestures to embodiment as a vehicle for observing qualities of cultural values. In the case of *nihon buyo* transmission, the distinct gaze in lessons manifests a particularly Japanese practice, permeated with traditions of lineage, hierarchy, spiritualism, and prescribed artistry, to name a few. The process of transmission via visualization of a sanctioned model transmits and reinforces continuity of a codified and specific practice of art. For me, the desire for dance embodiment that I have experienced all my life is enculturated. I have been trained to project my gaze a certain way, to visually attend in such an intense manner, and to follow, perhaps even to bond, for the sake of the art and group unity. The process of training the body has integrated with my personal desire to dance and to belong to such an organized group, magnifying the deeply connected relationship between modes of sensory practice, desire, and the body as self. In this sense, I see that the enculturated body becomes a sight and a site of cultural training (Leppert 1995) that is ritualized in the dance lesson.

Visual transmission forms a foundation for learning dance steps and establishing relationships, but also for how we see and envision our selves. Continuing our examination of transmission and the orientation of the body, the following section introduces tactile transmission, a sensory mode closely related to kinesthesia.

stretched

The grasp of a fan is particular, though there are many different ways to hold it. The hand clutches the fan gently, yet securely—"as if holding an egg in the palm of your hand," I remember Iemoto telling us. The end, where the bones are hinged together, is cradled in the well of the palm, the thumb against the metal finding. As my fingers comfortably spread out along the bones and stretch to conjoin with them, the fan becomes a huge hand that extends my limb outward.

touching arrays—tactile transmission, kinesthesia, and body space

We've all had the experience—while you are walking along a street, someone comes up from behind and pulls your arm back, changing the momentum of your walk. The hold on your arm imparts a flurry of information depending on the nature of the touch: Was the grasp forceful? firm? gentle? Was there an active pulling backward of your arm, imposing a physical stretch and contrasting movement quality on your body? How about the texture of the person's hand: Was it soft? rough? gloved? Was the person's hand hot or cold? This interaction probably changed the timing and direction of your walk—did you instinctively look back in response to see who was governing your movement? This simple example of a tactile interaction demonstrates the complexity of the sense of touch; it can transmit a wide array of information that the body interprets within the particular social context (Howes 2005).

Touch is used at Hatchobori as an active, direct means of teaching dance. This section turns to the sense of touch to discuss its role as an agent of movement and social information, with some attention to the related topics of kinesthesia and spatial orientation. I include a brief introduction of general characteristics of touch that are important for transmitting dance, followed by case studies from Hatchobori and an orientation.

Though the eyes are the perceptual organ of visual data, there is no single organ for sensing tactile information. Instead, tactile sensing occurs throughout the body; the receptors are cutaneous and connect to a web of nerves and muscles throughout the body. Touch is fully integrated into the body—cutaneous and subcutaneously—so the entire body is an organ of touch. This full-bodied feature of the sense is ideal for dance transmission, where the entire (receptive) body can feel and mediate movement qualities. The teacher can sensitively "read" a student's body through touch while a student simultaneously can be directly guided into place by the teacher.

Touch is a complex sense. Through touch we simultaneously perceive movement/kinesthesia, airflow, the temperature, pressure, and texture of an object or a living being that comes in contact with our body. The sense of movement via touch is particularly valuable for dance transmission. In fact, touch rarely occurs without movement.

When someone/something contacts our body we can perceive its movement quality, such as the speed and direction of its action. For example, if someone takes your hand, swings, and releases it in an upward toss, you experience this arm gesture through touch. The energy, or force, of the tactile encounter imparted a speed and direction of motion to your body. If this had been a lesson, could you reproduce the quality of this arm movement? As I will detail later, active tactile manipulation of the body is employed in dance lessons at Hatchobori to provide qualities of movement such as timing, flow, direction, and speed.

Active touch along the surface of an object can also verify its textural qualities, from smooth to rough, hard to soft. Edward Hall points out that Japanese have a predilection for subtlety, particularly nuances of texture (Hall 1966: 59). My experience in the traditional arts support this to a degree—for example, in tea ceremony lessons teachers encouraged me to feel the texture of a bowl or utensil, or in dance class, to notice the sensitive mixing of fabric textures in costume preparations.

Perhaps more than any other sensory parameter, the incorporation of touch in lessons reveals corporeality.[3] Tactile transmission exposes the union of dance and the corporeal body. Through embodiment, touch denies their separation—the body simultaneously exists as the art object for performance, as the direct transmitter of the art, and as an individual self. Touch is personal. The encounter negotiates the very boundaries of our physical self. During a tactile experience the boundaries of one body and another conjoin. Walter Ong framed touch as a gauge of what distinguishes us from other: "Touch, including kinesthesia, helps form concepts of exteriority and interiority. We feel ourselves inside our own bodies, and the world as outside" (Ong 1967: 119). Touch arouses and situates the body. Anthony Synnott stated, "Touching and the skin are therefore social and physical phenomenon, which cannot be separated: the physical is the social and vice versa" (Synnott 1993: 157). The skin not only contains the physical boundary of each individual; it locates the body *within* a context, *as* a context (a sense of the body's interior versus exterior), and it can distinguish a variety of tactile qualities to help individuals derive meaning from the outside world.

Touch is social. Tactile experiences between self and other inherently raise a variety of social issues depending on the individuals involved, culture, and context of the experience. A gentle stroke across the back, for instance, may be appropriate in one cultural context (between close friends or during a massage) yet completely inappropriate in others. Synnott pointed out, "Touching is instinctive, it is also culturally determined, with a wide variety of tactile interactive patterns in different societies and indeed in different families" (1993: 181). The socialized body physically holds, or embodies, knowledge concerning spatial coordination and "appropriate" contexts of touch. Through acculturation the body is socialized for sensitivities to touch in diverse contexts. The process of acculturation provides the body with a means for interpreting the tactile experience for that particular context.

Touch is polysemous. Contact signifies a range of intention, depending on the quality of touch, the emotional content, if any, and where on the body one is touched and by whom or what. It is no secret that, in general, Japanese respectfully allow ample personal space between themselves and acquaintances (Synnott 1993: 171; Hall and Hall 1987: 11–14). Of course, a variety of engagements of touch and allowances for personal space exist in Japan—from the Tokyo rush-hour subway, where strangers' bodies completely enter each other's personal body space; to a unisex hot spring where bathers are completely nude and actions of touch are select; to transmission processes in a dance studio. In these contrasting contexts the cultural codes for personal space accommodation have been socialized and are within peoples' embodied knowledge. How people navigate relative to others within a space are negotiations of personal body space gathered from past experiences and built on social norms.

Sukinshippu ("*skinship*") is a modern Japanese word created specifically to define the close physical/tactile mother-child relationship in Japan believed to develop well-being, security, and interdependence in a child (Caudill and Plath 1974; Hendry 1986: 98; Lebra 1976: 138). "*Skinship*" now circulates in everyday language to mean a "close relationship." The creation of this new term underscores the Japanese acknowledgment and use of touch as a means for acculturating individuals. Touch, or *skinship*, also pervades artistic traditions as a means for socializing the body, transmitting art and cultural values. The use of touch for dance transmission and such socialization of the body at Hatchobori will be a main focus of the following case study.

Touch is political. Tactile encounters signal actions of information flow and control. For example, in lessons at Hatchobori, touch is understood to be an appropriate and acceptable practice for teaching. I observed that touch often defined and reinforced the relationships of the dancers within the group. Teachers, in a superior rank, approach and touch students during lessons. Out of respect, students rarely touch their teachers. The tactile code here is culturally constructed, reflecting and reinforcing the hierarchical *iemoto* social system. It also illuminates the flow of artistic information from teacher to student. I recognize this cultural tactile code as an embodied manifestation of the deep respect that exists between individuals in the group and for their dance tradition.

Countless stories circulate concerning the practice of hitting during training in the Japanese performing arts, Buddhism, and martial arts.[4] In November 1993 Iemoto and Soke spoke freely to me about their disdain of hitting, revealing why I have not witnessed more than a tap during lessons at the Tachibana School. They expressed to me that hitting reflects the frustrations and impatience of a teacher rather than a sign of a student's inability. Iemoto mentioned that when she notices a student merely going through the moves with little concentration, then a tap on the arm might focus her/him to an alert state again.

Not all forms of dance in Japan (or around the world) incorporate touch as a means for teaching dance. I find it interesting to note when touch is incorporated into lessons as a transmission practice. At Hatchobori the interaction is common and reveals a number of fascinating qualities about teaching dance. Let's return to Hatchobori for two case study examples of touch used in transmitting movement.

case study in tactile transmission

I'm not sure which is more difficult, being the puppeteer or the puppet.
—Yamada Hisashi, Urasenke tea master
(Hahn field notes, 1992)

expanded field notes

Mid-way through my lesson today Iemoto ceased to guide me through the piece step by step. She darted from one side of me to the other as I danced—tapped me on the elbow; then a bit more firmly on my left shoulder; used her foot to push my left foot closer to my right during a pose; and then, suddenly disappeared from sight. I felt her completely envelop me from behind. She held onto

PHOTO 4. Tachibana Yoshie teaching through touch. PHOTO: WALTER HAHN

my hands and danced the next phrase herself. I experienced her dance through my own body, and I became a bunraku *puppet. A jolt of realization spanned my limbs and torso. The immediacy of actually feeling her dance that phrase conveyed much more than watching her steps in time and space.*

At a certain point in the learning process students are able to recall the movements, music, and choreography well enough to dance by themselves. Teachers are then freed from demonstrating dance and able to correct details through visual, tactile, and oral cues. At Hatchobori I experienced and observed tactile transmission employed as a direct approach for guiding movement, posture, and poses. As my field notes above intimate, the experience of guidance via touch introduces a dynamic to movement in space and time that conveys the fundamentals of movement, yet transcends the pragmatic to a deeper level of understanding dance. The immediacy of physical contact reveals a multidimensional field of body messages between the teacher and the student. Crossing the boundary of personal space, the intimate nature of touch forms relationships, connections, between teacher and student.

The examples in this section examine the employment of tactile transmission in two contexts: during static poses and while in motion. *Nihon buyo* choreography often features held poses, particularly at phrase endings. This distinctive element of the choreography presents a timely opportunity for a teacher to enter the dancer's space and adjust the body. The first example focuses on corrections made during this period of frozen time.

online tactile transmission example 5: December 1, 1993

A rather new student named Masako is learning the dance "Kishi no yanagi" (Willows along the Shore) in this example. Masako is standing on the left side of the video screen. She has studied this piece with Iemoto for several weeks at this point. Today they first reviewed the opening passage with taped music twice. Ten minutes into the lesson Iemoto walks through the dance with her, without the taped music. The quality of Iemoto's movements are now demonstrative in nature, emphasizing each step clearly within the phrase for Masako to follow easily. In the last phrase they stand motionless for a brief moment in a final pose.

In video example 5, time stamp (A), Iemoto looks over at Masako, turns, and, with her right arm extending toward Masako's fan, walks over to correct her pose. The quality of Iemoto's actions is no longer within the dance vocabulary but reflects her instructional manner. There is a sense of urgency in Iemoto's movements, as if she must catch Masako's pose at just the right instant. Often an incorrect pose or action is demonstrated for a student, in order to illustrate a clear contrast to the proper form. Iemoto first shifts the angle of Masako's fan and remarks, "Not like this," as she repositions the fan into an exaggerated unsatisfactory position. "Like this . . . ," and she corrects the angle.

Iemoto takes hold of Masako's left hand, removing her grasp of the fan, and repositions it lower, at the paper edge. Iemoto reaches around Masako's right side and lowers her arm. From here Iemoto sweeps her right hand down Masako's left arm to her wrist. By flexing Masako's wrist in a puppetlike manner, Iemoto corrects the grasp and angle of her *sensu*. For a moment, Iemoto's hands steady Masako's hands in this reformed position.

At time stamp (B) Iemoto circles around to Masako's left side and gently pats her left shoulder to lower it. Standing at her side, Iemoto reaches her right arm around to Masako's back and places a flat hand between her shoulder blades to straighten her posture. Iemoto runs this hand down Masako's spine to the *obi* (sash), emphasizing the proper upright carriage.[5] Standing in front of Masako, Iemoto again adjusts her hand position, then explains (and demonstrates) that if a dancer's arms are held up high in a pose, then her *kimono* sleeves will fall, revealing bare arms. Control of the costume is an important aspect of dance. Since it would be unladylike to expose one's arms, Iemoto instructs Masako to notice such details. Iemoto then guides Masako through the head movement by delicately gesturing her hand while singing "*hi fu mi*" (1-2-3) to conclude the phrase.

The passage detailed above lasts a brief two minutes. I have observed that beginners are taught through touch more often than advanced dancers. Since beginners are naturally less experienced and have a limited movement vocabulary, touch is employed pragmatically for both large-scale and subtle adjustments. Dancers come to apprehend the dance form directly by having their bodies directly moved into position by a teacher. A keener sensitivity to movement, space, and one's own body is gained through experiencing the repetition of tactile corrections. I have noticed that more experienced dancers draw on their previous dance vocabulary to learn new dances. They embody sensitivities to gentle touch, subtle cues, and nearly imperceptible prompting from a teacher standing across the dance floor.

In the above example Iemoto's corrections are typical for a beginner's lesson at Hatchobori but also common for a student at an early stage of learning a new piece. Several weeks later Masako would not need such large-scale adjustments. As a dancer becomes increasingly familiar with a particular piece, corrections become progressively refined, until she is ready to perform the dance.

The second example involves tactile transmission in midmotion, while a student continues to dance. Similar to a game of trading jump-rope partners, delivering tactile cues in midmotion requires a teacher to spring into the student's dance at the proper time, with the appropriate force and quality of touch. In order to grasp the constant physical interaction between teacher and student during an active passage, let us observe touch employed in another lesson at Hatchobori.

online tactile transmission example 6: September 17, 1993

At the beginning of Yuri's lesson Iemoto stood to one side, observing, as Yuri danced "Hokushu" (White Fan). Occasionally Iemoto cued Yuri—pointing across the room to direct her gaze, or singing a musical phrase. Several minutes into the lesson Iemoto interacted more physically, more demonstratively, yet she was not dancing full-out. Her movements suggested the bare minimum of the dance steps as an outline for Yuri to reference. At one point Iemoto's hands danced, curling in and out, to cue Yuri's timing. Later, just a subtle tilt of her head signaled a phrase ending. After the first eight minutes of the lesson, Iemoto's cues have become increasingly physical. The video footage begins at this point in the lesson.

In video example 6, time stamp (A), Iemoto points across the horizon with her right hand to direct Yuri's gaze into the distance. Simultaneously Iemoto strokes Yuri's middle back with her left hand to alter her posture. Yuri continues to dance. Iemoto gently places a hand on each of Yuri's shoulders and swings them from side to side, accentuating the shifting movement to coordinate with the timing of the music. Still kneeling, Yuri turns to her right, facing Iemoto, who releases her grasp. She continues dancing. Next, Iemoto bends down and nudges Yuri's right knee three to four inches back. Because most of Yuri's body weight leans on this knee, Iemoto's adjustment jogs Yuri's balance briefly, but the correction does change the angle of her kneeling position. The dance continues.

Several corrections via touch take place only a few steps later. At time stamp (B) Yuri spirals gently back and closes the phrase in a standing pose. As she settles into the position, Iemoto grasps each arm. She raises Yuri's right arm higher and draws her left elbow in to her waist. For a moment Iemoto holds Yuri in this position. Next Yuri circles to her left. Iemoto pushes her off into the turn by tossing Yuri's right arm into the direction of the turn, imparting the speed and quality of the rotation. After this turn Yuri steps forward three times. For each step her right hand, holding her *sensu*, undulates—palm up, palm down, palm up. Iemoto stands to her right for this passage. She clasps Yuri's right wrist with her right hand and actually moves Yuri's limb gracefully into place in a puppetlike fashion for the first two steps. At the same time she reaches across Yuri and straightens the position of her left hand. Iemoto then releases her hold and Yuri completes the third step, solo. Another example of teaching through touch occurs at time stamp (C). Here Iemoto again straightens Yuri's posture with a touch to her back. Next Iemoto alters her *sensu* position. One of the most powerful instances of contact can be observed when Yuri, balancing only on her left leg, holds the *sensu* high above her head. Iemoto steps into Yuri's dance. She envelops Yuri's body, clasps both of her hands, and continues to dance the passage. We can observe that this takes considerable effort for both women. Iemoto exerts just enough pressure to guide Yuri's arms through the movements. Because Yuri is balancing on one leg, however, too much force would be precarious. No fewer than fifteen instances of touch took place during Yuri's thirty-minute lesson. The example discussed above is an excerpt illustrating the most common instances of tactile transmission.

I have observed that dancers accumulate a vocabulary of tactile teaching cues in stages, in much the same way that they gain a visual vocabulary. For example, the most prominent instance of teaching through touch is the adjustment of posture, which occurs in both examples above. A teacher can straighten a student's posture merely by placing a flat hand between his/her shoulder blades. But how do students come to know this? In a beginner's lesson Iemoto can be heard saying, "Tighten these muscles, here . . ." as she strokes his/her back and repositions the rounded shoulders to an aligned position. Soon she need not verbally narrate the correction but can cue the adjustment with a subtle touch at this point on the dancer's back. I have noticed that over time I have become so accustomed to Iemoto's tactile cues that my back muscles kinesthetically fall into place at her slightest touch, or even as she approaches me.

Through touch, Yuri had an opportunity to actually feel Iemoto's dance directly. In the course of the lesson described above, Yuri's stiffened movements softened, grew larger and more distinct, as Iemoto puppeted her movements into place. Iemoto's guiding touch kinesthetically transferred several aspects of "Hokushu," such as the sensitivity to physical proportions, to depth and the use of space. Touch conveyed not only the basic movements but also the quality of her actions. Iemoto often physically urged Yuri forward, clarifying her timing by punctuating each step, yet maintaining a quality of movement that was soft and flowing. From personal experience I have come to understand the variety of Iemoto's tactile cues. The vocabulary is drawn from a wide palette of tactile instructions, including pressure sensitivity, touch (stroking, tapping, pulling), and enabling varying degrees of momentum. These multiple qualities of touch rarely exist separately from one another. Instead, they simultaneously transmit a dynamic range of movement, space, and timing to a student.

A fascinating aspect of the pedagogy is observing how a teacher decides when to make a correction and what kind of approach will be appropriate for that instance. For example, a teacher can observe a movement, realize a student's difficulties, and choose to verbalize the problem afterward. At this later point in time, however, the moment of the dance has passed. The teacher is faced with articulating what has physically transpired and also expressing what changes are necessary. For some types of movements or situations it is more appropriate to incorporate touch to guide the student just at the necessary moment. On the other hand, I observed that Iemoto often let a student continue a phrase without making corrections, then reviewed the passage later in a concentrated fashion to focus on detailed adjustments.

The use of touch in *nihon buyo* lessons involves two people; hence there exists a relationship of some sort. While I am moved through a dance by Iemoto, I find there is a strong sense of bonding. I realize that she is sharing her dance expression with me. Through attempting to feel and emulate the teacher's way of dancing there is also a sense of losing one's self. I recall what Iemoto said to me: "Do not to imitate me. That's boring. Learn the dance and then dance it with Samie's heart." Learning through touch starkly presents corporeal existence, but also self. Imitating a teacher challenges students to emulate her dance while also distinguishing themselves from her or the character portrayed, and finally to establish individual strength in their personal character.

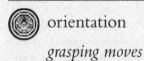

orientation

grasping moves

When is touch used to teach? What can touch impart? How does touch orient the body? When contemplating these questions I considered nondance situations in which I had experienced touch as a nonverbal teaching method.

As a child I studied Japanese calligraphy with Kan Shunshin, a Buddhist minister and *kendo* (fencing) master. During class he would walk around the room and observe the students' upright bamboo brushes mark wet black shapes on rice paper. I recall how he would occasionally stop behind me, take my hand and brush in his hand, and paint a character. His deliberate movements informed my body of complex brush techniques—my entire arm and shoulder moved as the bristles trailed ink across the page. The way he propelled my hand created a momentum that left lively brushstrokes: rolling the brush between our fingers left a chiseled corner; or downward pressure of the brush bristles at the beginning of a stroke, then a gradual lifting up, created a hooked shape. These are but a few examples of the "information" instilled by this tactile lesson of the brush. The process of grinding ink was also occasionally transferred in a similar way—sensory knowledge of the pressure, the speed, the methodical circular grinding of water with the ink stick, and the sensitivity of perceiving how thick the ink was at any given moment. The process could be meditative, especially if I let myself relax and understand how he approached creating ink. Repeated each week, these kinds of lesson experiences connected me to the brush, wet ink, paper, *kanji*, and Kan *sensei* (teacher). I remember watching him teach *kendo* (fencing) and, as if brush had transformed into sword, his guiding touch actively instructed students through sword maneuvers. Aerial strokes.

Touch is both an active and a passive engagement. A person actively touches and/or is passively touched by an object or person. Although varieties of relationships exist, generally teachers (as transmitters) actively touch, and students passively receive the tactile information.

Are there activities that come to mind that you learned via touch? For instance, when you learned to play a musical instrument, golf, or ride a bicycle, swim, sew, or canoe, did your instructor use touch to directly communicate some aspect? If so, did touch convey movement qualities such as direction, speed, and timing? What tactile pressure was involved? Was there an emotional content associated with the experience? What insights did you gain about the activity?

My interest in orientation, or a reorientation, of the body through touch centers on learning interactions. I have examined my own experiences and consider touch to impart a vast amount of varied information, depending on the task at hand. Touch is an intriguing sense that I feel is often taken for granted, or relegated as taboo for its manipulative or sexual connotations. It is this very social arena of heightened awareness and connotations that is important to take into consideration when observing how touch is used to teach. In your experience, has touch helped or hindered learning? Are there significant cultural associations with the encounter? In your life have there been particular situations deemed culturally appropriate for touch, and others that were not? How did you learn which situations were or were not appropriate?

To really engage in an orientation of touch, two people need to interact. For this orientation exercise enlist a partner to work with—one of you will play an active (teacher) role and one in a passive (student) role. If there is a simple movement familiar to the teacher, I suggest incorporating this into the orientation. Otherwise, utilize the following orientation as an activity that can be used to simulate how I experience touch in lessons at Hatchobori.

First, select a series of simple movements of one arm—for example, pointing to three spots along an imaginary horizon, followed by an abstract shape drawn in the air, such as a cursive *l*. Keep the phrase as simple as possible. The period of time where touch would occur in lessons is when the student can recall the basic sequence of movements. The teacher should decide, without telling the student, the qualities of each movement that will be imparted through touch. Providing gestures that have varied timing and a three-dimensional flow of movement is important. For example, the pace of the three points to the horizon could be slow-slow-fast, and each could have a nuance of movement quality; then the *l* movement might begin with the student's hand position close to her waist, then moving away from the body at the tip of the loop with a fully extended arm, and closing with a gently bent arm and wrist pose. The teacher should decide the nuances and keep them consistent for each run-through. Standing behind the student, the teacher should grasp onto the student's hand and allow contact along the arm when possible. As you dance the phrase for the student, how can you impart the nuances through touch? Do you swing her arm into place to emphasize momentum of movement? Use pressure in your grasp to imply a held position?

Meanwhile, from the student's perspective—move through the sequences decided on. As you move, allow the teacher to subtly guide the quality of your movements but continue moving through the phrase. What is different about the movement relative to your own manner of executing that phrase? Is there a sense of reorientation, as you tune in to the teacher's movement quality and make adjustments?

This orientation perhaps raises more questions than it answers regarding how bodies judge and learn spatial coordination. It is interesting to note, outside dance, how touch enables us to navigate through our daily rituals—closing a jar of jelly, turning the pages of a book, or washing our face, for example. Since these are all "tasks," the specificity as to how the activity is achieved is not usually critical as long as the end result is complete. However, in *nihon buyo* each movement is prescribed, and the transmission process reflects the specificity of direction. There is a clear idea of what constitutes a style and particular dance within each school—it is very important that the body appear and behave a certain way. There is no free "improvisation" in *nihon buyo*, as defined by contemporary practice (as in contact improvisation, for example). Therefore, clear transmission is valuable for the maintenance of the living tradition. Through touch, a teacher can transmit movement directly, allowing a student to "feel" and embody the tradition.

resounded

*Sight and sound intertwined today. A passage from "Komori" (The Babysitter) was
the focus of my lesson. Moving by Iemoto's side, I was keenly aware of the integration
of her body with the music—percussive claps, a head movement coordinated in time,
and her breathing through phrases. Vision became indistinguishable from sound
indistinguishable from vision. Why did I sense this? How does the body express
sound?*

*Several explanations come to mind. First, there is the notion of the body as musical
instrument. Choreographed stamps and claps incorporate the body within the musical
ensemble as a "player." When Iemoto dances to taped music, her movement sounds
coordinate to the tape, but in performance with live musicians her body clearly becomes
an equal instrumental member of the ensemble. I have seen her visually articulate
the music with her body. I sensed her firmly situated within the music, highlighting
particular instrumental and vocal passages. Simultaneously these musical lines were
highlighting her movements. It was as if each part of Iemoto's body aligned in time
with the music—sometimes her hands punctuated one instrumental line, her head
nodded to a different line, while her feet fluidly swept her across the room, marking a
larger level of the phrase. Her body, a moving visualization of the music, seemed to
provide overlapping sensory information for me—a synesthesia of sight and sound.
Body as sound as dance.*

*The lesson challenged my awareness, a dis-orientation and tangling of sensory
information. My own body, immersed in this complex musical stream, was guided
by her path through the sound. Conveyed in this guidance was the sensibility of the
musically articulate body situated in a complex sound world. I found myself considering
how bodies inhabit auditory scenes. In "Komori" each action coordinated with an
instrumental phrase embedded in the nagauta ensemble. As we playfully tapped
rhythms on the floor with long pole props, I felt as if Iemoto was leading me through
the movements as sound—and our taps blended into the ensemble as percussion.*

Iemoto sang "Ton-toko-ton." We were not only traversing a musical landscape; we were enacting it. We did not dance to the music; we embodied the music.

I also experienced very subtle relationships between body and sound. Since it is the custom to dance close to Iemoto in lessons, I am often aware of her breathing. The intimacy of lessons allows for this attention to detail. The rhythms of her breath were barely audible, barely visible. But today I noticed how her breath subtly cued my musical timing and phrasing—as she drew in a fresh breath, the swell in her chest cavity initiated a movement that rose from her torso and inched across her shoulders. Visually I could see her obi *become tight against her expanding rib cage, her* yukata *a taut sheath across her back. As she exhaled, this continuing movement if* ki *energy rippled down her right arm and extended through her hand and fingertips. Inhaling, exhaling—it was almost difficult not to kinesthetically harmonize with her breath as we danced together. Her body breathed the movements. If I am open and focused enough, I can breathe that same air.*

uttering expanses—oral/aural transmission

Immersed in a diverse blend of sounds every day, how do you make sense of the complexity? With your eyes closed, do you become attuned to sounds entering your ears, their motion, direction, timbre, intensity, rhythm, and pitch? How do you attend to sound, or parse sound events from one another in your attention? Sound's ephemeral quality sets it apart from vision and touch—there is nothing tangible to grasp—yet sound enters our bodies and touches us in a very real way. Sound and vision, according to Walter Ong, have different orienting effects: "Sound situates man in the middle of actuality and in simultaneity, whereas vision situates man in the front of things and in sequentiality" (1967: 128).

We have the capacity to hear something vibrating that is beyond our grasp and out of sight. Sound waves travel around corners, through walls, and for great distances. Sound is intimate, invasive even. Since we don't have earlids, sound waves indiscriminately enter the interior of our body—our head. But the ears are not the only body part that perceives sound waves. The entire body "feels" sound waves. Sound informs us of an energetic vibration being produced in a location, and we orient ourselves depending on our associations with the sound: sirens alert, doorbells announce, and stomachs gurgle (informing us of interior conditions), but what about a whistle, a chant, or hand clapping? Our experiences and associations help us shape meaning. While some sounds summon more innate responses, others are learned cultural constructions that help us to orient ourselves in a more abstract, social way. We learn to attend to specific aspects of sound—quality, dynamics, intensity, and rhythms—to acquire meaning of our sonic, musical, environment.

When you move through a space, are you assisted by an array of vibrations that convey where you are and how you can maneuver through the space? Consider an organized sonic palette, a musical scene, as it stirs your body to move. I imagine your current experience of the music brings forward prior listenings, prior experience with similar sonic events. How our bodies move to the music, too, is hinged on enculturated knowledge of sound and movement correspondences. We practice making sense of the many layers of complexity, and even learn to mask out some sounds in our selective attention. Experience and our various learned practices of sound and motion supply us with a field of sonic orientations, a vocabulary to draw on to connect sound and motion.[6]

Sound provides a dynamic, immersive "space" for dancers to orient themselves both within a physical space and within time. For example, the body can understand how large a room is, locate who or what is creating sound, and trace the order of events through time via the sounds within a room. Sound plays a major role in orienting dancers within a physical space as well as within a musical piece. Since dancers are masters of negotiating their bodies through space and time, it is important to understand how they are "trained" to tune in to sound for their specific artistic purpose.

The relationship between musical sounds and dance movement is culturally determined—for example, is the choreography based on precomposed music? Is the music composed to choreographic specifications? Are there cues for the musicians and/or for the dancer to coordinate? Is the dancer considered to be a member of the ensemble? Is there improvisation? Is there a direct correlation of sound to movement rhythmically? In pitch/movement content? In phrasing? Does music provide an accompaniment *for* dance? Does the music mark time for dancers with a regular pulse (such as a regular beat within the context of a phrase of four measures in 4/4 time)? How does music elicit a sonic setting for the dancer to move in? These are just some of the questions that reveal sight and sound relationships in dance and lend insight toward how to understand the moving body in a sonic setting.

practicing music

How music is transmitted in different cultures has long been a subject of ethnomusicological research. The focus on pedagogical practices has given us a wealth of cultural insights into how particular communities define and practice music, but also how music functions and orients individuals in their culture. Research on oral/aural transmission, notation systems, mnemonics, social structure, and teacher-student relationships has been a resource for understanding enculturation. Nearly every ethnomusicologist in the past three decades has taken on the task of learning an instrumental or vocal tradition as a participant-observer and, in the process, has learned what qualities are most important to becoming a musician in that culture. Analysis of transmission processes uncovers the essence of the tradition and the social networks that support it. It also helps us understand how music functions within a community.

During fieldwork in Ghana John Chernoff studied drumming. In *African Rhythm and African Sensibility*, he discusses how the sensibilities of the community are transmitted via musicking:

> Music is essential to life in Africa because Africans use music to mediate their involvement within a community, and a good musical performance reveals their orientation toward this crucial concern. As a style of human conduct, participation in an African musical event characterizes a sensibility with which Africans relate to the world and commit themselves to its affairs. . . . The development of musical awareness in Africa constitutes a process of education: music's explicit purpose, in the various ways it might be defined by Africans, is, essentially, socialization. An individual learns the potentials and limitations of participation in a communal context dramatically arranged for the engagement, display, and critical examination of fundamental cultural values. (Chernoff 1979: 154)

Michael Bakan, in his ethnography *Music of Death and New Creation*, provides a case study of Balinese pedagogy for gamelan called *maguru panggul* in a chapter titled "Learning to Play: Balinese Experiences." Bakan writes that the practice of *maguru panggul*, literally, "teaching with the mallet," reveals the "role of the mallet as a transmitter of musical information."

> Maguru panggul is an oral/aural tradition approach. No musical notation is employed, and the effectiveness of teaching is almost exclusively dependent on a holistic demonstration-and-imitation mode of transmitting musical knowledge from teacher to student. (Bakan 1999: 282).

One case I found particularly fascinating—a student, Wayan, studying with his teacher Sukarata through imitation. Bakan describes Wayan's intent visual focus on Sukarata's mallet motion:

> As "the music" is transported from Sukarata's mind through his body, through his hands, and into his mallet, ultimately being brought to life by the kendang itself, it enters Wayan's body and mind through an inverse process. As his mallet motion begins to approximate Sukarata's,

first hands, then arms and body follow suit. Before Wayan can play anything that sounds even remotely like "the actual notes" of the music, he
is in full command of a vocabulary of movement and a style of playing
that capture the essence of the musical passage while lacking most of its
structural and formal content (284–285).

When I read this passage I imagined a visual and kinesthetic dance
of learning supporting the oral/aural transmission process. The immediacy of learning to orient oneself within the soundscape, within the
learning system, and within the community, through imitation of a
teacher, seemed just like dance lessons I have experienced.

dancing in sound

The compositional elements in Japanese dance music are not centered
on chordal structures that vertically mark time and follow cultural
expectations of pitch-based elements as in Western music. Instead,
pitched and nonpitched elements of music mark a narrative, linear flow
of time to privilege the story line text. Music is not largely improvi-
satory, but is composed. The various instrumental and vocal lines of a
piece have horizontal relationships that are tied to the narrative text
and provide a sonic landscape for the dancer to move in. This might be
as specific as providing a segment of folk music during a narrative passage where a dance character comes upon an outdoor *matsuri* festival
while strolling down a busy street. In Japanese music the sonic landscape can also be created by abstract aural cues such as the constant beat
of a *taiko* (large barrel drum), a sonic metaphor that represents water
or snow elements in the landscape (similar to a leitmotif). There are
countless references to create sonic landscapes, each an instantiation of
a particular environment within a dance. These sound references are
woven into the music, and as a dancer "moves" a story, the musicians
convey the narrative in sound and text. The visual and sonic elements
complement each other to perform a rich, dramatic narrative.

How dancers become acquainted with music during lessons reveals a great deal about the sonically situated body. Music cues, much
like visual cues, are sonic associations that dancers learn through regular practice and regular immersion in a variety of sonic environ-
ments.[7] I have found that sound also provides a space to learn within.
The sounds that orient a student during a lesson—from Hatchobori's

front door chime to individual voices, vocables, and hand clapping in a lesson—immerse students in a familiar sonic space that is recognizable and conducive to learning. There is a complexity to the sounds at Hatchobori. In this section I provide a passage through the oral/aural sonic landscape of lessons.

case study in oral/aural transmission

expanded field notes

Early in my lesson today the taped music was turned off, and as we danced the passage again, Iemoto began to sing "toto hi fuya ton oi nao—ashi o yosete," a mixture of song, mnemonics, and instructions. Her "song" greatly informed my path through the complex music. The relationship of the movements and the music became clearer, and I experienced a sensation of dancing from within the music, or riding its contours. More importantly, as I kinesthetically followed her movements while hearing these instructions, I felt her physical use of space and time.

Oral instructions during *nihon buyo* lessons impart a wide range of directions to a student, from general to specific: fundamental dance movements, choreography, narrative story line, emotional content, and music. I found that teachers' articulations in lessons form a metalanguage, a unique dance instructional language reflecting a varied and deeply complex matrix of information. This "dance speak" comprises a fragmented yet completely fluid combination of the musical vocal line, instrumental vocables, emotive exclamations, and instructive speech.[8] A closer inspection of the oral transmission process reveals that the metalanguage created during lessons is spontaneously tailored for particular students' needs. In this section I parse the three basic categories of this metalanguage: movement instruction, emotive expression, and musical information. To convey how this dance speak informs dancers, I offer excerpted transcriptions of specific classes from my field video tapes (video examples 7–13).

moving sound

Teachers often verbally direct students' dance movements to state corrections or to introduce new material. These instructions are voiced for practical improvements such as body position, posture, carriage, space, and timing. For instance, when a teacher observes that a student's feet need repositioning, she might simply remark, "Feet, closer together." This direct verbal guidance assists the transmission of correct body movement in a clear and pragmatic manner.

As mentioned in chapter 2, *nihon buyo* dance vocabulary consists of small movement units, called *kata*. These set units are small enough to break down larger phrases, yet large enough to reference during lessons. Each individual *kata* carries a name that can be called out just prior to its execution. This verbal cue is particularly helpful for students who are learning a new piece, because they cannot anticipate the next move. For example, a teacher might call out "*oridatami*," allowing the student to anticipate a rather complex series of graceful movements. Specific *kata* are not precisely the same for every dance, however (for example, an *oridatami* will vary from dance to dance). Several factors affect this variance, including the type of character portrayed, the context of the *kata* within the phrase, and the dance genre. In other words, students need to remain alert when following, even if they are quite familiar with the *kata* vocabulary.[9]

A teacher sometimes talks the student through the dance narrative while gestures are pantomimed. A verbal description of movements contextualizes the mimetic gestures—"Look far away . . ." (*tooku mite*), Iemoto called out to me as I studied the piece "Seigaiha," for instance. Because this dance reflects the different phases of the sea during the year, the dancer's physical expression through a gaze far to the distant horizon can vivify the spirit of the seaside. Moments later I stepped back while looking downward, as if to avoid the incoming waves. Here Iemoto supplied, "*Aa nami ga kimasu*" (Oh, here come the waves), animating the narrative further. This type of direction informs in a literal sense. Her words elucidate the actions and gestural connotations, contextualizing the physical dance expression within the dance narrative.

During lessons Iemoto often sings small sections of the musical vocal line to emphasize the relationship of the movements to the ongoing narrative. For example, in my lesson Iemoto sang the lyrics "the sea is calm" (*nami o shizukani*) as I passed through the gestures—with palms down, my outstretched arms drew a continuous, smooth motion outward as my torso subtly lifted to pantomime the tranquillity of the water's surface. I found that hearing Iemoto orally accentuate the vocal text while I moved through the phrase connected aural and kinesthetic memories in my body—an essence of the sea's calmness embodied in action and sound.

storytelling

In many *nihon buyo* pieces, a single vocalist in the musical ensemble serves as a storyteller, singing the various characters' lines as well as the narrative. Although a tape recording of the music plays during dance lessons, Iemoto often vocally doubles the song, bringing the story to life.

In the opening scene of the dance "Komori" (The Babysitter) the dancer portrays a young babysitter chasing a bird flying off with her fried *tofu*. The babysitter, toting the infant on her back, takes a tumble and rubs her hurt knee. When I dropped to the floor and rubbed my knee (dancing the babysitter character) during my lesson, Iemoto sang with the tape-recorded vocal part, singing in the babysitter's voice—"Oh dear! What shall I do? . . . O-O-OUCH!" (*oya kana nanto shyo e . . . Aitatata!*) Iemoto's voice vivified the babysitter's exclamation as well as her boisterous character.

In late September of 1993, I watched Iemoto teach the dance "Mitsumen komori." In a very comical section of the dance narrative, the dancer assumes the role of a young girl who playacts several popular folk characters using masks. The dancer's challenge is to perform several contrasting characters while still portraying the main role (the young girl). During this animated lesson Iemoto interjected the comical folk characters' voices as they appeared in the dance:

> "*Nan da? Ha ha ha ha ha . . .* [What's this? Ha ha ha ha ha]," Iemoto called out in a low, gruff voice, impersonating Ebisu (patron of hard work and one of the seven gods of good luck).

> "*Oya oya oya ureshiina* [Oh, oh, oh, I'm so happy]." In very high-pitched, sweet voice, Iemoto cried out in Okame's voice (a woman who represents good fortune and happiness).

> "*Ano neisan to isshoni narimasu* [I want to marry that nice woman]." Iemoto knelt and uttered this hopeful prayer as the character Hyottoko (protector of fire).

With the dancer's face concealed behind masks, a large portion of her emotive expression is withdrawn. Therefore, movements in this piece must be distinct and particular to each (masked) character. Iemoto's dramatization of characters' voices enhances their presence, emphasizing the rapid role shifts for the student.

As illustrated by Iemoto's speaking each character in the example above, the quality of her voice is key to the emotive expression she imparts. Her high-pitched voice for the female character and low, gruff voice for the male character aurally project each character's identity, which a student must attempt to express in physical movement. Dancers are so conditioned to synchronize a sound and physical movement that I believe it would actually be difficult for a dancer to move in a feminine dance style while a male character's voice was portrayed, or as a farmer during a courtesan's exclamation. The quality of the voice embodies the inner spirit of the character as much as the dancing image. As a means for summoning movement qualities from a body culturally aware of movement vocabularies, sound invokes a physicalization of a character's identity during the transmission process.

Iemoto sometimes utters impromptu exclamations from the character's perspective (but not drawn from the musical vocal text) to personify the dance role a student is learning. In the process she creates an inspiration for the dancer's movements and reveals the emotional state of the character. I recall a lesson for the dance "Ame no shiki." Iemoto sat holding an open fan at arm's length before her. From the character's point of view she delighted, "Mmm looks tasty . . ." (*Aa oishisoo . . .*), and the fan transformed into a delicious watermelon slice. Her eyes and facial expression reflected the delight of seeing such a fruit. She bit off the tip and spit a seed to the side. To supply another example: during a lesson Iemoto and Soke were observing a student dance in a snow scene. Soke commented, "I don't see the snow." Running through the phrase again, Iemoto animated the character's inner voice—"Ah, snow . . . [is falling]"—fixing her gaze in the sky.

dancing music

Historically, most traditional Japanese instrumental music was transmitted orally. Each instrument has a separate set of mnemonics, or *shyoga,* that are incorporated into the transmission system.[10] As part of their dance training *nihon buyo* dancers often learn a musical instrument (such as *shamisen* or *tsuzumi,* a lute and shoulder drum respectively). Learning an instrument familiarizes dancers with the musical vocabulary, the compositional forms, as well as the mnemonic systems involved in the transmission. In dance lessons teachers primarily sing the *shamisen* mnemonics called *kuchijamisen* (*kuchi*, meaning "mouth" or "oral" *shamisen*) to supply a musical structure for the student when the recorded music is not playing.

Particular phrases or patterns in the music generally accompany certain choreographed movements or emotional gestures. These patterns and other verbal directions become students' aural dance vocabulary. Hearing these musical phrases each day while coordinating dance moves links the music and movements within the body, the two becoming inseparable in one's physical memory.[11] Tachibana Sahomi told me that, in the 1940s, Tachibana Saho (her childhood teacher in Fukushima) played the *shamisen* during her lessons. She recalled, "Saho used to play the *shamisen* and that's how I learned to sing. She used to sing the songs and lyrics and then when we got to a certain point where we could do it [the dance] by ourselves then she would pick up the *shamisen*. But if we didn't know the dance then she would only sing it. So this is why all of the songs are still stuck in my head" (interview, September 22, 1989). Soke and Iemoto both learned traditional instruments to prepare for their dance studies. Their knowledge of the music carries a depth that their dancing and teaching embody—movements that emanate from within the complex musical structures and exist as embodied cultural knowledge.

Today, dance teachers use recorded music for lessons, and musicians play live music for public performances. Several teachers have said that, with or without recorded music, they are aware of the vocal line and each of the instrumental lines as they dance. Further, this stream of musical lines in their memory enables them to clearly navigate within the musical soundscape.

Here I return to the topic of a teaching metalanguage for dance. During lessons teachers spontaneously sing a combination of instrumental mnemonics blended with fragments of the vocal line and verbal dance directions (instructional and emotive). The result is a unique dance language, a metalanguage patchwork of music and dance directions pieced together for the purpose of highlighting the salient cues within the music for the student. Though this language comprises parsed speech forms, teachers create a remarkably fluid line to maintain the time flow of the passage. Teachers supply this medley of verbal directions both with and without the taped music, although to varying degrees.

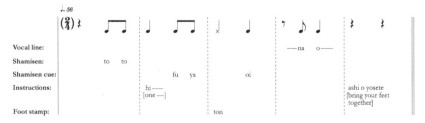

FIGURE 2. Transcription of teaching metalanguage. A lesson of "Matsu no midori."

When taped music accompanies a lesson, teachers continue to sing the *kuchijamisen* (*shamisen* vocables), to emphasize the crucial dance cues within the complex musical composition. Select mnemonics combine with verbal dance instructions and sounds (such as stamps and claps) to create a verbal interpretation of the music for the student. In the short example in figure 2 (from "Matsu no midori"), the rapid succession from singing the *shamisen* vocable "*to to*" is followed by a count "*hi*" ("one" implying "one-two-three-," etc.); next " *fu ya*," a vocal call used by *shamisen* players to cue the ensemble (here, a cue for a pickup to a downbeat); a foot stamp cue, "*ton*"; another *shamisen* cue, "*oi*"; one word of the vocal text, "*nao*"; and finally a verbal instruction for the student to keep her feet closer together, "*ashi o yosete*." Iemoto's single verbal line "*to to hi fu ya ton oi nao ashi o yosete*," when parsed by category, illustrates the complexity of this verbal cueing system.

In order to further demonstrate the role that this metalanguage plays in everyday practice within the dance studio, the following section offers two typical instances from my field experience.

online companion oral transmission example 7: verbal cueing, "Echigojishi"

The first case study example represents a typical passage of verbal cueing. During Yasuo's lesson Iemoto introduced a new section of the dance "Echigojishi." Because the dance steps are lively, Iemoto reduced the speed of the recorded music considerably. At one point she turned off the recorded music and walked through the steps at a slower pace for Yasuo. She alternately sang the *kuchijamisen* and vocal lyrics to supply a musical framework, and inserted a quick dance instruction here and there.

A transcription of Iemoto's verbal cues for this passage appears in

PHOTO 5. Tachibana Yoshie teaching "Echigojishi."

figure 3. This excerpt has been parsed by category in the transcription to include: (1) action sounds—nonverbal sounds that the dancers produce, such as hand claps and foot stamps; (2) vocal lyrics; (3) *kuchi-jamisen* and *shamisen*—calls for cueing the ensemble; and (4) dance directions—the verbal instructions specifically for Yasuo regarding his movements (see measure 21).

The transcription graphically illuminates Iemoto's flexible vocal shifting between categories of cues, particularly between the vocal lyrics and the *shamisen* line. She inferred the rhythm of the *shamisen* phrase occasionally, breaking down the (singer's) vocal passage into shorter rhythmic units during a sustained passage. For instance, the actual vocal text, from measure 11, follows: "*Botan wa motanudo Echigo no shishi wa . . .*" In the lesson however, Iemoto sang: "*Bota–a–n wa-a mo ta—a nu do–o–o Echi–i [g]o no–o shi shi–i wa.*" She emphasized the rhythm of the *shamisen* by drawing out and rearticulating syllables to accent the underlying *shamisen* rhythm. The most prominent case occurred in measure 14: "*do–o–o.*" Here Iemoto emphatically marked the two eighth-notes ("*do–o*") and the downbeat of measure 15 ("*o*"). In a sense she overlaid the *shamisen* rhythm onto the vocal part, imparting the fluidity of the arching vocal phrase simultaneously with the percussive rhythmic structure of the *shamisen* part.

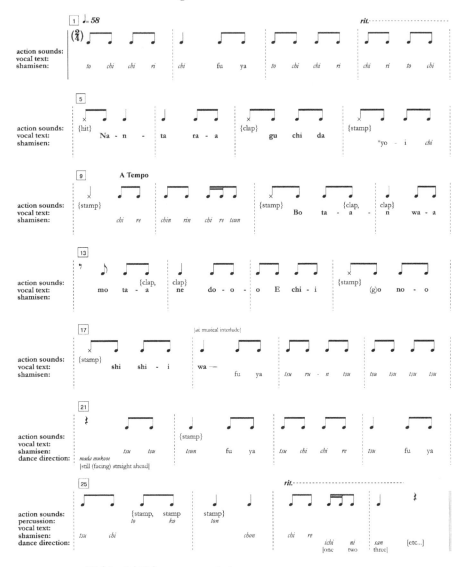

FIGURE 3. "Echigojishi" lesson transcription.

Iemoto's verbal patchwork of necessary musical elements and cues creates a structural musical setting for dancers to move in. In a sense, she can "hear" and reconstruct an entire dance and its music in her head—while teaching she selects from an ensemble of instruments (or voice) to highlight a path through the music. The complex music is pared to essentials. Each time a section is repeated during a lesson,

Iemoto creates a slightly different interpretation, stressing the vocal line in one instance, the *shamisen* in another, or dance cues in yet another. Perhaps we can liken her fluidity and complete awareness of the music and dance to that of a pianist who can brilliantly play a score reduction of a full orchestra by ear—consolidating the orchestral score to its bare essentials. In her verbal interpretation of the music Iemoto articulates the precise relationship of individual parts relative to the whole fabric of the ensemble. During one lesson a student might experience several of these varied interpretations—each a different musical and instructional pathway through the music. The next case study illustrates six of Iemoto's interpretations of a single passage that took place during one lesson.

online examples 8–13: verbal cueing, "Matsu no midori"

Audio examples 8–13 (transcribed in figure 4) are drawn from Kazue's first lesson of "Matsu no midori." During the lesson Iemoto introduced the opening passage (approximately two and a half minutes in length), and they repeated it five times together. At one point Iemoto singled out a difficult phrase to concentrate on. The transcription focuses on Iemoto's verbal teaching for the six reviews of this passage with particular attention to her musical cues.

This example also reveals a common format of lessons. In general, lessons can be broken down into three sections: (1) a review of what was covered in the last dance lesson or an introduction of a new dance; (2) an introduction of the next section of the dance and a detailed focus on the new movements and cues; and (3) a run-through of the entire passage from the beginning.

When a teacher introduces a new passage, recorded music generally accompanies the dance, providing the student with a concept of the musical context of the piece. In Kazue's lesson taped-recorded music was played for the first two reviews of the new section. Iemoto kept her verbal cues to a minimum at this point of the learning stage. She included only an occasional preparatory phrase cue such as "*fu ya*" and "*yo i*," which are similar to the pickup "and a—[one/downbeat]" (see figure 4, preparation to measure 1, and measure 5). These verbal cues are not mnemonics for pitches played on the *shamisen,* but preparatory cues (or calls) that players commonly employ to coordinate their timing with other ensemble members.

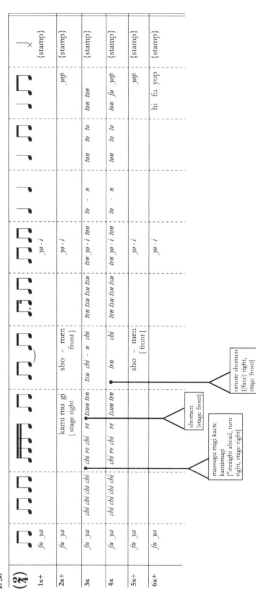

FIGURE 4. "Matsu no midori" lesson transcription.

Symbol key:

1x = Repetitions of phrases are represented by numbers in the far left corner.

+ = Phrase repetition numbers (see above) followed by "+" indicate those repetitions danced with taped music (repetition numbers 1, 2, 5, and 6).

= Time is momentarily suspended. Verbal instructions spoken during this time are inserted in a box below mnemonic text line.

Italicized text = *kuchijamisen* (*shamisen* mnemonics).

Non-italicized text = verbal instructions in Japanese (that are not mnemonics), translated in [ ] style brackets below Japanese text.

{ } = Text within these brackets indicate a sound that dancers make, such as a stamp or clap.

Iemoto stopped after the second run-through. Noticing less fluidity in Kazue's movements during the musical interlude, Iemoto reviewed only the difficult phrase. Without the taped music Iemoto verbally broke down the phrase carefully, singing the rhythms in detail and clarifying the direction of movements. Note on the transcription the detailed *kuchijamisen* Iemoto provided in the third and fourth review of the phrase, relative to other interpretations. Without the recorded music, she supplied a musical framework with *kuchijamisen* to reinforce how the dance movements coordinate with the music.

An important aspect of the oral transmission process lies in the teacher's control of time. Without the recorded music playing, Iemoto can manipulate the musical time—from a subtle nuance, a pause, to a momentary suspension of the music altogether. Adjustment of the musical time allows Iemoto to create a musical setting tailored to individual students' needs and abilities.

A case of time suspension occurs in figure 4, phrase repeat numbers 3 and 4, in the transcription (note: verbal directions spoken during time suspensions are enclosed in boxed areas). In the third repetition, on the third and fourth beats, Iemoto suspends the music for a moment to insert a lengthy dance direction, then smoothly reenters the music to continue the passage. On beat three of this example, Iemoto directs Kazue, "straight ahead, turn right, stage right" (*massugu. migi kaete. kamimugi*), suspending the time. Iemoto continues with the *kuchijamisen* mnemonics, "*chire chire*"; then, on beat four, she squeezes in the comment "[face] front stage" (*shomen*), followed by the remainder of the musical phrase sung in *kuchijamisen*.

Iemoto's varied vocal interpretations of a phrase offer another level of musical flexibility. When dancers perform onstage with live music, the rendition of the piece varies. Often the contemporary dancer's first experience with live music occurs during a dress rehearsal, and the rehearsal musicians might not be the same as those who play for the actual performance. Iemoto's changing vocal interpretations during class help students develop flexibility in their conception of the music. Students' insights regarding the music thus include variables beyond the confines of the set recorded music.

The vocal interpretations sung in lessons also serve the purpose of highlighting instrumental and vocal parts heard in the recorded music. The singing of various interpretations of the music without recorded music creates a highlighted musical structure. Later, when the recorded music is reintroduced, the specific cues from individual instruments within the ensemble stand out prominently.

Curiously, dance metalanguage sung in classes persists beyond spe‐ cific lessons. One of my childhood teachers, Tachibana Sahomi, told me during a lesson in 1987, "Every time I dance this piece I can hear Saho [her own childhood teacher] sing the song and *kuchijamisen*." She smiled and looked off in the distance for a moment. I imagined she was fondly remembering her own dance lesson. Then, without another word, she turned and continued my lesson, singing the vocal line and mnemonics. All at once I realized that, while dancing, I hear Saho‐ mi's voice in my mind. Because Sahomi learned the piece from Saho, it is in part Saho's voice I hear. In a way, dancers' aural memories cap‐ ture a lineage of dances and music, transmitted through generations of dancers' voices. I find that a particular teacher's manner of "singing a dance" endures in my memory in tandem with the dance. The process of teaching, transmitted from generation to generation along with a dance, is as personal an expression as the dance itself.

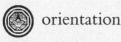 orientation

moving sounds

Upon a casual listening to *nihon buyo* music, it is impossible to fully appreciate the depth of enculturated meanings this music has for dancers. However,
we can attempt to understand and appreciate its complexity and the way in
which dancers orient themselves through music and dance. To that end, this
orientation will reveal Iemoto's fluidity in traversing and transmitting the
many levels of the soundscape to students—we will listen to and become sen-
sitized to the various components of the music alone, then listen to Iemoto
sing the composition back to us.

One of the pleasures of listening to music is the experience of listening on
different levels, of hearing something different on each listening. As an anal-
ogy, imagine a forest landscape. There are different levels of observing the
vista—for example, viewing the general outline of the forest, then an individual mountain, a stand of trees, an individual tree, the leaves on the tree,
and the forest floor. Similarly, separate listenings to a passage of music may
yield a variety of paths through a sound world. For this orientation listen to
and watch video example 14, a lesson of the dance "Echigojishi." It is an excerpt from the same lesson and dance phrase as example 7. However, in example 7 Iemoto provides the music and dance cues orally, whereas recorded
music for that same passage can be heard in example 14.

In your mind's ear, step back and listen to the whole texture as one sound
mass, not making an effort at this point to focus on any individual musical
line. In this excerpt, there are a variety of individual sounds that together create a unified, multilayered composite texture. On separate listenings we can
unfurl the rich complexity of the music to focus on different characteristics
of the music, such as the words, the vocal line, individual instruments, phrasing, form, or nuances of sound quality. As we become aware of details of the
sound it is important to keep in mind how they contribute to the complexity of the whole.

Let's continue, allowing our ears to travel from one level to another. In
the ensemble there are three groups of instruments and a vocalist—a drum
(*shimedaiko*), a bell (*kane*), and a three-string lute (*shamisen*). On the first listening concentrate solely on the drum. Its regular beat establishes a firm
rhythmic structure and maintains a steady, forward momentum for the en-

semble. Does the drum help you to anticipate the next downbeat? How does the drum contribute to the ensemble sound? What is its function? How might it help to orient the moving body?

Next listen to the bell. Listen to how the nature of the bell's bright sound pierces through the overall ensemble. The bell's function within the ensemble as a punctuator of rhythm is linked to its sharp clarity of timbre. Direct your ears to the relationship of the bell and drum. Do the parts overlap? The combined bell and drum sounds create a foundation of regular rhythm—perhaps a view of the landscape floor and trees from a distance.

Focus on the *shamisen* part. In many ways this three-stringed instrument also functions as a percussion instrument because of the manner in which it is played. A plectrum is used to pluck the strings but simultaneously strikes the skin face and edge of the *shamisen*'s wooden resonating body. This action produces a percussive slapping sound that can be quite loud. The "Echigojishi" excerpt is a fine example of virtuosic *shamisen* playing. Notice that the melody is very quick yet fluid. The percussive nature of the *shamisen* adds a precise quality to the rhythms. Focusing on the *shamisen* alone, what does its fluid, rapid line convey to you? What role do you find it plays in the ensemble? Does its virtuosic speed hasten the music forward? Does the *shamisen* line convey a different sense of time to you than the drum or vocal parts? What part of a forest landscape would this part play?

Finally, direct your ears to the vocal line. Draw your attention to how the vocal melody seems to float above the ensemble in long, arching phrases. This floating quality is partly due to the continuous, fluid sound of the voice, which rides above the intricate, nonsustaining sounds of the percussive instruments and plucked *shamisen*. The phrasing of the vocal line is based on textual structures that arch across the undercurrent of rhythms provided by the instruments. The steady downbeats provided by the drum, bell, and *shamisen* allow the voice great freedom to float freely above the precise rhythmic structure. Notice how the vocal line consistently avoids the downbeat on each entrance. Since the narrative story is conveyed by the text, the ability for the words to be clearly audible is vital.

Stepping back and taking in the whole musical vista again—which sounds do you perceive as driving the music ahead, and which are scenery? Are there certain aspects of the music propelling time forward for you? The rhythmic drive of the instrumental parts provide this momentum, and the vocal line a lush scenery. The text remains primary, and its clarity is fully supported by the strong rhythmic foundation. Does the vocal line provide a perspective like that of individual leaves and trees in the overall forest scene?

Now that we have familiarized ourselves with the components of the musical excerpt, let's return to Iemoto's oral transmission of this same passage (example 7). It is important to point out that Iemoto does not sing the dance structure exactly the same way for every run-through but creates an impromptu setting appropriate for the pedagogical purpose. Her fluidity with the components of the music and dance enables her to capture the essential structure of the music in time, while simultaneously moving and instructing. At this point in the lesson Iemoto has turned off the recorded music, and she vocally provides the musical structure for the student to dance within. Notice she has slowed the time of the excerpt, allowing her to focus on the precision of the normally fast dance steps at a more relaxed pace. Iemoto also manipulates the speed within the phrase to clarify relationships of movement to sound. In Iemoto's oral interpretation, or dance metalanguage, notice how she deliberately switches between ensemble vocables and dance instructions. Compare examples 7 and 14 and notice how Iemoto's metalanguage highlights particular musical characteristics to provide an aural orientation through the (recorded) music. Do you experience the immersive sound "space" that she sets for the student? When you observe the student following Iemoto, can you see/hear how oral transmission enables him to physically orient his body inside the sonic environment?

propelled

Fans are electric machines. Conveyances. Plugged in. Somehow they have transfigured from a simple paper object for "fanning" to a mechanical device—though both propel currents of air. Can we still dance with this whirring and buzzing machinery? This new-age fan seems to move on its own. It is motored by an energy source beyond my limbs. What can these conveyances articulate? I might lift one someday to see what gestures it suggests.

mediating sense—notation and video

Rapidly, we approach the final phase of the extensions of man—the technological simulation of consciousness, when the creative process of knowing will be collectively and corporately extended to the whole of human society, much as we have already extended our senses and our nerves by the various media.
—Marshall McLuhan (1964: 19)

Imagining life without media is difficult. Media have extended our sensorium and become fully integrated into our daily lives. Certainly media, as it mediates art and ideas, changes the way the performing arts are transmitted (see Williams 2001). With McLuhan's spirit, this chapter includes media as sensory devices for transmitting dance and examines the ways in which media are incorporated into teaching practices. Though the transmission of *nihon buyo* relies primarily on human interaction, some teachers find media useful, such as written notation, audio (including phonographs, tape cassettes, and compact discs), and video cassettes.

It is interesting to note the strong attitudes that teachers have regarding recording devices. Their opinions reveal a wariness of technology, largely because of the effects it might have on the traditions they practice. However, I find that the strength of many teachers' convictions—their misgivings about media—is conveyed so clearly to their students that it actually allows media to be utilized in innovative ways. For the most part, media are permitted within the pedagogical system primarily as a device for extending memory, as a memory aid.

dancing paper

Dance notation is not considered to be essential for transmitting *nihon buyo*. I have observed dance notation used by contemporary dancers in two situations: private notation created by individual dancers as a memory aid, and as a document of established choreography distributed to teachers within a school.

Japanese dance notation exists in a variety of styles. A dancer's objective for notating a piece greatly influences the notational system employed. For example, if the notation is to be used solely as a memory aid by an active dancer, then the notation must be easily read for quick reference. The impracticality of holding a text while dancing, or pausing a phrase in order to refer to a stationary dance text, indicates the cumbersome nature of notated dance. Specifically, a notational style that demands prolonged visual observation interrupts the fluidity of dance. For that reason, notation written in a condensed style is not only practical but preferred by active dancers who notate dances to recall choreography. On the other hand, for researchers who aim to clearly "record" the dance in detail, the inscription of every nuance in the dance notation is crucial. Machida Kasho, in *Hyoju nihon buyo fu* (Standard Nihon Buyo Notations), points out this dichotomy in a paradox—the notation that is easily read is not precise or detailed, and notations that are detailed are not easily read (Machida 1967: 28).

The history of *nihon buyo* notation has not been documented well. This is in part due to the lack of published dances, a common system for notation, and the function of notation within the context of dance. Prior to the twentieth century, personal dance notations were more common than published documents. I surmise that, for teachers, dance notation might appear to undermine the strong teacher–pupil transmission system. Notation creates a paradox because it is a fixed object representing a living, changing art form that exists in space and time. The vivid qualities of the lived learning experience so vital to lessons cannot be translated to paper. However, notation need not become a rigid text that stands for the definitive, authoritative dance. Rather, I have noticed a flexible view of what notation represents within the transmission process for a school, a teacher, or a student.

I observed Iemoto refer to her father's notes during a lesson (although this was rather unusual). In this case the purpose of checking his notes was to reference the original choreography. The use of notation in this instance manifests the *iemoto* system, revealing the deep respect for Tachibana Hoshu's choreography. On a more pragmatic level, his notation served as a memory aid for his choreography, to extend the tradition beyond his lifetime.

Underlying the basic problems concerning *nihon buyo* transmission via notation is the fact that individual schools seldom intermingle (particularly prior to the establishment of the Nihon buyo Kyokai [Japanese Dance Association] in 1931). It is widely known that individual schools protect their secret artistic techniques and choreography, and caution dancers not to reveal the "tricks of the trade" via notated texts. The coherence of a particular school's style is greatly influenced by the strength of the school's interior social network, the *iemoto* structure, and student allegiance. Notations were (and currently still are in many cases) meant for individuals within the school only. For example, Nishikawa Koizaburo's *Nishikawa ryu hidensho* (Secret Notations of the Nishikawa School) of 1854 was an unpublished text circulated only within the Nishikawa School as a sort of "tricks of the trade" booklet.

This "secrecy" of schools' artistry and transmission is present in virtually every art tradition in Japan. It is one of the factors that strengthens the schools' transmission and social bonding, and shapes the distinct styles of individual schools. At the close of Zeami's *Kakyo*, an inscription (attributed to his student, Komparu Zenchiku) cautions the reader of the seriousness of the document:

> This teaching was passed on by Zeami himself for the succeeding generations of this house and should not be shown to actors from other troupes. Luckily, thanks to the Will of Heaven, which knows that my heart reveres the art of no, this manuscript has come into my hands. This secret teaching forms the very core of the art of our school, and it is a text of fearsome power. Thus it must not be shown carelessly to others. (Rimer and Yamazaki 1984: 110)

No doubt both the writer and the owner of these printed objects were aware of the liabilities of permanent texts. The concern about who might read the texts reveals the serious attitude toward the transmission process and the allegiance of these artists to their craft and school.

After World War II many dance styles (including *nihon buyo*) gained popularity and prompted a practical means for notation for the public. The recording and publishing industries were now technically capable of providing interesting products for the masses. A boom in recorded dance music on 45 and 78 rpm records facilitated rapid transmission of dance music (and established musical standards of the dance repertory). Often records included dance steps on the dustcover, or as an insert.

In the 1940s, magazines (such as *Nihon buyo*) specifically catering to dance audiences were published. The magazines included photographs of performers, costumes, and props; articles; reviews; and interviews. These publications fed hungry dance-going crowds. Dance stars emerged. Amateur dancers flocked to dance halls and lessons, and bought up fashionable publications. This excitement in the general public created a demand for greater quantities of information on all facets of *nihon buyo*. The rekindled interest in dance, coupled with growing media facilities (phonograph, film, and written publications), greatly influenced the notation of dance pieces. *Nihon buyo* magazine published dance instructions that included step-by-step, or rather frame-by-frame, photographs of dances, including dance directions and song lyrics.

A range of notational styles was published in Machida's brief collection of notational styles, from highly abstract symbolic systems to stick-figure styles. This variety of notation styles illuminates the diversity of notation practices as well as the pragmatic use of the notation. On the one hand, dancers (novice and professional) can easily comprehend the stick-figure style because it so closely represents the body engaged in motion. On the other hand, the less accessible and intuitive symbolic notation systems are capable of greater detail in their inscription of movements. Also, the latter notation style takes a commitment of time, requiring a dancer to learn a new vocabulary in order to notate and read it fluently. One senior Tachibana teacher pointed out to me that the stick-figure notation style can be read at a distance or handheld, a practical and very necessary feature for dance notation. Which style a dancer or school elects to employ ultimately must be based on its functional purpose and for whom the notations are geared.

One of the most comprehensive published works on *nihon buyo* notation is Hanayagi Chiyo's *Jitsu nihon buyo no kiso* (The Practical Skills of Basic Nihon Buyo Movement). She provides a valuable introduction to the Hanayagi style of dance and her own approach to notating the repertory (in a stick-figure style notation). The book illustrates *nihon buyo* extensively in photographs and illustrations and is a fine document of the *nihon buyo* vocabulary in text.

Within the Tachibana School dancers create notations for their personal reference. Several times I have stepped into the dressing room to find a dancer focused on notating a dance. Most everyone uses *ningyo* (stick-figure) notation style. When I asked about their notations, several students mentioned that they regularly make only a few quick notes directly after the lesson but fill them out on the subway ride home. Once they arrive home, they notate the passage with greater detail. I have not witnessed a student taking notes during his/her lesson or when observing another student's lesson.

Some dances are skillfully notated by a dancer within the school. A copy of the dance is issued to the teachers so that they may teach their students the Tachibana choreography. This notation is primarily *ningyo* (stick-figure) style, with added graphic symbols to impart the sense of

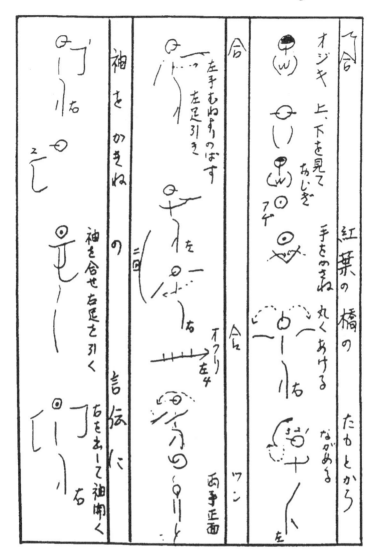

FIGURE 5. Tachibana notation, an excerpt of "Momiji no hashi."

motion. The vocal line and instrumental cues are also included so that the dancer can coordinate the movements with the music. An example of this notation is illustrated in figure 5. This figure represents one of the four pages of an unpublished Tachibana notation for the dance "Momiji no hashi" (Bridge of Maple Trees) choreographed by Tachibana Hiroyo, notated by Tachibana Hosen, March 11, 1995. A general explanation of the first line of this page may be seen in figure 6.

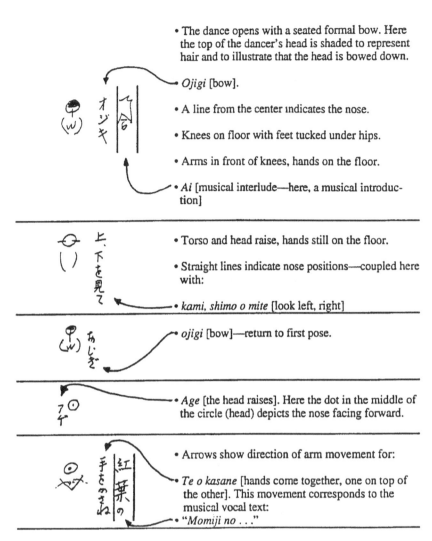

- The dance opens with a seated formal bow. Here the top of the dancer's head is shaded to represent hair and to illustrate that the head is bowed down.

- *Ojigi* [bow].

- A line from the center indicates the nose.

- Knees on floor with feet tucked under hips.

- Arms in front of knees, hands on the floor.

- *Ai* [musical interlude—here, a musical introduction]

- Torso and head raise, hands still on the floor.

- Straight lines indicate nose positions—coupled here with:

- *kami, shimo o mite* [look left, right]

- *ojigi* [bow]—return to first pose.

- *Age* [the head raises]. Here the dot in the middle of the circle (head) depicts the nose facing forward.

- Arrows show direction of arm movement for:

- *Te o kasane* [hands come together, one on top of the other]. This movement corresponds to the musical vocal text:

- "*Momiji no* . . ."

FIGURE 6. *(Above and opposite)* Tachibana notation example translated. Reprinted by permission.

- Stand (the full body is depicted).

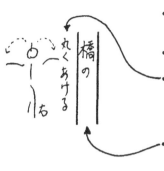

- *migi* [right] written next to the foot marks that the right foot is forward.

- The head raises (note the nose is now up].

- *Maruku akeru* [open (arms) in circles): The hands open from the previous position outward in a circular movement—note dotted lines indicating the direction of the arm movements.

- These movements correspond to the musical vocal text: "*hashi no . . .*"

- Body now faces right.

- Right hand curves down and then up to a position with the hand, flat with fingers together, shading eyes. Note how the thumb position is included, showing that the hand is palm down.

- Left hand under right elbow (keeping sleeve back).

- *Nagameru* [look far away].

- 1 2 3: looking in the distance, the head moves from left to right in three moves.

- *hidari* [left] written next to the foot marks that the left foot is forward.

- These movements correspond to the musical vocal text: "*tamoto kara.*"

While there is ample evidence of *nihon buyo* notation through history and in contemporary dance life, it is not considered to be a "true" means of transmission. It is not intended to be utilized as the sole method for learning dance. Virtually every dancer I spoke to strongly remarked that his/her personal notations were merely a memory aid. Further, teachers remark that notes are wonderful references but cannot possibly convey the essence of a dance. I have attempted to present a general background of *nihon buyo* notational styles, problems, and practices in this chapter; however, it is clear that these notations are documents of dance, lacking the embodied spirit so crucial to this genre.

dancing tape

We can not rely on machines to remember what our bodies
should know, even if we do use tape recorders.
—*Noh* performer Mori Tsuneyoshi
    (Hahn field notes, November 18, 1993)

The practice of employing videotape as a means of transmitting *nihon buyo* is uncommon. However, not to include a brief mention recounting its occasional use would neglect a fascinating aspect of contemporary Japanese society. Further, the strong attitudes and controversies concerning the use of modern recording technologies unmistakably demonstrate artists' enduring commitment to the lived experience for maintaining the art form.

One summer Iemoto visited New York for a week, and I had an opportunity to study the dance "Kyo no tsuki" with her. Several of the lessons were videotaped so that other dancers and I could review the dance in Iemoto's absence during the year. The following summer I traveled to Hatchobori to study dance. At my first lesson we reviewed "Kyo no tsuki." Soke and Iemoto seemed surprised that I recalled the dance after only a few dance lessons the previous year. I naively revealed, "I watched the videotapes." To this remark Soke promptly responded, "You cannot get emotion from a videotape" (Hahn field notes, August 1, 1991).

Soke's statement greatly influenced my thoughts about *nihon buyo* transmission. Despite the various methods of transmission—such as taking part in dance lessons, personal notations, or videotaping—the personal, one-on-one method of transmission continues to be the most vital. Further implied in this statement is that, for Soke, dance is not dance without presence—emotion, heart (*kokoro*). Successfully executing dance steps in the correct form and order does not necessarily produce good dance.

While videotapes supply visual images, personal contact provides emotion and individual nuance. Further, video has numerous limitations that clearly disembody dance from the lived experience. For example, video is a medium viewed on a screen that presents figures within a flat image, losing the spatial qualities of dance; and the medium is limited to visual and aural senses, while other sensate experiences (such as smell or touch) are not represented.

The use of a technology such as video or audio taping during lessons differs from teacher to teacher. All teachers in the Japanese performing arts whom I spoke to voiced strong opinions about the use of technology in the context of learning art. While observing *tsuzumi* (shoulder drum) lessons at Toshya Rosen's studio I noticed a tape recorder positioned next to the student. However, several times during the lesson Toshya Rosen instructed the student to turn the machine off, then would discuss the musical passage. Other times he would inquire, "Is the [tape] machine off?" In these lessons it was clear to me how conscious he was of the taping process and and how sure he was about its proper use within the lesson. Uchikata Keizo, a performer of *noh kan* (the transverse flute played in *noh* ensembles) said he does not allow tape recorders in his lessons. He said, "Students who learn using a tape recorder sound like robots imitating the machine. For example, students who study *rakugo* (traditional comic storytelling) with a tape recorder—when they perform, no one in the audience laughs, because they sound like a machine!" (Hahn field notes, November 18, 1993).

Incorporating a recording medium within the pedagogical practice challenges the ways of tradition. Not one teacher with whom I spoke fully approved of using audio or videotapes for learning. However, acknowledgment of videotape as a valuable documentary medium is unquestioned. Performances are often videotaped professionally. Also, tapes of television interviews and performances by well-known artists and performers are considered valuable documents.

Nevertheless, videotapes provide a convenient visual and aural reference for those students living a great distance from a main Tachibana school. Over the years I have observed that this is the only circumstance in which videotapes are permitted for learning. Through videotapes, for example, the New York City Tachibana group has the opportunity to view current Tokyo choreography as well as newly created works. In such cases dances have been learned in person first so that the videotapes (usually of the lessons or performances) merely reinforce what physical knowledge has already been passed down. In subsequent lessons with Iemoto these dances will be reviewed and properly corrected. Transmission via videotape presents difficulties, however, as one Japanese American dancer pointed out: "What is problematic about learning dances from these tapes is that if performers in Japan have made mistakes during the performance, we have no way of knowing. We copy everything, maybe even their mistakes—until someone from Japan points out that we're doing it incorrectly" (Hahn field notes, May 12, 1990).

In October of 1995, while I was setting up my video camera for practice, Iemoto teased me and said jovially, "It used to be that dancers needed a fan to dance, now it seems we need a video camera!" (Hahn field notes, October 13, 1995). Through the years I have noticed dancers becoming accustomed to the presence of video cameras. Many manage themselves comfortably before a camera. During my fieldwork, dancers even spoke directly to the camera as if it were a living entity. Iemoto occasionally walked off the dance floor and spoke directly to my camera in the middle of my lesson.

When I was analyzing my videotapes in New York I was astounded when I came upon footage of Iemoto speaking to me in the future. Apparently I had left the video camera on record mode in the dance studio while I was changing in the dressing room and she had seized the opportunity to extend my lessons. Iemoto spoke directly into the camera, "Remember this [movement] when you're in New York," and later, holding up a stage prop, "See, this is how long the pole should be."

Walter Ong, a student of McLuhan, observed that the "sensorium becomes narrowed" as new media for communication are created and that "the movement through the sequence of media is of course not merely a matter of successive reorganizations of the sensorium. It involves a host of social, economic, psychological, and other factors" (Ong 1967: 53). I believe that *nihon buyo* teachers have the foresight to envision the complex repercussions that the inclusion of media technologies may bring to their traditions, hence their cautious incorporation of these devices within their daily practice. As teachers are attempting to open their students' awareness through sensoria, misuse of these media could possibly "narrow," or defeat, the practice.

While Soke and Iemoto both acknowledge the practical aspects of video technology, they are very clear, even passionate, about its limitations. The strength of *nihon buyo* transmission lies in human contact to convey the vitality of this very personal, physical, art form.

caught

A childhood memory of a fan stays fastened in my mind. I was listlessly playing in my
seat during a performance, not quite focused on the stage I admit, when a flutter of a
fan caught my eye. Immediately the dancer stopped moving and, as she imperceptibly
turned the fan in her palm, the image of a pine branch on the sensu face mutated.
It was as if the branch slowly contracted to a single pine needle—the limb somehow
swallowed by the folds.

    The transformation occurred just as the sound of a noh kan hit a shrill pitch. I did
not know at the time that this was a dance passage borrowed from noh, a tradition of
transformations, and that the flute was my wake-up call.[12]

five

transforming sensu—presence and orientation

November 21, 1993

Today I witnessed Iemoto transform from a modern Tokyo woman to
the character of a child, to perform the piece "Komori" (Babysitter).[1]
Although I videotaped her making up and changing costume backstage, these were only surface features—the embodied transfiguration
would not be captured through my lens. But the transformation occurred. A small fifty-two-year-old woman, once clothed in layers of
undergarments, *kimono*, and makeup, emerged onstage as a tough nine-
year-old babysitter. Not so simply.

Transfiguration came gradually. Arriving at Mitsukoshi Theater,
Iemoto could have been anyone. As she approached the dressing room,
however, there were clues that this was no ordinary individual, nor ordinary day. People within the theater abruptly halted their conversations and bowed deeply as Iemoto passed by; others, upon seeing her.
immediately knelt on the floor in a formal bow. In her dressing room,
a parade of visitors arrived every few minutes to greet her—the wig
dresser, costume man, musicians, dance acquaintances, and Mitsukoshi
Theater directors. Beautiful flower arrangements also poured in, filling
the already small room with color and the scent of freesias and roses.
At one point a television camera crew from NHK even entered, set up
bright lights, and interviewed Iemoto. I had no idea her dressing room
would be so lively.

The room calmed after the visitors left. Iemoto and her assistant turned their attention to costume and makeup preparations. She changed from a colorful pantsuit to stark white cotton and red silk *kimono* undergarments. Next she laid out the makeup carefully in front of the mirror, and I noticed that there was a logic to the placement of each object according to its order in the makeup process—*bin* (beeswax), a bowl of water, *oshiroi* (white makeup), small containers of pigment in red and black, several shapes of brushes, sponges, powder, towels, and countless other accessories. The color, smell, and textures of these objects were familiar to me. I moved so that I had a direct view of Iemoto's face reflected in the mirror. As I watched her put on a *habutai* (a purple silk fabric to cover the hair under a wig) and begin to apply layers of makeup, an empathetic sensation came over me, as if I could feel the makeup on my face too. The makeup has a certain feel, and smell, and particular motions that are used for applying it—sticky beeswax to seal pores and create a smooth canvas for the layers of pigment to follow, red pigment applied with quick strokes with the middle fingertip in a triangular region from eyebrow to nose, the sound of makeup boxes opening and closing. These familiar sensations streamed from my memory. The room was warm. The assistant drew a fan from her *obi* and pulsed a constant stream of air toward Iemoto to keep her face cool and dry.

Iemoto mixed the *oshiroi* with water to a thick consistency, dipped a wide, flat brush in the mixture, and whitewashed her face, ears, upper chest, arms, and the front of her neck. Again, although I was standing three feet away, I vicariously felt the sensation of the wooden brush in my hand, dipping it in the bowl filled with white liquid and then feeling its soft hair, damp and heavy with *oshiroi*, sweeping cool pigment across my face. Iemoto patted her painted skin evenly with a dry brush, then repeated with a second coat of *oshiroi*—white on white—softening all lineaments of her face. Iemoto's ghostly white appearance seemed neutral in character. As the *oshiroi* dried, the undercoat of brilliant red makeup around her eyes and nose emerged as a faint pink hue, adding depth to her now stark-white flesh. She dusted red above her eyes, deepening the contours. Iemoto seemed to disappear beneath the whitewash.

The assistant painted the back of Iemoto's neck and repeated the patting. Then, with steady hands, Iemoto painted the outer edges of her eyes with red using the middle fingertip of her left hand while holding a handled mirror close to her face with her other hand. With a small brush she painted small eyebrows—her own long vanished beneath

PHOTO 6. Tachibana Yoshie applying makeup. PHOTO: YONEZU TAKASHI

layers of *oshiroi*. Then, tapping the pigment with her fingertip, the sharp edge of the black line became diffused, and two gently curved eyebrows emerged. Iemoto turned her attention to shaping a babysitter's pouty lips in a brilliant red color with a small brush.

Her precise movements contoured her new features like jet-black calligraphy ink on white rice paper. The clarity of each brushstroke was no different from the decisive movement qualities I knew in her dance. Distinct. Unwavering. Unlike dance, however, tangible marks remained after each of these movements to compose the semblance of a babysitter. Iemoto edged back from her makeup area and, after wiping her shins and feet, painted them with *oshiroi* as well. The babysitter wears *geta* (wooden clogs) without *tabi* (socks)—and Iemoto's exposed feet and lower legs had to be painted to match the white skin tone of her face and hands. Iemoto paused before standing up to dress, and for a moment I caught a glimpse of the babysitter character reflected in her mirror, but Iemoto's own voice and movement quality betrayed this illusion.

The wig dresser arrived. Putting on a *katsura* (wig) requires a great amount of skill. Dance wigs, rigid and helmetlike, fit snug against the head. Iemoto held a sheet of plastic film to her forehead as the wig dresser slid the wig onto her head from back to front. The plastic sheet kept her makeup intact but also drew the wig forward to her forehead as she slid it out. Two cotton cords attached to the interior of the wig were pulled back, around Iemoto's ears to the nape of her neck, tied firmly, and tucked under the back of the wig. A delicately shaped long-handled wood comb appeared in the hand of the wig dresser, and she combed the unruly locks into place. The wig for the babysitter is cute—flaunting a big red bow puffed up at the crown, several round ornaments, a red lacquer comb at the front, and short tassels of hair hanging at each temple. Iemoto noticed me teetering nearby with my video camera and shot me a playful grin and laughed.

Next, a professional dresser and two assistants wrapped layers of costume onto Iemoto's body fastened with *himo* (ties) and an *obi*. The dresser was a jovial, elderly gentleman who arrived while Iemoto was applying makeup. I noticed that his slight frame was not much larger than Iemoto's as he stepped forward to dress her. He first bound cotton padding around her torso, then scarlet silk undergarments with white abstract designs, followed by a yellow and black plaid *kimono* with a black collar. Over this colorful costume he wound a red, white, and purple *obi* around her and tied it securely in a bow on her back. After Iemoto was in costume, the wig dresser stepped forward and tied a white *hachimaki* (cotton headband) around Iemoto's head with the knot atop her forehead so that the ends stood up.

Finally, the "baby" (a doll prop) was bundled onto her back under a green and yellow silk jacket. The eyes of the baby seemed to peer over Iemoto's shoulder. The babysitter was still not present, though all the surface features of the *komori* character stood before me. When Iemoto went backstage for her entrance, I left to take a seat in the audience. As we walked in opposite directions down the corridor, I looked back at her one more time. In this fleeting glance I witnessed a profound instance of transformation—Iemoto was scurrying down the corridor *as* the child babysitter. Her embodied expression was a dramatic metamorphosis. It was as if Iemoto had vanished in that instant, leaving *komori* to take the stage. Elegant codeswitching.

From my seat in the audience the vivid nature of the babysitter appeared. Each step of the choreography was impeccable and seemed effortless. But beyond her physical execution of movement, the babysitter's presence shined through—penetrating layers of makeup and costume. I had to remind myself that this doll-like figure was the same woman who, moments ago, had been joking backstage with the NHK interviewer.

orienting culture

Extraordinary experiences are situated somewhere between reality and the constructs of our beliefs. We experience these unusual moments in part because they extend the realm of our orientation in "ordinary" life and are enculturated possibilities. With this remark I am not denying the existence of such experiences, but proposing that beliefs and desires frame them. Because they are *extra*ordinary experiences, we depart from the ordinary and find ourselves transformed. Concerning the relationship of ordinary and extraordinary experiences, Roger Abrahams notes:

> The very flow of the everyday assures the continuity between routine activities and the more extraordinary ones. We have become aware of the continuities between the ordinary and the "deeper" or "higher" events through performed mimetic experiences, which openly imitate (and stylize) everyday acts and interactions. Far from exhausting the relationship between the ordinary and the otherwise, such imitational play only begins the discussion. Indeed, *how* the disruption of the patterns of expectation in ordinary interactions are remedied, even transformed and used in play events, may prove to be the most important point of connection between the different states of apprehension and understanding. (Abrahams 1986: 68, italics in original)

I find performance, as well as fieldwork, to be an encounter that heightens awareness and draws our attention to the "continuity between routine activities and the more extraordinary ones." In particular, performance can construct an extraordinary experience to affectively precipitate a sense of shared experience in a community. Though performance itself is an extraordinary experience for many people to witness, for performers it is their craft, or medium of expression. I intimated my jarring and quite physical experience of Iemoto's transformation backstage because it offers insights on dance transmission, culture, and ethnography. Transmission trains us to learn the craft of setting the stage for expectation and, perhaps, moving the audience.

Consider an occasion that tested your sense of reality, perception, or orientation. It can be an everyday event that transformed to an extraordinary or unusual moment. Have you seen a performance that caused you to focus differently? What made this an extraordinary experience? I imagine that the experience had an impact on you, since you recognized it as extraordinary and set it apart from what you deem to be "ordinary." When you were experiencing this event, do you recall if it caused you to stop and consider the situation in depth? To figure it out sensibly? logically? Were there sensations that were unknown to you? Did the extraordinary and ordinary overlap? How? Did you need to resolve the experience before turning your attention to something else? Did you question or deny the experience?

Extraordinary encounters are disorienting, particularly if they summon sensations we previously have not physically experienced. I am purposely vague in my use of "extraordinary experience" because I believe that everyone and every culture defines what sits outside their realm of "ordinary" experience. Of course, each person has a different set of life experiences. Extraordinary events occur because they test our perception and sense of reality within our frame of cultural beliefs. Our senses are triggered, yet during such an experience we might question the reality of what we sense. What qualities of sensation would be necessary for you to deem an event extraordinary? A visual apparition? A sound or smell? Touch? Taste? Returning to the experience you considered above, can you detail the experiential elements of sense that marked that event as out of the ordinary for you? Does an examination of the experience reveal why the encounter disoriented you? Transformations, on any level, are informative in that they provide us with opportunities to recognize boundaries that define our patterns of orientation, patterns of reality.

It seems to me that ethnographers are in the business of (cultural) disorientation by consciously situating themselves within particular contexts and searching for ways to comprehend these experiences from a variety of perspectives. These contexts may be disorienting because they are completely unfamiliar. But extraordinary experiences in familiar settings can be twice as disorienting because they are unexpected and cause us to experience sensory displacement (as in my "backstage" experience). Some of these disorientations can be resolved as cultural differences, while other episodes are perhaps truly out of the ordinary. But, as ethnographers, what do we make of these unusual events in the field? Do we hide them and only analyze and present hard data? How might we integrate these experiences into our academic work and attempt to convey their transformative effects on us? (See Hahn 2006b.)

A collection of articles in *Being Changed by Cross-cultural Encounters: The Anthropology of Extraordinary Experiences* describes extraordinary experiences that ethnographers have had in the field and discusses the issues that arose from them. The editors, David Young and Jean-Guy Goulet, assert that these experiences need to be included in ethnographic texts:

> Good ethnographic reports, whatever their subject matter, jolt us into new awareness, for they are derived from lived experiences that challenge our own conventions and assumptions in life. Good ethnographic reports evoke a realm of human experience and in the process lay the groundwork for its explanation within anthropology. (1994: 20–21)

Ethnomusicologist Deborah Wong observed spirit possession in Thailand while conducting fieldwork on the *wai kruu* (a ritual to honor teachers). In particular, she witnessed the "Old Father" spirit enter the body of ritual participants. In *Sounding the Center: History and Aesthetics in Thai Buddhist Performance*, Wong writes, "My time in Thailand fundamentally changed my own beliefs. I didn't plan on that" (2001:·254). Acknowledging encounters with the Old Father's presence, she writes:

> Having encountered him so many times and in so many places, I can't not believe, as my mask maker acquaintance said to me . . . The fields of anthropology, ethnomusicology, and cultural studies (to name a few) have so thoroughly problematized ethnographic authority that one necessarily addresses the construction of cultural reality through the lens of particular subjectivities, and the fact is, my subjectivity changed in the course of my research . . . I can not tell you at what point, precisely, I felt that the Old Father was touching me—at what point I felt his blessing as something tangible. I can say that there is no retreat from the moment when subjectivity shifts, no going back . . . (2001: 255)

Wong's subjectivity shift interests me. Although my experience of Iemoto's transformation backstage was not spirit possession or trance, I identify with Wong's encounter with a different sense of reality and her experience of a subjectivity shift. My own experience transmitted a sensibility of presence that changed my perspective, my orientation.

Disorienting encounters during fieldwork can be challenging, leaving us vulnerable. Writing about such encounters and changes in our beliefs poses further challenges, as Wong offers—"If experience is accessible only through a certain loss of control, then the moment of threshold-crossing, when experience folds into belief, is even more difficult to write." In a provocative book, *Deep Listeners: Music, Emotion, and Trancing*, Judith Becker discusses how legitimacy is a factor in the experience and reception of trance. She proposes that believability, or faith, plays a large role in a community's practice of trance (2004: 30–34). Believability teeters on an edge that Western research is uncomfortable to embrace. And that edge is where the extraordinary resides.

In *Between Theater and Anthropology*, performance studies scholar and theater director Richard Schechner included a section titled "Transformation of Being and/or Consciousness," and proposed:

> Either permanently as in initiation rites or temporarily as in aesthetic theater and trance dancing, performers—and sometimes spectators too—are changed by the activity of performing . . . While watching the deer dance of the Arizona Yaqui in November 1981, I wondered if the figure I saw was a man and a deer simultaneously; or, to say it in a way a performer might understand, whether putting on the deer mask made the man "not a man" and "not a deer" but somewhere in between. (1985: 4)

Disorienting encounters pose challenges to our experiential knowledge. Believability is called into question, and through the process of sorting out the experience there is a possibility for growth.

I realize that the ease of Iemoto's transfiguration in that spellbinding moment backstage was the result of decades of practice in the studio. Still, I was left with an extremely moving experience that I could not immediately "make sense" of logically. The extraordinary can easily be explained away. For example, one could say that the nature of performance itself is an art of illusion and that Japanese performers are trained to transfigure on cue. Since I have been enculturated through dance training to believe in artistic transfiguration, one might conclude that my cultural expectations created my experience backstage. To a degree this is true, because dance training includes transformation as part of the movement vocabulary, and transformation is also part of the folklore narratives.

For example, I grew up listening to Japanese bedtime stories with shape-shifter protagonists. Japanese folklore is filled with stories of *henge* "transformation," such as an animal transfiguring to an object or another living being. The most well-known *henge* tales star a shape-shifting fox, or *kitsune*, who has supernatural powers to transfigure, most often into a woman such as a nun or a mother. Badgers, or *tanuki*, are also masters of transfiguration. The most famous tale is of a *tanuki* transforming into a teapot to escape the wrath of taunting children. My elaboration of *henge* in folklore here is meant to provide examples of how the notion of transformation is not unusual in Japan. Transformation itself is considered to be extraordinary, but it is not an unusual concept.

How are dancers enculturated to the notion of transformation through dance? And how does transmission play a role in the process? In the following section I offer a glimpse into how transmission practices provide an essence of performance that reaches beyond the rudiments of codified dance. Believability remains at the core.

transfiguring on cue

Orientation through disorientation occurs as a disruption of normalcy, followed by a clarity that signals a reorientation and comprehension of one's sense of place, literal or otherwise. Let's examine a *nihon buyo* performance practice in which transfiguration—the narrative shifting between characters—is choreographed into dance.

As mentioned earlier, *nihon buyo* pieces most often follow a narrative form. Depending on the piece, dancers either portray a single character or shift between several characters within a single dance. In both structures, the embodied shift from one's self (identity) to a performed character can be a disorienting experience. Recall the footage of Hideo's first dance lesson, where his movements continue to project his own character rather than the performer in "Matsu no Midori." Performers must learn to articulate each persona with expressive clarity so that the characters appear distinct for the audience.

Iemoto's direction to me, "without experiencing life, without personality, you have no dance, no *kokoro* [heart, spirit, or soul], and you are invisible . . . but if you have a sense of self, then you can become any character onstage—a woman, a young boy, an old man," conceptually links performance and the formation of a dancer's identity (see the opening to chapter 3 for the full conversation). Her comment reveals the notion that strength in one's self (identity) provides a freedom and ability to be flexible in dance. I believe there is a correspondence between Iemoto's idea of a stable yet flexible self; the metaphoric, shifting self in dance; and the Japanese philosophical/spiritual conception of self being capable of change. One gestures to the other through practice, revealing the notion that one might comprehend the essence of life's ephemeral nature in an actively embodied way (Yuasa 1987, 1993; Varela, Thompson, and Rosch 1991). In the following paragraphs I provide an example of how this concept of shifting identity (or codeswitching), choreographed in dance, provides dancers with an opportunity to playfully embody multiple identities in dance.

The piece "Ame no shiki" ("Rain in the Four Seasons," choreographed by Tachibana Hoshu) provides a clear example of character-shifting techniques. It poetically depicts a traveler encountering seasonal rains in picturesque Edo. The performer must make an embodied shift between numerous contrasting roles throughout the dance. With only a simple paper fan in hand, a dancer must also convincingly animate and transform the prop into a variety of objects to tell the narrative. The following is a description of the opening six-minute passage of "Ame no Shiki" to illustrate the use of character shifting.

First emerges the male traveler, the main character. The dancer holds a male carriage, feet shoulder-width apart; toes pointed slightly out; legs in an open (vs. turned inward) position; elbows away from the body; and a broad, erect torso. The traveler shields his face from the rain with a straw hat, conveyed by an upturned fan. Facing away from the audience, he peeks out from under his hat to see rain still falling. He walks along a path, sidestepping puddles. Facing the audience, he peers out again and sees that the rain has stopped. Removing his hat with a shake (the fan closes), the traveler continues along his way. Several sights along the road amuse him, such as birds soaring in the sky. The traveler's *kimono* sleeves transform to wings as he flutters his arms as a bird. The character shifting becomes more complex as the dancer portrays a traveler who then mimes a bird within the dance.

Several minutes into the passage the dancer transforms into a contrasting character—a mother with her child in tow. Now the dancer's movements are feminine in nature, elbows close to the body; knees bent and legs together; and feet pointed slightly inward (keeping the line of the *kimono* trim and composed). The open fan, held by the paper tip in her right hand, represents the woman's child at her side. She stands for a moment holding the child's hand and looks off in the distance. The mother adjusts her hair with gentle movements and then

PHOTO 7. Tachibana Yoshie (*in black*) teaching a student the
role of the male traveler in "Ame no shiki." Tachibana School,
Tokyo, Japan.

gestures to attract her child's attention. She points ahead, showing the
child where they will visit. After walking forward the mother notices
that the moon has appeared and points it out to the child. They continue to walk together and come to a series of vendors along the street.
The child sees *miso dango* (a sweet dumpling served on a stick, dipped
in a fermented bean paste) being sold by a peddler and wants one. The
mother purchases the *dango*, dips it in *miso*, and feeds it to the child.
Immediately following this vignette the dancer turns and shifts into
the character of a candy peddler.

The vendor appears balancing his wares on his head (the dancer
mimes this by balancing an open fan atop her head) and makes his
presence known by hitting a gong, mimed by the dancer with her left
hand held above her head. The candy man finds a customer, takes the
money with his right hand, and puts it into his left *kimono* sleeve. He
takes down a stick of candy and passes it to the customer. Smoothly,
the dancer now shifts to portraying a series of four fruit peddlers in
rapid succession. First the dancer mimes the peach seller with her gestures—holding the luscious large peach cupped in the left palm while

PHOTO 8. A student following Tachibana Yoshie during a quick
change of character. "Ame no shiki" lesson, Tachibana School,
Tokyo, Japan.

her right hand polishes it with a circular movement. The vendor displays to customers how juicy the fruit is by wiping his mouth with
one swift sweep followed by a second shake of the hand to fling the
peach juice off his fingers. The dancer then places her hands inside her
sleeves. This movement abstractly represents the mandarin orange and
apple vendors. Finally the dancer tosses the fan from her head to her
hand and, by closing it, transforms the fan into a banana that the vendor holds high in the air as he circles the area.

The closed *sensu* (fan) transforms from banana to a pestle as a sesame
seed peddler appears. The dancer kneels facing the audience and rapidly grinds the sesame seeds in a mortar. The dancer points to the distance at more vendors. Out comes the watermelon hawker. The *sensu*
becomes a watermelon slice as the dancer swings the fan open. She
mimes holding a knife and cuts the melon in two, then picks up half
(the fan) and takes a bite, roughly spitting the seeds off to the ground.
The dance continues, and many more characters appear. With these
codeswitching examples in mind, let us continue the examination of
how codeswitching techniques foster orientation.

shifting selves

Research on codeswitching in linguistics and social anthropology has been helpful to my understanding of the character-shifting process in dance. The research reveals that verbal codeswitching patterns enable individuals access to a number of social identities. In cultures where codeswitching is prevalent, individuals negotiate multiple frames of reference, with multiple roles and role relationships within the society.[2] Carol Myers Scotton, in her analysis of verbal codeswitching in East Africa, noted: "It is as if the switch is made to remind other participants that the speaker is a multi-faceted personality, as if the speaker were saying 'not only am I X, but I am also Y.' This ploy, in and of itself, is a powerful strategy because the speaker 'enlarges' himself/herself through marked choices in a mainly unmarked discourse, asserting a range of identities" (Scotton 1988: 170).[3]

Borrowing concepts from linguistic theories on codeswitching, I applied codeswitching analysis to the choreographic language of dance. I acknowledge that the practice of switching between identities in dance is not impromptu as in the everyday speech analyzed by Scotton and others. However, the linguistic framework provides a useful starting point for analysis of codeswitching. As seen in the brief description of "Ame no Shiki," codeswitching is consciously employed and honed as a codified formula to convey a narrative, and so it is a practice that is trained into the body. I find that the embodied "shifting," or codeswitching, between characters in dance metaphorically mirrors a social coordination of self that is present and respected in daily life in Japan, where clear delineations between social circles, between men and women, between young and old are reflected in impromptu behavior and speech. In the past two decades, research on "self" in Japanese culture has received a great amount of attention.[4] Social anthropologists propose that the conceptual flexibility of self enables individuals to orient themselves and interact in a wide variety of social levels. Identity is relational—contextually based. Concerning the nature of Japanese social interactions, Jane Bachnick wrote, "Japanese choose appropriate behavior situationally, from among a range of possibilities, resulting in depictions of the Japanese self as 'shifting' or 'relational'" (Bachnick 1992: 152).

The practice of codeswitching in daily life in Japan can easily be observed—levels of speech from familiar to honorific are chosen situationally, as is the pitch of speech, manner of dress, body language (such as bowing and other social coordinations within a space), and the different names individuals acquire in their artistic practices. In dance, as in daily life, the patterns of codeswitching are transmitted through embodied practices—lessons of orientation and agency enabled by the practice of dance.

I find that the continuous codeswitching exemplified in the dance "Ame no shiki" is conceptually similar to the codeswitching one may experience outside the dance studio. By this statement, I am not saying that Japanese dance is drawn directly from everyday life, but that codeswitching is a common practice in everyday life and in that respect it is within Japanese dancers' daily vocabulary, inside and outside the dance studio, to enact identity shifts. This does not make the practice of training the body to codeswitch on cue any less disorienting, however. Like codeswitching in everyday life, the codeswitching in dance is founded on a common vocabulary of communication. Shared physical, expressive vocabulary is vital in any narrative artistry in order for the audience to comprehend the story line and the development of a plot. It can be argued that the codeswitching experienced in daily life is founded on social, ethical, and moral situations an individual must spontaneously interact within, whereas dance is a choreographed artistic practice. What I find fascinating is that in both settings codeswitching reveals social structures through metaphor. I believe that the complex sensitivities needed in contrasting social relationships in everyday life form the foundation of choreographic structures in many *nihon buyo* dances. Dance serves as a valuable model of embodied metaphors that inform how techniques of the body in motion are culturally and historically situated.[5]

I have noticed that switching between characters can have a disorienting effect on students. The switch requires a dancer not only to embody the proper carriage and movement for each role but to portray the essence of each character so that each persona is distinct. In my experience of learning "Ame no shiki" and observing other students learning the dance, I find that focusing one's attention on the subtleties of character portrayal and shifting is crucial.

Iemoto calls our attention to the details of each character portrayal, including carriage, gesture, eye gaze, sound, facial expression, costume, and prop use. She often takes time to clearly describe the character and the context of his/her appearance. Iemoto is particularly attentive to the moment of transformation between characters. The clarity of the shift is vital. She teased me one day and made her point clear: "You can't be the [male] vendor but still have feminine feet [from the previous character]!" When I learned the sesame seed vendor passage, Iemoto commented: "Do you know what you're doing? Have you ever ground sesame seeds?" Although the portrayal of grinding the seeds is performed in a stylized manner, the mimetic act must convey the process of grinding to the audience; otherwise, "How will they know what you are doing?" Not until the character being portrayed is fully understood, in both intellectual and physical ways, can a deeper transformation occur. Believability must be rooted in the body.

I am often asked if learning to embody stylized stereotypes in dance constricts dancers' sense of individual identity. From personal experience as a dancer and researcher, I actually find the opposite to be true—that physical expression in dance and everyday life provides an abundant palette of performed selves to express the diversity of one's inner sense of self. I believe that Iemoto's illustration, "without experiencing life, without personality, you have no dance, no *kokoro* (heart, spirit, or soul), and you are invisible . . . but if you have a sense of self, then you can become any character onstage—a woman, a young boy, an old man," resonates the profound relationship between a dancer's sense of self and character both inside and outside dance. Only from a solid core of realized identity can flexibility arise. As the headmaster of the Tachibana School, it is Iemoto's obligation to transmit the school's way of dance to her students. Her guidance reaches far beyond dance to a deeper level of comprehending one's self relative to others and the world.

There are contrasting perspectives on the topic of multiplicity and self. Some view multiplicity as a fragmentation, or distortion, of a person's sense of self (and self-image), while others see multiplicity as a vibrant marker of plural identity.[6] Philosophers Catriona Mackenzie and Natalie Stoljar state, "Diversity critiques parallel postmodern critiques in challenging the assumption that agents are cohesive and unified. Such critiques claim that each individual has a 'multiple identity,' which reflects the multiple groups to which the individual belongs" (Mackenzie and Stoljar 2000: 11). In the case of codeswitching in Japanese dance, it may be argued that the highly stylized portrayal of characters in many Japanese dances restricts the repertoire of identity representations to a narrow vocabulary of stereotypes that reinforce male-dominated hierarchical social systems. I find, however, that dance lessons, where women are encouraged to physically enact roles beyond their daily repertory of identities, provide a rare setting to "imagine oneself otherwise," to borrow Catriona Mackenzie's phrase:

> I contend that our ability to imagine ourselves otherwise—that is, our ability to imaginatively distance ourselves from our habitual modes of self-understanding and to envisage, in imaginative representations, alternative possibilities for ourselves—plays an important role in practical reflection and deliberation about the self, and hence in self-definition. (Mackenzie and Stoljar 2000: 139)

Building on her idea, I propose that physical activity through role-playing significantly reinforces an expanded image of self through the vocabulary of embodied memories in dance. The *process* of cultural embodiment, the enactment of a wide variety of characters, has a powerful effect on dancers' identities. Extreme role-playing—such as playing a witch, a demon, or a rude, spoiled child—can provide an emotional outlet as well as an expanded vocabulary of identity. Further, dance lesson contexts are a socially acceptable and "safe" haven to playact expressive modes not deemed appropriate outside the dance studio in Japanese public life.

There is, however, a complex set of traditional social obligations attached to *nihon buyo* life. The strict *iemoto* (headmaster) system, which enforces the continuity of the oral tradition and dance family heritage, for example, overlies yet another complex web of multiplicity. I am sure that added obligation and perceived confinement of behavior must dissuade many women from entering into the *nihon buyo* world. I acknowledge that these pressures exist, though I personally find them outweighed by the deep bonds I experience in the Tachibana dance family. The commitment of these women to the art inspires me to move and write.

Performance provides a vehicle for expressing complex identities, and even for broadening personal expressive vocabularies. Richard Bauman sees performance as a means "for the encoding and presentation of information about oneself in order to construct a personal and social image" (Bauman 1984: 21). I see performance as a process where cultural boundaries of identity are negotiated metaphorically. Through the structures of choreographed codeswitching, I believe it is possible to transgress the boundaries of our everyday identities and to reorient self through practice. The potential of enacting multiplicity through performance is so clearly stated by Tachibana Sahomi: "When you're dancing you can be anyone." In such play enactments, dancers perform codified identities—cultural sensibilities of learned, embodied agency. Is this a part of "believability"?

The direct physical transmission of multiple characters in the dance studio teaches stylized roles, yet it also imparts a way of knowing self and character through the body, which reaches beyond superficial mimicking. *Nihon buyo* offers all dancers, but women in particular, powerful expressive means to transcend the boundaries that might confine them in daily life in Japan.[7] Strict social rules and expectations within the society restraining women's behavior can create a high level of pressure. Dance provides an opportunity to act out a variety of roles. This can be a liberating and even playful activity—consider a daily practice of embodiment that includes transforming into a warrior, monkey, lower-class character, ghost, drunkard, or bold, demonic witch. Dancers learn from a very early age how to express a diversity of character portrayals, and as a result a wide vocabulary of embodied cultural ideologies is transmitted.[8]

The tradition of metaphoric shifting provides students with abilities to negotiate and comprehend multiple identities on the dance floor. I believe that the metaphoric shifting present in *nihon buyo* choreography empowers women through the transformative, shared, embodied experience of multiple identities as well as flexible notions of self, within a society that has historically restricted their expression. As one might imagine, codeswitching between a complex series of characters can be disorienting at first. In a sense, codeswitching is a practice of orientation through disorientation—the transformation into "other" necessitates a clear knowing and establishing of self.

performing passion

When I told dancers at Hatchobori that I was studying how dance is taught they nodded, but smiled with blank faces. On one occasion someone exclaimed, "Oh you're here to learn to dance!" I replied, "Yes, but I'm also here to learn *how* we learn." More puzzled faces. "We watch and listen," someone else chimed in. At this point even I began to question myself. After all, the gist of my study was exactly what this dancer said—to show how we see, hear, feel touch, and put it all together. But "putting it all together" seemed too simplistic. I have seen many dancers proficiently execute the codified steps of a dance, yet something was lacking. All the steps were there, timing great, costuming impeccable, but the passion and heightened awareness in the performance nonexistent. On the other hand, I have watched dancers miss a few steps yet embody a wonderful essence of artistry. *Putting it all together* is not enough, I thought . . . I must have missed something in the transmission process.

I believe it is presence.

Presence, as ephemeral as the body, remains an elusive quality of dance. Ineffable. Presence is vital to a dancer's artistry. I wondered how presence could be transferred from teacher to student—is it in the steps? In the relationship between teacher and student? In the eyes of the observer? Is it active believability? Early on, presence eluded my scorecard of observable transmission modes, yet I found it integrated into every lesson. I am not certain it is possible to definitively provide a formula for the transmission of presence. Presence is transmitted in the folds of lessons, when dancers learn to orient themselves via the senses during lessons; when they learn to expand their awareness; learn to transfigure on cue; and understand the flow of embodied *ki* energy available to them. Heightened awareness and sensibilities are not only absorbed through practice; dancers embodying such a depth of awareness and orientation can project this *ki* energy out to the audience.

My disorienting moment backstage as Iemoto transfigured into the babysitter drew me to the idea of presence as a trained sensibility. The practical features of learning dance movement through the senses preoccupied me at the time—how we learn to heighten our visual, tactile, and aural/oral awareness in order to absorb dance. This had been my primary focus in fieldwork. A flash of insight on presence grabbed my attention when I witnessed Iemoto backstage. As dance students we absorb the tradition through honed awareness, but as performers we project awareness outward. Iemoto's back was turned to me as she scampered down the hallway, so I saw no gaze, no emotive facial expression; her projection of the babysitter's presence was an embodied one. This is difficult to describe, but permit me to try.

Throughout this book I have detailed an inward motion, a taking in of sensory information to train the body. But once apperception occurs, assimilation and realized embodiment, the very sensory paths that were the vehicles of transmission now enhance presence. We become present through visual awareness, through our tactile and kinesthetic awareness, through our listening awareness, through our life force, or *ki* energy. What was absorbed can be projected *if* the dancer draws on her embodied sensibilities and *ki* energy. The audience can observe the dancer's heightened awareness as the performing body projects presence. This is what Zeami, the fourteenth-century originator of *noh*, termed "*hana*" (flower)—the essence of dramatic artistry.

Iemoto described a flow of awareness between dancer and audience: "In Japanese performance the house lights are left on. This way performers can see the audience—I mean really see them—and [the dancer can] draw on their energy to intensify [her] performance." I admit that at the time her instruction seemed logical and interesting, but it would soon change the way I understood presence and *ki* energy flow onstage. The energy that performers can tap from seeing, feeling, and hearing the audience cannot be quantitatively measured; however, comparing the opposite setting—when the stage lights are on and the audience is in the dark—reveals a very different perspective. With the house lights turned off, the flow of communication is muted; the anonymous audience gazes on the performer, and the performer looks out at darkness. When a performer has the opportunity observe the audience, she can draw on their energy and subtly craft nuances of her performance to the unfolding context, or mood. In other words, a dancer can read the audience and work with its emotions on the spot.

Awareness of the audience is not a simple task. It demands much more than just looking in the correct location when dancing. It demands confidence in one's dancing abilities, self, and the role one is portraying. Performers must project their energy stemming from the *hara* area, the abdominal region considered to be the center of energetic and spiritual strength. The *hara* is where *ki* energy, or power, resides. The flow of *ki* energy is practiced repeatedly in dance class via *haragei* (the art of visceral communication, introduced in chapter 3) and is used to connect with an audience. Ben Befu points out the connection between *haragei*, the body, and transmission: "*haragei* (visceral communication) which lies very near the end of the spectrum of non-verbal communication" is connected to the Japanese aesthetic of suggestion as a form of communication using empathetic readings of others' facial expressions and other nonverbal forms of communication (Befu 1991: 110). In *nihon buyo*, movement must originate from the *hara* center and ripple up the torso, out the arms, legs, head, and even the gaze of the eyes. In fact, the choreography demands that movement must flow from the *hara* and project outward. Transmission practices reinforce the *hara* as the central source of energy, an area that is trained repeatedly to project movement, character, awareness, and resilience.

flowing transmission

When a dancer effortlessly executes the many requirements of a dance while projecting a keen awareness of multiple sensory modes, a vibrance of energy, or presence, arises. I believe that this state is what Mihaly Csikszentmihalyi refers to as "flow," an optimal experience of consciousness and focused awareness. He states that, "to pursue mental operations to any depth, a person has to learn to concentrate attention. Without focus, consciousness is in a state of chaos" (1997: 26). He provides an example of a flow experience:

> Imagine, for instance, that you are skiing down a slope and your full attention is focused on the movements of the body, the position of the skis, the air whistling past your face, and the snow-shrouded trees running by. There is no room in your awareness for conflicts or contradictions; you know that a distracting thought or emotion might get you buried facedown in the snow. And who wants to get distracted? The run is so perfect that all you want is for it to last forever, to immerse yourself completely in the experience. (1997: 29)

Dancers can easily identify with this state of flow, where the intensity of dancing before an audience under stage lights parallels the dramatic in-the-moment flight on the slope. Onstage, when mental and physical coordinations effortlessly "flow," a dancer can use the heightened state of focused energy to project that awareness. I believe that this is the ultimate embodiment of dance. Every dance lesson is about gaining flow. Csikszentmihalyi provides insights on flow and learning: "Flow tends to occur when a person's skills are fully involved in overcoming a challenge that is just about manageable" (1997: 30)—and several pages later, "the flow experience acts as a magnet for learning—that is, for developing new levels of challenges and skills" (33). In a sense, Iemoto teaches students to focus and heighten their awareness. She is conscious of the edge where introducing too much material will overwhelm a student and too little will lead to boredom. But there is much beyond the basic memorization of movements and choreography. Once rudimentary dance material is learned, the next stage is to rehearse the dance so that movements and energy are fluid. This "putting it all together" is perhaps the most difficult stage of learning dance.

Throughout this book I have detailed the stages of learning and students' struggles with new information. We can observe different stages of students' embodied fluidity with the learning process—a continuum of potential flow experiences for the beginner, intermediate, and experienced dancers. If you were to visit a dance studio and watch lessons over a period of time you would see how the process of gaining embodied knowledge is very gradual. In some cases, painfully slow. While a dancer may intellectually comprehend how to move, the body is generally slower to realize the essence of the dance. Repetition encourages flow.

Dance transmission actively invites flow experiences. The physical and mental multitasking required of a dancer during lessons (as well as during performances) is challenging—a setting where flow experiences can potentially occur. These multitasking events have been detailed in this book, but to review a few—coordinating the steps; listening to the music and orienting the body in time; orienting within space; facial expression; character shifting; costume management; choreography; and energy flow. During a lesson these tasks expand to other sensory negotiations—visual awareness (following the teacher), tactile awareness, and oral/aural awareness (listening to the teacher and the music).

For each individual the ability to focus attention and awareness is different. I believe that experiences of flow and the projection of presence can arise during the early stages of a dancer's development, although they may not be as apparent as they are when an advanced dancer beams energy and confidence while fluidly performing in class.

One of the most fascinating aspects of flow that Csikszentmihalyi introduces is the relationship of flow and self: "Following a flow experience, the organization of the self is more *complex* than it had been before. It is by becoming increasingly complex that the self might be said to grow" (1991: 41). I do not believe that dancers' sense of personal growth is something observable, or even a sensibility that can be measured in any way. Yuasa clarifies some of these intangible aspects of self and embodiment in Japanese training: "the tradition of Eastern self-cultivation places importance on entering the mind from the body or form. That is, the mind is not simply consciousness nor is it constant and unchangeable, but rather it is that which is *transformed* through training the body" (Yuasa 1993: 26), and a page later, "a characteristic of Japanese artistry is that its fundamental emphasis is placed more on the *standpoint of the performer* than in that of the audience . . .

The artist requires the catharsis and enhancement of his or her mind in pursuit of beauty, just as does the cultivator in pursuit of satori [enlightenment]" (27).

At Hatchobori there is a passion for dance and there is a passion for teaching. Iemoto and Soke teach with an enthusiasm that is compelling. Transmission of presence exists through the intimate sharing of *kokoro* (heart, spirit) and *ki*. Sensational knowledge. The experience is transformative.

orienting folds

An uneasy question: where does emotion fit into the transmission process? Deidre Sklar, in her essay "Five Premises for a Culturally Sensitive Approach to Dance," inspired me to grapple with this problematic question: "beneath concepts, movement inevitably involves feeling. Simply to move is to feel something as the body changes. More important, habitual patterns of movement are colored with associated emotions" (2002: 31). Dance literally transforms our bodies. We rehearse movements linked with sounds, linked with emotions, and these physical and emotional associations become enculturated—embodied. Presence rides this energetic path of associations and offers a way to connect with others. If dance is a "way of knowing," it is also a way of expressing what we know, what we embody, and who we are.

Splayed open, one can see that a fan's outermost bamboo "bones" differ from the rest. These two bones bear the pressure of opening and closing the fan, so they are slightly heavier. Here, in the closing bone of this book, I return to a more personal reflection of the type that appeared most strongly only in the opening chapter. Dance classes have been personally transformative for me, filled with lessons of the social and performing body, energy, and presence.

Sensory "sensational" knowledge orients. Clearly, embodied identities rise from the wealth of sensory information we encounter in our daily lives. It is disturbing that in such a sensory-rich world, visible surface qualities of the body—such as skin pigmentation, hair color, eye shape, cranial contour, height and weight—establish the yardstick of embodied sameness/difference with which to essentialize racial/gender boundaries.[9] Absent in this prioritized fixation on mere surface is the essence of deeply embodied experience and sensory knowledge sustained through transmission practices. As a multiracial individual I

168 » *Sensational Knowledge*

find this notion particularly charged, and I ask, What stories are told by bodies that differ? . . . bodies that rupture the lineage of reproduction/ transmission in their very presence and perhaps alter the course of the stories through misread reception of such a (different) moving body? It is not possible to definitively answer these two questions, since each multiracial person has a different orientation due to his/her upbring-ing, appearance, and social life. Below I provide my own orientation to offer one experience in this complex negotiation.

Throughout my life Japanese and Americans from a variety of back-grounds have boldly questioned me: "Why are you studying *Japanese* dance? Why not ballet? You could easily pass [as white]." Within the Tachibana group my Eurasian appearance has never been an issue, and I have always felt a strong sense of belonging and acceptance. This at-titude may be particular to my school, however. Unfortunately there are many cases of rejection of foreigners practicing Japanese traditional arts. A genre termed "Japanese dance," while it embraces and embod-ies Japanese culture, can simultaneously reject outsiders. It is an art ex-pressed by the human form, but must one be Japanese to perform it? The aesthetic components of the style reinforce this to some degree: the attire, the mimetic movements drawn from Japanese culture, the aesthetic of the physical movements, and the physique itself. Of course, these aspects of performance were well established specifically for the Japanese physique hundreds of years prior to contact with the outside world. *Kimono* and other traditional costumes are constructed to com-fortably fit the compact, petite Japanese body.

The movement qualities are (logically) tailored to complement the Japanese stature as well. This is not unusual; many if not all dance communities across the globe base their movement aesthetics on ideal concepts of their native physique. So, what reactions come about when outsiders attempt to perform these world traditions? If the aesthetics and concepts of the body within a performance genre are intrinsically flexible so that a variety of body types can be included, then the issue of outsiders performing the tradition may not create a conflict. A cul-ture's philosophies of the body and how philosophical/spiritual prac-tices inform the aesthetic style embodied by the performer are also important factors to consider. Outsiders remain outsiders when such differences are found crucial to a performing tradition.[10]

These considerations can be quite painful for performers involved in traditions outside their (physical) heritage. This brings me to the ques-tion, What are "natural" bodies? If a culture deems bodies as (biologically) natural or naturally talented, then essential ethnic or national body traits can be defined and idealized. In turn, "authentic" performances can be constructed from these, and only these, bodies. But if dance is seen as a system of representations that are culturally coded, then "outsiders" practicing the tradition can be included on some level. If an "authentic" performance consists only of insiders to the tradition, then when outsiders perform, is it considered to be blurring or destroying the art? A colleague related a tale of a Japanese teacher commenting that an American dancer's style was "*bata kusai*" (reeking or stinking of butter). As butter is associated with Western cuisine, and with the distinct odor of those who eat meat and dairy, this was not meant as a compliment. Distasteful. Clearly the essence of the art was altered by the very presence projected by the foreign dancer in this teacher's eyes. Several non-Japanese colleagues practicing traditional Japanese arts have confided to me that they receive strong reactions from Japanese audiences, particularly to aspects of their physical appearance, which they believe reflect Japanese nationalism. I find it interesting that many *gaijin* visual artists, tea ceremony practitioners, and monks have been more readily accepted within Japanese communities yet performers, whose bodies are displayed in public as instruments of their art, are often discouraged, ignored, or merely included as a novelty.

During my fieldwork Soke and Iemoto stated very strongly to me that "this is *nihon buyo*, and *kokoro* is the most important thing . . . it is about a *human* feeling, a *human* experience. It does not matter if you are Japanese or not." I remember how they emphasized the word *human* (*ningen*) to make this point. However, outside the Tachibana group I often experienced rude awakenings to my *gaijin* identity. Once, three Japanese women came up after seeing me dance and, as if I was invisible, carried on a conversation before me: "Oh she dances so well . . . and she's not even Japanese! Most Americans just don't look right." On the other hand, both Japanese and Americans have asked if I believe that my dance abilities are due to Japanese blood. I commonly reply that, while my petite physique and Asian features have not hindered my training, I do not believe that Japanese art practices naturally flow through my veins but, rather, exist because of my upbringing. The explanation of my identity can be a daily performance—embodiment of biracial performativity is full-time.

Multiracial individuals complicate and confuse the constructs of race. We do not easily fit into statistic census categories in an orderly manner. Marginalized by the mainstream and by the marginalized themselves, living double enforces a continual critical perspective of the "politics of difference" (West 1993) and a lived flexible (flexed?) sensibility of agency. This "double consciousness" (Du Bois 1993) has been enacted through the body—ironically, the notion of shifting identities has been not only a metaphor within the dance style I have been trained in, but also an embodied practice I negotiate in my daily life as a biracial individual. Through experience I have come to understand that the notion of a flexible sense of agency and the enactment of shifting identities can be a positive aspect of an individual's well-being.[11] I found that the codeswitching that I finessed and deployed defensively between diverse communities as I grew up was fortified by the practice of dance, nurturing strength in fluid plurality. As a child I played at becoming different characters onstage. This continues to offer me pleasure, yet I currently also see the process of embodied transfiguration/transformation as a powerful way of *dis*-orienting myself and experiencing different cultural orientations, physical sensibilities, and perspectives.

Curiously, learning to enact multiple identities in dance has leveled the polarity of my biracial "halves" and redeployed "doubleness" as a viable presence to project. By orienting within plurality I understand that embodiment allows for a cohabitation and enactment of multiple identities. I have a strong sense that biraciality is in itself a haunting performance that disrupts discrete racial boundaries for others.[12] Mixed-race individuals, by their very presence, display and broadcast the sexual "act" of race mixing. The taboos of racial boundary crossing are embodied, so that our daily lives, our very presence, can become confrontational performative enactments. The (not so noble) savage/ethnologist stares back, and what does she see? A postmodern embodiment quandary that messes with well-established notions of an ethnographic order of whole and bounded communities. Mixed-race, mulatto, mestizo, hapa, criollo, biracial, multiracial—these are all designations of mixture, not a "one drop" either/or racial classification. Like panels on a fan, each identity exists relative to the whole scene.

The experience of shifting between identities is something many people negotiate in everyday life. While not the same as the identity shifting of one who is multiracial, the subtle dance between anyone's various personae—student, teacher, daughter, wife, friend, coworker—draws on knowledge of relational social experiences. Each of us is socially enculturated to orient in various situations with certain people, whether it is through dance training or other cultural practices.

closing fans

I would like to expand John Berger's insight, "The way we see things is affected by what we know or what we believe" (Berger 1972: 8), replacing "see" with "sense." The way we sense and experience the outside world is surely affected by constructs of our culture. For me, the key word in Berger's sentence is "way," for it is not so much the biological capacity to sense that draws my attention, but the cultural construction of the *way* we are trained to sense. "Way" also denotes a manner, path, or practice that imparts activity. Learning through the body is the practice of active *attendance* to particular sensory inputs. Embodiment of "sensational knowledge" is "the way" we consume experience to grow as individuals and as members of a community.

The flow of transmission is the flow of energy between dancers.

I find that the very shaping of our bodies through dance transmission is an ongoing process of sensual orientation that reveals the constructs of our individual realities. Bodies, situated by sense, are transformed by the very stories we live and dance. Soke's straightforward direction, "Know with your body," speaks to the simplicity of transmission yet simultaneously gestures toward a complexity of what is embodied within.

enfolded

Sensu close with the defined percussive snapping of bamboo and paper. Appressed together, the bones become one solid unit. When not in use we store the compact, quiescent fan close to our body—enfolded between layers of obi, under the left breast and below the heart.

Swordlike, they are ready to be drawn and enact a story.

notes

preface (page xiv)

1. Concerning the body as both the *subject* and *object* of culture in anthropology, see Csordas (1990).

1. introduction: sensual orientations (pages 1–22)

1. See Howes and Classen (1991: 257–285) for a "sensitive" approach to fieldwork and ethnography.
2. For further readings on the premise of the senses as a formative development of cultures' "worldview" see Stoller (1989); Bull (1997); Classen (2005, 1991); Hahn (1997, 2000); Howes (2005, 1991); Synnott (1993).
3. *Sensu* and *kankaku* are both used for "sense." The use of Euro-American words in Japan has fostered a fascinating syncretic vocabulary (also known as "Japanglish," "Jenglish," "Japanese English" or "Japlish"). In many cases words are only loosely tied to their English counterpart or do not correspond at all to the original meaning. A few I am particularly fond of: *skinship* for a close relationship with someone; *punk* for a flat tire; and *smart* for slender or thin. Contemporary language in Japan is mobile, and one need only look up "Japanglish" on an Internet search engine to find lists of borrowed words.
4. *Sensu* are the most common fans used in lessons, though other types such as *ogi* and *uchiwa* are also used. See Hutt and Alexander (1992) for more information on the history of Japanese fans.
5. Unfortunately, the information of which dance school (*ryu ha*) we studied in was lost.
6. In search for notions of the ethnographically situated body, I pursued research in contrasting field sites in order to jar my embodied perspective and to engage in fieldwork outside my previous experience. Research in interactive electronic music and Monster Truck rallies in the United States supplied me with dramatically contrasting, yet equally physically immersive, sites to survey and comprehend. Imagine the contrast—the delicate subtlety of hand

and wrist movements in Japanese dance relative to the intensity of a Monster Truck rally, where ten-thousand-pound trucks flying into the air create deafening soundscapes; or an interactive electronic music studio, where gestural controllers are utilized to extend the capabilities of musical instruments and make bodies aural. The contrasting dynamics of the situated body in these three field sites magnified the rich and diverse sensibilities essential to each of these performance practices. I became fascinated by how performers talked about their artistic sensibilities and related the sensations of sound and motion they experienced while performing. The stories they told, combined with observations, presented me with multiple perspectives from which to comprehend embodiment and the senses relative to performance and the fieldwork experience. In a sense, the navigation between these diverse field sites offered me the opportunity to experience multiple sensual orientations not unlike the codeswitching in my everyday life or between characters in dance. As a number of ethnographers have noted, sometimes we need to go away to understand more about home. See Hahn (2006a, 2006b, 2000); Hahn and Bahn (2003); Bahn, Hahn, Trueman (2001).

7. Also of great influence are the essays contained in *The Anthropology of Experience* (Turner and Bruner 1986). The authors of these works focus on the lived experience of being in the field and strive to make sense of the varieties of human experiences in the world and, as ethnographers, the process of writing about fieldwork experiences.

8. See Allison (2000) and Traubitz (2000) for a variety of perspectives, as well as critiques, on books about *geisha*.

9. See Varela, Thompson, and Rosch (1991) for Eastern and Western theories of embodiment and the practice of "mindfulness."

10. For an interesting perspective of order and chaos reflected in American writing see Slethaug (2000). For creative ethnography see Herbst (1997).

2. moving scenes (pages 23–40)

1. See Gunji (1956, 1985).

2. See Nishikata (1988: 52).

3. See Tokumaru (1991) for background on the complexities and nuances of intertextuality in Japanese *shamisen* music.

4. For more extensive readings in English see Malm (1963).

5. Nishikata (1988: 80).

6. See Masuda (1987) numbers 513 and 1137.

7. Unlike a graduation ceremony in the United States, the student's parents do not participate in or even observe this ceremony, establishing a distinction between the student's nuclear family and her fictive family.

8. According to Nishiyama (1962: 67–68), this places the teacher in a superior position.

3. unfolding essence (pages 41–69)

1. I use the word *flow* to reference Mihaly Csikszentmihalyi's ground-breaking body of works concerning a concept he terms "flow" regarding consciousness, states of awareness, and exceptional experiential moments. See Csikszentmihalyi (1991, 1996, 1997).

2. Poem and translation in Addiss (1992: 73).

3. Poem and translation in Tsuge (1983: 81).

4. revealing lessons (pages 70–145)

1. See Barry (1997) concerning issues of visual orientation and visual intelligence.

2. Concerning performers' manipulation of attention, see MacAloon (1984), who writes, "Whatever performers do, or are meant to do, they do by creating the conditions for, and by coercing the participants into, paying attention" (10).

3. See Hahn (1996).

4. A strike, or hit, is not uncommon when training the body; see Phim and Thompson (2001: 46–49).

5. This view behind Masako is hidden from the camera. However, since this kind of correction is so commonplace, and I have physically experienced it, I have included it in the description.

6. For ways of listening see Oliveros (1970, 1984, 2005) and Bamberger (1994). For a background on attention and parsing of auditory events see Jones and Yee (1993); Handel (1989).

7. Research in ethnomusicology on the cultural construction of music is extensive. See Seeger (1987) and Feld (1982, 1991) for examples of research on cultures that privilege sound. See McLean (1968) for the use of music as a system of cues.

8. For a variety of readings on oral transmission, vocables, and dance see Frisbie (1980); Halpern (1976); Furukawa (1972); Kineya (1932); Kikkawa (1989); Motegi (1984); Tokumaru (1991); Tokumaru, Yamaguchi, and Otani (1984); Yokomichi and Gamo (1978).

9. While basic *kata* do not change from dance school to dance school, each school cultivates subtleties, nuances, as well as some *kata* that are particular to the school. In this fashion, dancers become accustomed to (and indoctrinated in) a school's movement vocabulary, strengthening the sense of group feeling. For background on *nihon buyo* pedagogy see Kikkawa (1989); Nishikata (1980).

10. For research on *shyoga* and singing of dance music see Motegi (1984); Tokumaru, Yamaguchi, and Otani (1984); Yokomichi and Gamo (1978).

11. Noemi and Avner Bahat (1981) observe that "while learning, the child watches the hand movements of his teacher, each of which becomes associated in his mind with a particular accent in the text" (20), and "[these movements are] used as mnemotechnical aids in the reading of the scriptures" (21). I find this a fascinating example of hand gestures used as a memory aid, contrasting with *nihon buyo shyoga*, which are mnemonics used to cue movements. Both systems utilize oral, kinesthetic, and visual mnemonic systems concurrently to reinforce memory of a piece.

12. In *noh* plays often characters undergo a spiritual transformation during the story. The plays can be several hours in duration, and it is common for audience members to fall into a half-wakened state. The startling sound of the shrill *noh kan* can strategically arouse the audience during exciting moments such as a climactic transformation.

5. transforming *sensu* (pages 146–172)

1. I employ the words *transformation* and *transfiguration* to convey a blurring of embodied boundaries on a number of levels. While *kabuki onnagata* actors have been known to transform and "become women" on and off stage, *nihon buyo* dancers do not. See Jennifer Robertson's chapter "Conceptualizing Androgyny" (1998: 47–88) for a thorough discussion of the concepts of (gender) transformation in *kabuki* and the Takarazuka Revue.

2. See Heller (1988: 8).

3. For codeswitching in music and performance see Slobin (1993).

4. To list a few: Bachnik (1992); Clammer (1995: 59–97); DeVos (1985); Doi (1973, 1980); Kasulis (1993); Kondo (1988, 1990, 1992); Rosenberger (1992); Yuasa (1987, 1993).

5. See Holledge and Tompkins (2000) for approaches to studying (intercultural) performance by women, including constructions of space, ritual, narrative, and economic markets.

6. For more on multiple identities see Whitehead and Conaway (1986); King (1988); Lugones (1991); Mohanty (1991); Kondo (1992); Griffiths (1995); Meyers (1997); Maciszewski (2001).

7. See Carothers (1990) concerning black mothers teaching daughters the sensibilities critical for "learning to be black and female" in society.

8. Concerning cross-dressing in the popular all-female Takarazuka Revue, Jennifer Robertson proposes that "ambiguity and ambivalence can be used strategically as grounds for containment (resolution, control) *and* as a basis for parody that draws attention to the artifices that uphold the status quo" (1998: 40).

9. See Wiegman (1995) for theoretical concerns regarding "visibility" of gender and race.

10. The collection of essays *Performing Ethnomusicology: Teaching and Representation in World Music Ensembles*, edited by Ted Solis (2004), provides many accounts of ethnomusicologists grappling with teaching non-Western ensembles (and dance) and the reception of nonnative performances. In particular, the articles by Locke, Kisliuk, and Gross, and Trimillos, raise fascinating issues regarding "staging authenticity."

11. Anne Wilson (1987: 36), in her study of mixed-race children, wrote: "It would be rather far-fetched to suggest that mixed race children in Britain can be 'black all the time and white all the time' without experiencing any identity conflict. But it may well be that black and white are both elements in their racial identity which can be played up or down according to context. Being of mixed race need not mean feeling torn between the black and white groups all the time; the concept of being of mixed race may provide a viable secondary identification in its own right which gives the child a sense of belonging and self-esteem."

12. For other articles on multiracial individuals see Root (1992, 1996); Tizard and Phoenix (1993); Kilson (2000). See Yamamoto (1999) for issues concerning Japanese American women, identity, and their bodies. Trinh's (1989) work has been helpful to me for understanding alternative ways of writing about difference and "other."

glossary

ainote	Musical interlude.
bakufu	Shogunate.
bharatnatyam	A style of South Indian Classical dance.
bin	A makeup made of beeswax used for the undercoat in Japanese traditional theatrical makeup.
bonsai	Dwarf potted trees.
bunraku	Japanese traditional puppet theater.
chanoyu	Tea ceremony.
eri	The collar of a *kimono*.
furi	Pantomime movements.
furoshiki	A square cloth used to wrap and carry things.
furyu	Popular dances.
gaijin	Foreigner.
geisha	Female teahouse entertainers of music and dance.
geta	Japanese wooden sandals.
goshugimono	A formal, celebratory dance.
habutai	A scarf-like covering for the head, worn under a wig.
hachimaki	Cotton headband.
haiku	A poetic form with a verse form of 5-7-5 syllables per line.
hara	(1) Belly, bowels, stomach. (2) Mind or heart.
haragei	Visceral communication, implicit mutual understanding.
hikinuki	A quick costume change executed on stage, whereby the outer layers of a *kimono* are dramatically removed to reveal a second layer but also to reveal that character's true identity.
hone	Bone, or, in the context of dance fans, the individual bamboo ribs of the fan.
iemoto	Master or leader of a school. The *iemoto seido* is the hierarchical headmaster system.
jo-ha-kyu	A three-part compositional structure used in the performing arts.
kabuki	Japanese traditional dramatic genre.

179

kamigata mai	Dance pieces from the *geisha* tradition.
kaname	Pivot. In the context of dance fans, this is the area of the fan where the ten ribs intersect, fastened with a metal finding.
kane	A bell, gong, or chime.
kanji	Board members, supervisors, managers.
kanji	Chinese character (used in Japanese writing).
kata	Secretary or manager.
katachi	Shape, form, or, in the context of dance, posture or carriage.
katsura	Traditional wig.
keikoba	Practice hall (or dance studio in the case of *nihon buyo*).
kekkai	Spiritual boundary.
kendo	Japanese fencing, swordsmanship.
ki	A flow of energy or power in the body (in Chinese, *chi* or *qi*).
kimono	Traditional Japanese costume worn by men and women.
kokoro	Heart, mind, spirit, or soul.
komai	Short dances (genre).
komori	Babysitter.
kotan	Refined simplicity.
koto	A traditional Japanese thirteen-string zither played with finger picks.
ko tsuzumi	"Small *tsuzumi*," a traditional Japanese hourglass-shaped drum held on the shoulder and played with the fingers and hand.
kouta (or *hauta*)	"Short songs," a genre associated with *geisha*.
kuchijamisen	"Mouth *shamisen*" or vocables used to sing a *shamisen* part.
kyogen	Japanese traditional comic drama.
ma	A temporal and spatial artistic concept of "emptiness."
mai	Japanese dance, particularly the Kyoto style of dance.
matsuri	Festival.
miko	A temple priestess.
minzoku geino	Folk arts.
mon	Family crest.
nagauta	"Long song," the genre of music that accompanies *kabuki* theater.
natori	Accredited or licensed performer, one who has received a stage name. In the phrase *natori shiki*, *shiki* pertains to the licensing ceremony or ritual.
nembutsu odori	Buddhist dances.
nihon buyo	Japanese traditional dance, often referred to as Japanese "classical" dance.
ningyo-fu	Stick-figure-style notation.

nisei	Second-generation Japanese American.
noh	Japanese traditional dance-drama in which the actors wear wooden masks.
noh kan	Flute used for *noh* theater.
noren	A short, split curtain hung in doorways.
obi	A sash worn with a *kimono*.
odori	Dance. Pertains to a lively style of dance such as folk dance or *kabuki*.
okeikogoto	Practiced arts, including tea ceremony, *nihon buyo*, flower arrangement, and archery.
omote	Surface, exterior, front.
onnagata	A female dramatic role played by a man.
oshiroi	"White," a white makeup used by performers of *nihon buyo* and *kabuki* (and *geisha*).
rakugo	Traditional Japanese comic storytelling.
riji	Director or chairman.
ryu ha	School or guild.
sabi	A term referring to an aesthetic of quiet, rustic, unadorned beauty.
sake	Rice wine.
samurai	Warrior.
sarari-man	Salary man, a white-collar worker.
satori	Spiritual awakening, enlightenment.
seishin	Spiritual strength.
seiza	A proper manner of sitting on one's heels on the floor or *tatami*.
sensei	Teacher.
sensu	The standard fan used for Japanese dance.
sensu (or *sense*)	Japanese borrowed term for "sense."
shamisen	A Japanese traditional three-stringed lute, played with a plectrum.
shihan	Master instructor, licensed teacher.
shimedaiko	A traditional drum with laces for tuning. It sits on a frame and is played with wooden sticks.
shinjin ichinyo	The oneness of body-mind, *satori*.
shinobue	A Japanese traditional bamboo transverse flute with six or seven holes (generally seven).
shinsaku buyo	Newly created dance.
shitamachi	The traditional shopping and entertainment district of a city, specifically "downtown" Tokyo.
shoji	A sliding door made of wood and rice paper.
shomen	Front area of the stage.
shugyo	Enhancement of the personality, or self-cultivation.

shyoga	Mnemonics, or vocables.
skinship	See *sukinshippu*.
soke	Previous headmaster (*iemoto*).
sukinshippu	(Also *skinship*.) A word that means a "close relationship." Originally it referenced the close physical/tactile mother-child relationship in Japan, believed to develop well-being, security.
suodori	Dances performed in *kimono* but without full costuming.
suriashi	A "sliding feet" style of walking.
tabi	Socks worn with traditional clothing in which the large toe is separate from the other four, enabling *zori* (thong sandals) to be put on easily.
taiko	Large traditional Japanese barrel drum.
takebue	A Japanese traditional bamboo transverse flute (*shinobue*), the onstage *nagauta* flute.
tanka	A poetic form with a verse form of 5, 7, 5, 7, 7 syllables per line.
tatami	Thick grass matting covering the floor of traditional homes or buildings.
terakoya	A private school in the Edo period.
tsuzumi	A traditional Japanese hourglass-shaped drum held at the hip and played with the fingers and hand. (*O tsuzumi*: large *tsuzumi*.)
ura	Hidden side.
wabi	A term referring to an aesthetic of subdued elegance.
wakashu kabuki	"Youth" *kabuki*.
yugen	A term referring to an aesthetic of profound sublimity.
yukata	An informal cotton *kimono*.
zori	Thong sandals worn with traditional clothing. *Zori* are easily slipped on or off. Since Japanese traditionally take off their shoes when entering homes or temples, *zori* are convenient.

references

Abrahams, Roger. 1986. "Ordinary and Extraordinary Experience." In *The Anthropology of Experience,* edited by Victor Turner and Edward M. Bruner, 45–72. Urbana: University of Illinois Press.

Abu-Lughod, Lila. 1991. "Writing against Culture." In *Recapturing Anthropology: Working in the Present,* edited by Richard G. Fox, 137–162. Santa Fe: School of American Research Press.

Addiss, Stephen. 1992. *A Haiku Menagerie: Living Creatures in Poems and Prints.* New York: Weatherhill.

Addiss, Stephen, Gerald Groemer, and J. Thomas Rimer, eds. 2006. *Traditional Japanese Arts and Culture: An Illustrated Sourcebook.* Honolulu: University of Hawaii Press.

Allison, Anne. 2000. "Book Essay: *Memoirs of a Geisha." Education about Asia* 5, no. 2: 42–44.

Bachnik, Jane. 1992. *"Kejime:* Defining a Shifting Self in Multiple Organizational Modes." In *Japanese Sense of Self,* edited by Nancy R. Rosenberger. Cambridge: Cambridge University Press.

Bahat, Noemi and Avner. 1981. "Some Notes on Traditional Scriptural Reading Hand Movements as a Source to the Dance of the Yemenite Jews." *The World of Music* 23, no. 1: 20–25.

Bahn, Curtis, Tomie Hahn, and Dan Trueman. 2001. "Physicality and Feedback: A Focus on the Body in the Performance of Electronic Music." In *Proceedings of the International Computer Music Conference.* Havana, Cuba: ICMA.

Bakan, Michael. 1999. *Music of Death and New Creation: Experiences in the World of Balinese Gamelan Beleganjur.* Chicago: University of Chicago Press.

Bamberger, Jeanne. 1994. "Coming to Hear in a New Way." In *Musical Perceptions,* edited by Rita Aiello with John Sloboda, 131–151. New York: Oxford University Press.

Barry, Ann Marie Seward. 1997. *Visual Intelligence: Perception, Image, and Manipulation in Visual Communication.* Albany: State University of New York Press.

Bauman, Richard. 1984. *Story, Performance and Event: Contextual Studies of Oral Narrative*. Cambridge: Cambridge University Press.

Becker, Judith. 2004. *Deep Listeners: Music, Emotion, and Trancing*. Bloomington: Indiana University Press.

Befu, Ben. 1991. "Yugen: Aesthetics and Its Implications in Global Communication." In *Rethinking Japan*, vol. 1, *Literature, Visual Arts and Linguistics*, edited by Adriana Boscaro, Franco Gatti, and Massimo Raveri, 110–116. New York: St. Martin's Press.

Behar, Ruth. 1996. *The Vulnerable Observer: Anthropology That Breaks Your Heart*. Boston: Beacon Press.

Berger, John. 1972. *Ways of Seeing*. New York: Viking Press.

Browning, Barbara. 1995. *Samba: Resistance in Motion*. Bloomington: Indiana University Press.

Bull, Cynthia Jean Cohen (aka Cynthia Novack). 1997. "Sense, Meaning, and Perception in Three Dance Cultures." In *Meaning in Motion: New Cultural Studies of Dance,* edited by Jane Desmond, 169–287. Durham, N.C.: Duke University Press.

Carothers, Suzanne C. 1990. "Catching Sense: Learning from Our Mothers to Be Black and Female." In *Uncertain Terms: Negotiating Gender in American Culture,* edited by Faye Ginsburg and Anna Lowenhaupt Tsing, 232–247. Boston: Beacon Press.

Caudill, William, and David W. Plath. 1974. "Who Sleeps by Whom? Parent-Child Involvement in Urban Japanese Families." In *Culture and Personality: Contemporary Readings*, edited by R. Levine, 125–154. Chicago: Aldine Publishing Company.

Chatterjee, Ananya. 2004. "Contestations: Constructing a Historical Narrative for Odissi." In *Rethinking Dance History, A Reader,* edited by Alexandra Carter, 143–156. London: Routledge.

Chernoff, John. 1979. *African Rhythm and African Sensibility: Aesthetics and Social Action in African Musical Idioms*. Chicago: University of Chicago Press.

Clammer, John. 1995. *Difference and Modernity: Social Theory and Contemporary Japanese Society*. London: Kegan Paul International.

Classen, Constance. 1991. "Creation by Sound/Creation by Light: A Sensory Analysis of Two South American Cosmologies." In *The Varieties of Sensory Experience,* edited by David Howes. Toronto: University of Toronto Press.

———. 1993. *Worlds of Sense: Exploring the Senses in History and across Cultures.* London and New York: Routledge.

———, ed. 2005. *The Book of Touch.* Oxford: Berg.

Clifford, James. 1986. "Introduction: Partial Truths." In *Writing Culture: The Poetics and Politics of Ethnography*, edited by James Clifford and George Marcus, 1–26. Berkeley: University of California Press.

Coaldrake, William. 1990. *The Way of the Carpenter*. New York and Tokyo: Weatherhill.

Cowan, Jane. 1990. *Dance and the Body Politic in Northern Greece.* Princeton, N.J.: Princeton University Press.

Csikszentmihalyi, Mihaly. 1991. *Flow: The Psychology of Optimal Experience.* New York: HarperPerennial.

———. 1996. *Creativity: Flow and the Psychology of Discovery and Invention.* New York: HarperCollins.

———. 1997. *Finding Flow: The Psychology of Engagement with Everyday Life.* New York: Basic Books.

Csordas, Thomas. 1990. "Embodiment as a Paradigm for Anthropology." *Ethos* [Journal of the Society for Psychological Anthropology] 18, no. 1: 5–47.

DeVos, George. 1985. "Dimensions of the Self in Japanese Culture." In *Culture and Self: Asian and Western Perspectives,* edited by Antony Marsella, George DeVos, and Francis Hsu. New York: Tavistock Publications.

Doi, Takeo. 1973. "Omote and Ura: Concepts Derived from the Japanese 2-fold Structure of Consciousness." *Journal of Nervous and Mental Disease* 157: 258–261.

———. 1980. *The Anatomy of Dependence* [Amae no kozo]. Trans. John Bester. Tokyo: Kodansha International.

Du Bois, W. E. B. 1993 (1903). *The Souls of Black Folk.* New York: Penguin.

Elkins, James. 1996. *The Object Stares Back.* New York: Simon and Schuster.

Feld, Steven. 1982. *Sound and Sentiment: Birds, Weeping, Poetics, and Song in Kaluli Expression.* Philadelphia: University of Pennsylvania Press.

———. 1991. "Sound as a Symbolic System." In *The Varieties of Sensory Experience, A Sourcebook in the Anthropology of the Senses,* edited by David Howes, 79–99. Toronto: University of Toronto Press.

Fernandez, James. 1974. "The Mission of Metaphor in Expressive Culture." *Current Anthropology* 15, no. 2: 119–133.

Fine, Elizabeth, and Jean Haskell Speer, eds. 1992. *Performance, Culture, and Identity.* Westport, Conn.: Praeger Publishers.

Forrester, Michael. 2000. *Psychology of the Image.* Philadelphia: Routledge.

Foster, Susan Leigh. 1995. "An Introduction to Moving Bodies: Choreographing History." In *Choreographing History, Unnatural Acts, Theorizing the Performative,* edited by Susan Leigh Foster, 3–21. Bloomington: University of Indiana Press.

———. 1997. "Dancing Bodies." In *Meaning in Motion: New Cultural Studies of Dance,* edited by Jane Desmond. Durham, N.C.: Duke University Press.

Foucault, Michel. 1977. *Discipline and Punish: The Birth of the Prison.* Trans. Alan Sheridan. New York: Pantheon Books.

Frisbie, Charlotte J. 1980. "Vocables in Navaho Ceremonial Music." *Ethnomusicology* 24, no. 3: 347–392.

Furukawa, Mari. 1972. "Nihon dento ongaku no denshyo keitai ni okeru seido kenkyu: ongaku shokai no ikadaito shite" [Forms of Transmission in

Traditional Japanese Music: A Study into Institution as a Problem in Sociomusicology]. *Ongaku gaku* 18: 174–184.

Gamman, Lorraine, and Margaret Marshment. 1989. *The Female Gaze: Women as Viewers of Popular Culture*. Seattle: Real Comet Press.

Gates, Henry Louis, Jr. 1987. *Figures in Black: Words Signs, and the "Racial" Self*. New York: Oxford University Press.

———. 1988. *The Signifying Monkey: A Theory of Afro-American Literary Criticism*. New York: Oxford University Press.

Geertz, Clifford. 1973. *The Interpretation of Cultures*. New York: Basic Books.

Golden, Arthur. 1998. *Memoirs of a Geisha*. New York: Vintage/Random House Books.

Griffiths, Morwenna. 1995. *Feminisms and the Self: The Web of Identity*. London and New York: Routledge.

Gunji, Masakatsu. 1956. *Kabuki to Yoshiwara*. Tokyo: Asaji Shobo.

———. 1960. *Odori no bigaku* [Aesthetic of Dance]. Tokyo: Engeki shuppan shu.

———. 1970. *Buyo: The Clasical Dance*. New York: Walker/Weatherhill.

———. 1985. *Kabuki*. Tokyo: Kodansha International.

Hahn, Tomie. 1996. "Teaching through Touch: An Aspect of the Kinesthetic Transmission Process of Nihon Buyo." In *The Body in Dance: Modes of Inquiry, Paradigms for Viewing Artistic Work and Scientific Inquiry*. Congress on Research in Dance, 1996 Conference Proceedings.

———. 1997. "Sensational Knowledge: Transmitting Japanese Dance and Music." Ph.D. dissertation, Wesleyan University, Middletown, Conn.

———. 2000. "Sensual Orientations: Considering the Sensibilities of Fieldwork." Paper delivered at Musical Intersections, an interdisciplinary musical conference, Toronto.

———. 2004. "Shifting Selves: Embodied Metaphors in Nihon Buyo." In *Women Voices across Musical Worlds*, edited by Jane Bernstein. Boston: Northeastern University Press.

———. 2006a. "Emerging Voices—Encounters with Reflexivity, an Article on Reflexivity as a Feminist Practice." *Atlantis: A Women's Studies Journal / Revue d'etudes sur les femmes* 30, no. 2.

———. 2006b. "'It's the RUSH': Sites of the Sensually Extreme." *The Drama Review* 50, no. 2 (T190), Summer.

Hahn, Tomie, and Curtis Bahn. 2003. "Pikapika—the Collaborative Composition of an Interactive Sonic Character." *Organised Sound* 8, no. 8.

Hall, Edward. 1966. *The Hidden Dimension*. New York: Doubleday.

Hall, Edward T. and Mildred R. 1987. *Hidden Differences*. New York: Anchor Press/Doubleday.

Halpern, Ida. 1976. "On the Interpretation of 'Meaningless-Nonsensical Syllables' in the Music of Pacific Northwest Indians." *Ethnomusicology* 20, no. 2: 253–271.

Hanayagi, Chiyo. 1981. *Jitsu nihon buyo no kiso* [The Practical Skills of Basic Nihon Buyo Movement]. Tokyo: Shoseki.

Handel, Stephen. 1989. *Listening: An Introduction to the Perception of Auditory Events*. Cambridge, Mass.: MIT Press.

Hanna, Judith Lynne. 1988. *Dance, Sex and Gender: Signs of Identity, Dominance, Defiance, and Desire*. Chicago and London: University of Chicago Press.

Heller, Monica. 1988. *Codeswitching: Anthropological Sociolinguistic Perspectives*. Berlin: Mouton de Gruyter.

Hendry, Joy. 1986. *Becoming Japanese: The World of the Pre-school Child*. Manchester: Manchester University Press.

———. 1995. *Wrapping Culture: Politeness, Presentation and Power*. Oxford: Oxford University Press.

Herbst, Edward. 1997. *Voices in Bali: Energies and Perceptions in Vocal Music and Dance Theater*. Middletown, Conn.: Wesleyan University Press.

Holledge, Julie, and Joanne Tompkins. 2000. *Women's Intercultural Performance*. London: Routledge.

Howes, David, ed. 1991. *The Varieties of Sensory Experience: A Sourcebook in the Anthropology of the Senses*. Toronto: University of Toronto Press.

———, ed. 2005. *Empire of the Senses: The Sensual Cultural Reader*. Oxford: Berg.

Howes, David, and Constance Classen. 1991. "Sounding Sensory Profiles." In *The Varieties of Sensory Experience: A Sourcebook in the Anthropology of the Senses*, edited by David Howes, 257–288. Toronto: University of Toronto Press.

Hsu, Francis. 1975. *Iemoto: The Heart of Japan*. New York: Schenkman Publishing Company.

Hutt, Julia, and Helene Alexander. 1992. *Ogi: A History of the Japanese Fan*. London: Dauphin.

Johnson, Mark. 1987. *The Body in the Mind: The Bodily Basis of Meaning, Imagination, and Reasoning*. Chicago: University of Chicago Press.

Jones, Mari Riess, and William Yee. 1993. "Attending to Auditory Events: The Role of Temporal Organization." In *Thinking in Sound: the Cognitive Psychology of Human Audition*, edited by Stephen McAdams and Emmanuel Bigand, 69–112. Oxford: Clarendon Press.

Kasulis, Thomas P. 1993. "The Body—Japanese Style." In *Self as Body in Asian Theory and Practice*, edited by Thomas P. Kasulis, Roger T. Ames, and Wimal Dissanayake, 321–346. Albany: State University of New York Press.

Kasulis, Thomas, Roger Ames, and Wimal Dissanayake, eds. 1993. *Self as Body in Asian Theory and Practice*. Albany: State University of New York Press.

Kealiinohomoku, Joann W. 1974. "Review Number One, Caveat on Causes and Correlations" (a review of Allan Lomax's *Folk Song Style and Culture:*

A Staff Report). Congress on Research in Dance News 6 no. 2: 26–27. New York: CORD.

———. 1979. "Culture Change: Functional and Dysfunctional Expressions of Dance, a Form of Affective Culture." In *The Performing Arts: Music and Dance*, edited by John Blacking and Joann W. Kealiinohomoku. The Hague and Paris: Mouton Publishers.

———. 2002 (1969). "An Anthropologist Looks at Ballet as a Form of Ethnic Dance." In *Moving History/Dancing Cultures: A Dance History Reader*, edited by Ann Dils and Ann Cooper Albright. Middletown, Conn.: Wesleyan University Press. (Originally published in *Impulse Magazine*.)

Keene, Donald. 1981. *Appreciations of Japanese Culture*. Tokyo: Kodansha International.

Kikkawa, Shuhei. 1989. "Nihonbuyo no riron, buyo no yoso, kozo, dosa no bunseki" [Theory of Japanese Dance, Analysis of Dance Elements, Structures, and Movements]. In *Nihon no ongaku, Aija no ongaku*, edited by Gamo Satoaki et al., vol. 5: 155–184. Tokyo: Iwanami shoten.

Kilson, Marion. 2000. *Claiming Place: Biracial Young Adults of the Post–Civil Rights Era*. Westport, Conn.: Greenwood Press/Bergin & Garvey.

Kineya, Eizo. 1932. *Nagauta no utai kata* [The Singing of Nagauta]. Osaka: Sogensha.

King, Deborah K. 1988. "Multiple Jeopardy, Multiple Consciousness: The Context of a Black Feminist Ideology." *Signs* 14, no. 1: 42–72.

Kishibe, Shigeo. 1984. *The Traditional Music of Japan*. Tokyo: Ongaku no tomo sha.

Kisliuk, Michelle. 1998. *Seize the Dance! BaAka Musical Life and the Ethnography of Performance*. New York: Oxford University Press.

Komparu, Kunio. 1983. *The Noh Theater: Principles and Perspectives*. New York: Weatherhill/Tankosha.

Kondo, Dorinne. 1985. "The Way of Tea: A Symbolic Analysis." *Man* 20, no. 2: 287–306.

———. 1988. "Dissolution and Reconstruction of Self: Implications for Anthropological Epistemology." *Cultural Anthropology* 1: 74–88.

———. 1990. *Crafting Selves: Power, Gender, and Discourses of Identity in a Japanese Workplace*. Chicago: University of Chicago Press.

———. 1992. "Multiple Selves: the Aesthetics and Politics of Artisanal Identities." In *Japanese Sense of Self*, edited by Nancy R. Rosenberger, 40–66. Cambridge: Cambridge University Press.

Lakoff, George, and Mark Johnson. 1980. *Metaphors We Live By*. Chicago: University of Chicago Press.

Lebra, Takie Sugiyama. 1976. *Japanese Patterns of Behavior*. Honolulu: University of Hawaii Press.

Leppert, Richard. 1995. *The Sight of Sound: Music, Representation, and the History of the Body*. Berkeley: University of California Press.

Lin, Lynda. 2005. "The Mystique of a Geisha Packaged, Available for Sale." *Pacific Citizen, The National Publication of the Japanese American Citizens League*, Oct. 21: 1, 4.

Lugones, Maria. 1991. "On the Logic of Feminist Pluralism." In *Feminist Ethics*, edited by Claudia Card. Lawrence: University Press of Kansas.

MacAloon, John. 1984. "Cultural Performances, Cultural Theory." In *Rite, Drama, Festival, Spectacle: Rehearsals toward a Theory of Cultural Performance*, edited by John J. MacAloon. Philadelphia: Institute for the Study of Human Issues.

Machida, Kasho, comp. 1967. *Hyoju nihon buyo fu* [Standard Nihon Buyo Notations]. Tokyo: Tokyo Kokuritsu Bunkazai.

Maciszewski, Amelia. 2001. "Multiple Voices, Multiple Selves: Song Style and North Indian Women's Identity." *Asian Music* 32, no. 2: 1–40.

Mackenzie, Catriona, and Natalie Stoljar, eds. 2000. *Relational Autonomy: Feminist Perspectives on Autonomy, Agency, and the Social Self.* New York: Oxford University Press.

Malm, William. 1963. *Nagauta: The Heart of Kabuki Music.* Tokyo: Charles E. Tuttle Company.

Masuda, Koh, ed. 1987. *Kenkyusha's New Japanese-English Dictionary.* Tokyo: Kenkyusha.

Mauss, Marcel. 1979. "The Notion of Body Techniques." In *Sociology and Psychology: Essays*, translated by Ben Brewster. London and Boston: Routledge & Kegan Paul.

McLean, Mervyn. 1968. "Cueing as a Formal Device in Maori Chant." *Ethnomusicology* 12, no.1: 1–10.

McLuhan, Marshall. 1964. *Understanding Media: The Extensions of Man.* New York: McGraw-Hill Book Company.

Mendoza, Zoila S. 2000. *Shaping Society through Dance: Mestizo Ritual Performance in the Peruvian Andes.* Chicago: University of Chicago Press.

Meyers, Diana Tietjens, ed. 1997. *Feminists Rethink the Self.* Boulder, Colo.: Westview Press.

Mohanty, Chandra Talpade. 1991. "Under Western Eyes: Feminist Scholarship and Colonial Discourses." In *Third World Women and the Politics of Feminism*, edited by Chandra Talpade Mohanty, Ann Russon, and Lourdes Tores. Bloomington: Indiana University Press.

Moriji, Ichiro. 1992. *Nihon buyo kyoku shuran* [Collection of Nihon Buyo Compositions]. Tokyo: Hogaku-sha.

Motegi, Kiyoko. 1984. "Shyoga (kanafu) nitsuite no ichi kosatsu" [Shyoga (kanafu): An Observation about Japanese Traditional Notation of Instrumental Music]. *Ongaku gaku* 24, no. 2: 155–166.

Motzafi-Haller. 1997. "Writing Birthright: On Native Anthropologists and the Politics of Representation." In *Auto/Ethnography: Rewriting the Self and the Social,* edited by Deborah E. Reed-Danahay. Oxford: Berg.

Nagatomo, Shigenori. 1993a. "Translator's Introduction." In Yuasa Yasuo, *The Body, Self- Cultivation, and Ki-Energy*. Albany: State University of New York.

———. 1993b. "Two Contemporary Japanese Views of the Body: Ichikawa Hiroshi and Yuasa Yasuo." In *Self as Body in Asian Theory and Practice*, edited by Thomas Kasulis, Roger Ames, Wimal Dissanayake. Albany: State University of New York Press.

Nakane, Chie. 1970. *Japanese Society*. Berkeley: University of California Press.

Ness, Sally Ann. 1992. *Body, Movement and Culture: Kinesthetic and Visual Symbolism in a Philippine Community*. Philadelphia: University of Pennsylvania Press.

Nishikata, Setsuko. 1980. *Nihon buyo no kenkyu* [Studies of Japanese Dance]. Tokyo: Nansosha.

———. 1988. *Nihon buyo no sekai* [The World of Japanese Dance]. Tokyo: Kodansha.

Nishiyama, Matsunosuke. 1962. *Gendai no iemoto* [Iemoto Today]. Tokyo: Kobun-do.

———. 1982. *Iemoto no kenkyu* [Research on Iemoto]. Tokyo: Yoshikawa Kobunkan.

Novack (Bull), Cynthia. 1990. *Sharing the Dance: Contact Improvisation and American Culture*. Madison: University of Wisconsin Press.

Oliveros, Pauline. 1970. *Sonic Meditations*. Baltimore: Smith Publications.

———. 1984. *Software for People, Collected Writings, 1963–80*. Baltimore: Smith Publications.

———. 2005. *Deep Listening: A Composer's Sound Practice*. Lincoln, Neb.: iUniverse.

Ong, Walter. 1967. *The Presence of the Word: Some Prolegomena for Cultural and Religious History*. New Haven, Conn.: Yale University Press.

Phim, Toni Samantha, and Ashley Thompson. 2001. *Dance in Cambodia*. Oxford: Oxford University Press.

Qureshi, Regula Burckhardt. 1987. "Musical Sound and Contextual Input: A Performance Model for Musical Analysis." *Ethnomusicology* 31, no. 1: 56–86.

Rimer, J. Thomas, and Masakazu Yamazaki, trans. 1984. *On the Art of the No Drama: The Major Treatises of Zeami*. Princeton, N.J.: Princeton University Press.

Robertson, Jennifer. 1998. *Takarazuka: Sexual Politics and Popular Culture in Modern Japan*. Berkeley: University of California Press.

Root, Maria, ed. 1992. *Racially Mixed People in America*. Newbury Park, Calif.: Sage Publications.

———, ed. 1996. *The Multiracial Experience: Racial Borders as the New Frontier*. Thousand Oaks, Calif.: SAGE Publications.

Rosenberger, Nancy R., ed. 1992. *Japanese Sense of Self.* Cambridge: Cambridge University Press.

Said, Edward. 1978. *Orientalism: Western Conceptions of the Orient.* New York: Pantheon Books.

Sapir, E. 1921. *Language: An Introduction to the Study of Speech.* New York: Harcourt, Brace, and World.

Savigliano, Marta. 1995. *Tango and the Political Economy of Passion.* Boulder, Colo.: Westview Press.

Schechner, Richard. 1985. *Between Theater and Anthropology.* Philadelphia: University of Philadelphia Press.

———. 2003. *Performance Studies: An Introduction.* New York and London: Routledge.

Scotton, Carol Myers. 1988. "Codeswitching as Indexical of Social Negotiations." In *Codeswitching: Anthropological Sociolinguistic Perspectives,* edited by Monica Heller. Cambridge: Cambridge University Press.

Seeger, Anthony. 1987. *Why Suya Sing: A Musical Anthropology of an Amazonian People.* Cambridge: Cambridge University Press.

Sellers-Young, Barbara. 1993. *Teaching Personality with Gracefulness: The Transmission of Japanese Cultural Values through Japanese Dance Theater.* Lanham, Md.: University Press of America.

Shelemay, Kay Kaufman. 1991. *A Song of Longing: An Ethiopian Journey.* Chicago: University of Illinois Press.

Singleton, John. 1998. "Situated Learning in Japan: Our Educational Analysis." In *Learning in Likely Places: Varieties of Apprenticeship in Japan,* edited by John Singleton. Cambridge: Cambridge University Press.

Sklar, Deidre. 2001. *Dancing with the Virgin: Body and Faith in the Fiesta of Tortugas, New Mexico.* Berkeley: University of California Press.

———. 2002. "Five Premises for a Culturally Sensitive Approach to Dance." In *Moving History/Dancing Cultures: A Dance History Reader,* edited by Ann Dils and Ann Cooper Albright. Middletown, Conn.: Wesleyan University Press.

Slethaug, Gordon. 2000. *Beautiful Chaos: Chaos Theory and Metachaotics in Recent American Fiction.* Albany: State University of New York Press.

Slobin, Mark. 1993. *Subcultural Sounds: Micromusics of the West.* Hanover, N.H.: Wesleyan University Press.

Smith, Linda Tuhiwai. 2004. *Decolonizing Methodologies: Research and Indigenous Peoples.* London: Zed Books.

Smyth, Mary M. 1984. "Kinesthetic Communication in Dance." *Dance Research Journal* 16, no. 2: 19–22.

Snyder, Allegra Fuller. 1974. "The Dance Symbol." In *Congress on Research in Dance (CORD) Annual VI: New Dimensions in Dance Research: Anthropology and Dance—the American Indian,* edited by Tamara Comstock. New York: CORD.

Solis, Ted, ed. 2004. *Performing Ethnomusicology: Teaching and Representation in World Music Ensembles.* Berkeley: University of California Press.

Stoller, Paul. 1989. *The Taste of Ethnographic Things: The Senses in Anthropology.* Philadelphia: University of Pennsylvania Press.

Sullivan, Lawrence E. 1986. "Sound and Senses: Toward a Hermeneutics of Performance." *History of Religions* 26, no. 1: 1–33.

Suzuki, Daisetz T. 1973 (1959). *Zen and Japanese Culture.* Princeton, N.J.: Princeton University Press.

Synnott, Anthony. 1993. *The Body Social: Symbolism, Self, and Society.* New York: Routledge.

Takashina (Rosen). 1988. "The Sermon without Words." In *A Second Zen Reader: The Tiger's Cave and Translations of Other Zen Writings,* edited and translated by Trevor Leggett, 177–180. Rutland, Vt.: Charles E. Tuttle Company.

Taylor, Julie. 1998. *Paper Tangos.* Durham, N.C.: Duke University Press.

Tizard, Barbara, and Ann Phoenix. 1993. *Black, White or Mixed Race? Race and Racism in the Lives of Young People of Mixed Parentage.* London and New York: Routledge.

Tokumaru, Yoshihiko. 1991. "Intertextuality in Japanese Traditional Music." In *The Empire of Signs: Semiotic Essays on Japanese Culture,* edited by Yoshihiko Ikegami. Amsterdam/Philadelphia: John Benjamins Publishing.

Tokumaru, Yoshihiko, Osamu Yamaguchi, and Kimiko Otani, eds. 1984. *Koto-densho no hikaku kenkyu* [Studies of the Oral Tradition: An Interdisciplinary Approach]. Tokyo: Academia Music.

Traphagan, John W. 2000. *Taming Oblivion: Aging Bodies and the Fear of Senility in Japan.* Albany: State University of New York Press.

Traubitz, Nancy. 2000. "Suggestions for Comparing *The Life of an American Woman, Moll Flanders,* and *Memoirs of a Geisha.*" *Education about Asia* 5, no. 2: 33–39.

Trinh, T. Minh-ha. 1989. *Woman, Native, Other: Writing Postcoloniality and Feminism.* Bloomington: Indiana University Press.

Trouillot, Michel-Rolph. 1991. "Anthropology and the Savage Slot: The Poetics and Politics of Otherness." In *Recapturing Anthropology: Working in the Present,* edited by Richard G. Fox, 17–44. Santa Fe: School of American Research Press.

Tsuge, Genichi. 1983. *Anthology of Sokyoku and Jiuta Song Texts.* Tokyo: Academia Musica.

Turner, Victor W., and Edward M. Bruner, eds. 1986. *The Anthropology of Experience.* Urbana: University of Illinois Press.

Varela, Francisco, Evan Thompson, and Eleanor Rosch. 1991. *The Embodied Mind: Cognitive Science and Human Experience.* Cambridge, Mass.: MIT Press.

West, Cornel. 1993. *Keeping Faith: Philosophy and Race in America.* New York: Routledge.

Whitehead, Larry, and Mary Conaway, eds. 1986. *Self, Sex, and Gender in Cross-Cultural Fieldwork.* Urbana and Chicago: University of Illinois Press.

Whorf, B. 1956. *Language, Thought, and Reality.* Cambridge, Mass.: MIT Press.

Wiegman, Robyn. 1995. *American Anatomies: Theorizing Race and Gender.* Durham, N.C.: Duke University Press.

Williams, Sean. 2001. *The Sound of the Ancestral Ship: Highland Music of West Java.* Oxford and New York: Oxford University Press.

Wilson, Anne. 1987. *Mixed Race Children: A Study of Identity.* London & Winchester, Mass.: Allen and Unwin.

Wong, Deborah. 2001. *Sounding the Center: History and Aesthetics in Thai Buddhist Performance.* Chicago: University of Illinois Press.

Yamamoto, Traise. 1999. *Masking Selves, Making Subjects: Japanese American Women, Identity, and the Body.* Berkeley: University of California Press.

Yamazaki Kazuko. 2001. "Nihon Buyo: Classical Dance of Modern Japan." Ph.D. dissertation, Indiana University, Bloomington.

Yano, Christine. 2002. *Tears of Longing: Nostalgia and the Nation in Japanese Popular Song.* Cambridge, Mass.: Harvard University Asia Center.

Yokomichi, Mario, and Satoaki Gamo. 1978. *Kuchijamisen taikei* [Solmization of Japanese Instruments] (album included). Tokyo: CBS Sony.

Yoshikawa, Mako. 1999. *One Hundred and One Ways.* New York: Bantam Books.

Young, David, and Jean-Guy Goulet, eds. 1994. *Being Changed by Cross-cultural Encounters: The Anthropology of Extraordinary Experiences.* Peterborough, Ontario, Canada: Broadview Press.

Yuasa, Yasuo. 1987. *The Body: Toward an Eastern Mind-Body Theory.* Albany: State University of New York.

———. 1993. *The Body, Self-Cultivation, and Ki-Energy.* Albany: State University of New York.

index

MUSIC/CULTURE

A series from Wesleyan University Press

Edited by Harris M. Berger and Annie J. Randall

Originating editors: George Lipsitz, Susan McClary, and Robert Walser